LAW FOR SALE

LAW FOR SALE

A Philosophical Critique of Regulatory Competition

JOHANNA STARK

OXFORD
UNIVERSITY PRESS

OXFORD
UNIVERSITY PRESS

Great Clarendon Street, Oxford, OX2 6DP,
United Kingdom

Oxford University Press is a department of the University of Oxford.
It furthers the University's objective of excellence in research, scholarship,
and education by publishing worldwide. Oxford is a registered trade mark of
Oxford University Press in the UK and in certain other countries

First Edition published in 2019

Published in the United States of America by Oxford University Press
198 Madison Avenue, New York, NY 10016, United States of America

British Library Cataloguing in Publication Data
Data available

Library of Congress Control Number: 2018961283

ISBN 978–0–19–883949–1

ACKNOWLEDGEMENTS

This book is based on my doctoral thesis, which was written at Ludwig-Maximilians-University in Munich in the years 2012–15. The conceptual beginnings of the book date back to my involvement in a research programme titled 'Law as a Product', which was sponsored by LMU Munich under the 'Excellence Scheme' of the German Research Foundation.

Special thanks are due, first and foremost, to Horst Eidenmüller, who encouraged me to embark on philosophical thinking about regulatory competition, supervised the manuscript's creation, and provided invaluable suggestions for its improvement. I also owe thanks to Martin Fries, for being a constant source of collegial advice, patience, and support throughout the whole writing process. Erasmus Mayr gave much needed feedback regarding some of the philosophical arguments presented here; my debt to him calls for explicit mention, although I doubt that his standards of clarity and precision have been met after all.

Among the many other people whom I want to thank for lending help and support to this project at its various stages are Gregor Bachmann, Sara Dietz, Birke Häcker, Alexander Hellgardt, Jens Kersten, Marina Javid-Mamasani, Ralf Michaels, Florian Möslein, Christine Osterloh-Konrad, Maria C. Schweinberger, Stefan Vogenauer, Marc-Philippe Weller, and Petra Wittig. Franziska Reich deserves special thanks for meticulous research assistance, as does Conor McLaughlin for linguistic polishing.

Parts of this book have been presented at conferences and workshops, and I wish to thank the participants of those events for their beneficial questions and criticisms, as well as two anonymous referees for OUP for their insightful comments.

I further wish to express my gratitude to the German National Academic Foundation (Studienstiftung des deutschen Volkes), for supporting me with a scholarship and generously funding research stays at Yale Law School as well as at the Institute for European and Comparative Law at the University of Oxford. Thanks are also due to the Mentoring Programme at LMU Munich for financial support with conference travel and language editing, and to

LMU Munich's Law Faculty for awarding the thesis one of 2016's Faculty Prizes.

The final version of the manuscript was revised while I was working as a Senior Research Fellow at the Max Planck Institute for Tax Law and Public Finance in Munich. I am indebted to Wolfgang Schön in particular for providing a research environment one can only wish for, and to all of my wonderful colleagues there for their open ears, helpful advice, and encouragement when things don't go as planned.

I dedicate this book to my family, to whom I owe more than I can say.

Johanna Stark
Munich, October 2018

CONTENTS

Table of Cases xi
Table of Legislation xiii

Introduction 1

1. Regulatory Competition 9

A. A Competitive Law Market 9
1. Law as a Market Good: Product or Service, Public or Private? 12
2. The Competitive Cycle: Supply and Demand 15
3. Structural Preconditions 17
(a) Legal diversity 18
(b) Physical mobility 19
(c) Legal mobility 22
4. Incentives 25
(a) Political incentives 26
(b) Economic incentives 27
5. Dimensions of Regulatory Competition: Proactive versus Passive 30

B. Regulatory Competition as a Real World Phenomenon 31
1. Tax Law 34
2. Corporate Law 37
(a) Origins of the debate: charter competition in the US 37
(b) The race to Europe: Limited, GmbH, and UG 38
(c) Corporate governance issues: employee representation 41
3. Contract Law 44
4. Labour Law 46
5. Insolvency Law 48
6. Dispute Resolution 51
(a) Judicial services 52
(b) Adjudication versus alternative dispute resolution 53

C. Conclusion 55

2. The Economic Case for Regulatory Competition 57

A. Promises of Regulatory Competition 57
1. Discovery of Efficient Legislative Solutions 58
2. Acceleration of Law Reform 60

3. Taming of the Leviathan State 61
B. Dysfunctional Regulatory Competition 62
1. Market Failure and Externalities 63
(a) The 'race to the bottom' 63
(b) Externalities 65
(c) The selection principle 66
2. Asymmetrical Influence of Interest Groups 67
3. Bundling and the Price Mechanism 68
C. Conclusion 69

3. Regulatory Competition and Utilitarianism 71
A. Regulatory Competition as an Imperative of Utilitarian Politics 71
1. Subjectivist Welfare 72
2. Legal Utilitarianism 74
3. Regulatory Competition as a Means to Preference Satisfaction 76
B. Philosophical Arguments against Political Utilitarianism 77
1. Illegitimate Preferences and Individual Rights 77
2. Insensitivity to Distributive Justice 79
3. Lack of Regard for Special Relationships and Past Commitments 81
C. Arguments against Particular Instances of Regulatory Competition 82
1. Tax Competition and Redistribution 83
2. Residual Debt Discharge in Insolvency Law 87
D. Conclusion 89

4. Political Values under Competitive Pressure 91
A. Regulatory Competition and Democracy 91
1. Demand Rule versus Majority Rule 92
(a) Open conflict between market demands and majority view 94
(b) Indirect erosion of majority rule 95
(c) Devolutionary erosion of majority rule 99
2. Democracy and Equality 101
B. Regulatory Competition and State Autonomy 103
1. Autonomy as a Political Concept 104
(a) Autonomy as an ideal 106
(b) Autonomy versus self-sufficiency 107

2. State Autonomy under Competitive Pressure 107
(a) Choice of law opportunities and formal state autonomy 108
(b) Substantive state autonomy under competitive pressure 109
3. State Autonomy and Democracy 110
C. Regulatory Competition and Political Authority 115
1. The Legitimacy of Political Authority 117
2. Perfectionist Authority and Regulatory Competition 118
(a) Perfectionist authority versus personal autonomy 120
(b) Diverging conceptions of human flourishing 121
3. Proceduralist Authority and Regulatory Competition 122
D. Conclusion 123

5. Law as a Contested Commodity 125

A. Law as a Market Product 126
B. The Evaluative Logic of the Market 128
1. The Price Mechanism 128
2. Crowding Out: Consequences of Market Exposure 129
C. Contested Commodities 132
1. Historical Origins: *res extra commercium* 134
2. Distributive Justice: Access to the Good Life 134
3. Corruption of Moral Character 137
4. Market Valuation versus Social Meaning 142
D. Market Logic and the Law 148
1. Law as a Price versus the Price of the Law 149
2. The Moral Character of Law 151
E. Social Meaning and Functions of Law 153
1. Law as Order and Stabilization of Expectations 156
2. Expression of Communal Value Decisions 162
(a) Expressive law and regulatory competition 164
(b) Which values? 166
(c) Mobility for some, mandatoriness for others 168
(d) Philosophical externalities of regulatory competition 169
3. Law Markets and Spheres of Justice 170
F. Conclusion 172

6. Conclusion 175

A. Summary of Critical Arguments 175

B. Regulatory Competition as a Symptom of Globalization 176
C. Law and the State: Philosophical and Cultural Differences 178
1. Individual Well-Being 179
2. Cultural Traditions 181
3. Agreeing to Disagree 182

Bibliography 183
Index 205

TABLE OF CASES

EUROPEAN COURT OF JUSTICE

Centros Ltd v Erhvervs-og Selskabsstyrelsen [1999] ECLI:EU:C:1999:126 .... 23, 38–39
Überseering BV v Nordic Construction Company Baumanagement GmbH (NCC) [2002] ECLI:EU:C:2002:632 38–39
Kamer van Koophandel en Fabrieken voor Amsterdam v Inspire Art Ltd. [2003] ECLI:EU:C:2003:512.......... 38–39
Laval un Partneri Ltd v Svenska Byggnadsarbetareförbundet [2005] ECLI:EU:C:2007:809 47–48
International Transport Workers' Federation and Finnish Seamen's Union v Viking Line ABP and OÜ Viking Line Eesti [2007] ECLI:EU:C:2007:772..... 47–48

US

Louis K. Liggett Co. V. Lee [1933] 288 US 517, 558-59 63–64
Moore v Regents of the University of California [1990] 271 Cal.Rptr. 146, 51 Cal.3d 120, 793 P.2d 493 132–33
Carnival Cruise Lines v Shute [1991] 499 US 585, 593-94 (1991) 53
Caspi v Microsoft Network [1999] 732 A.2d 528, 531 (NJ Super Ct 1999) 53

TABLE OF LEGISLATION

EUROPEAN UNION LEGISLATION AND TREATIES

Council Directive 2001/86 (EC) supplementing the Statute for a European Company with regard to the involvement of employees [2001] OJ L294/22 43
Council Regulation (EC) 1346/2000 on insolvency proceedings (Insolvency Regulation) [2000] OJ L160/1 49–50
Council Regulation (EC) 2157/2001 on the Statute for a European Company (SE) [2001] OJ L294/1 43
Council Regulation (EC) 593/2008 on the law applicable to contractual obligations (Rome I Regulation) [2008] OJ L177 . . . . 24, 44
European Parliament and Council Directive (EC) 2005/56 on cross-border mergers of limited liability companies [2005] OJ L310/1 43
European Parliament and Council Directive (EU) 2017/1132 relating to certain aspects of company law [2017] OJ L 169/46 43
Treaty on the Functioning of the European Union [2012] OJ 326/47 (TFEU)
Art. 34 . . . . 20, 96–97
Art. 45 . . . . 20, 96–97
Art. 49 . . . 20, 23, 38–39, 47–48, 96–97
Art. 56 . . . . 20, 96–97
Art. 63 . . . . 20, 96–97
Art. 288 108

US

Internal Revenue Code 1986, 26 US Code §877A 35

GERMANY

2005 Code of Civil Procedure (*Zivilprozessordnung*, ZPO)
§38 53
2006 German Judicial Systems Act (*Gerichtsverfassungsgesetz*, GVG)
§184 54–55
2008 Limited Liability Companies Act (*Gesetz betreffend die Gesellschaften mit beschränkter Haftung*, GmbHG)
Sections 5a(1), 5(2) 40–41
2012 Act on Further Facilitating the Restructuring of Distressed Companies (*Gesetz zur weiteren Erleichterung der Sanierung von Unternehmen*, ESUG) . . 49–50
2014 Insolvency Code (*Insolvenzordnung*, InsO)
§287(2) 50
§300(1) 50

FRANCE

Loi n° 2003-721 du 1 août 2003 pour l'initiative économique, 13449 40–41

NETHERLANDS

2012 Act for Simplification and Flexibilisation of Private Company Law (*Wet Vereenvoudiging en Flexibilisering BV-Recht*) . . . 40–41

OTHERS

New York Convention on the Recognition and Enforcement of Foreign Arbitral Awards (1958) 53–54

UN Convention on Contracts for the International Sale of Goods (CISG, 1980) 159

INTRODUCTION

Imagine the unlikely: you have bought a ship, a large vessel, and need to register it in order to put it into use. Apart from your home country, you could register it under a so-called 'flag of convenience' of another state, deserving that name by offering regulation leading to significantly reduced operating costs for your ship. Advantages such as comparatively low minimum wages for crew, lax handling of fisheries and other environmental regulation, as well as opportunities to conceal beneficial ownership for reasons of tax avoidance are the reasons that the majority of merchant ships operate under convenient flags.[1]

Chances are high that you would end up with the flag of either Panama, Liberia, or the Marshall Islands, whose flags together account for about 40 per cent of the world's registered tonnage.[2] You might then end up filing documents with the Liberian Registry LLC, 'a wholly U.S. owned and operated company'[3] based in Virginia, glad to hear that one of the 'unique advantages' of your choice is a 'tax sensible jurisdiction'.[4]

The annual and tonnage-dependent fees to be paid by ship owners have been the principal source of dollar revenue in Liberia since the 1990s.[5] This gives us a clear picture of why the Republic

[1] An overview of the reasons for and the extent of convenient flagging is given, eg, by DD Murphy, 'The Business Dynamics of Global Regulatory Competition' in D Vogel and R Kagan (eds), *Dynamics of Regulatory Change: How Globalization Affects National Regulatory Policies* (University of California Press 2004) 84, 95–6; see also E Bonacich and JB Wilson, *Getting the Goods: Ports, Labor, and the Logistics Revolution* (Cornell University Press 2008) 85.

[2] United Nations Conference on Trade and Development, *Review of Maritime Transport 2017* (United Nations 2017) 43.

[3] 'About the Liberian Registry' <http://www.liscr.com/about-liberian-registry> accessed 1 August 2018.

[4] 'Unique Advantages' <http://www.liscr.com/unique-advantages> accessed 1 August 2018.

[5] DD Murphy, *The Structure of Regulatory Competition: Corporations and Public Policies in a Global Economy* (OUP 2006) 61 with an estimate of €20–150 million per year.

of Liberia would have an interest in offering a set of legal rules that make its flag as convenient as possible for ship owners. As already noted, Liberia is competing with other states for this kind of 'registration business'. Not surprisingly, European countries have responded to the challenge from the emergence of convenient flags by adjusting their shipping laws, mainly by establishing 'second onshore registers' (fulfilling the function of free trade zones), lowering tonnage taxes, and cutting registration fees.[6]

The context of merchant vessel registration illustrates a competitive dynamic among states tailoring their law to the interests of potential buyers of their services, albeit one rather removed from most people's everyday reality. It is, however, by far not the only example of such legislative behaviour. In many fields and areas of law, choice options of individuals and states' incentives to have their law applied combine into a scenario that has been termed 'regulatory competition', in the course of which states compete against one another for the favour of consumers of their legal products. Associated with this situation is the idea of a 'market for law', of law as a product that is being marketed by suppliers to potential demanders, who then 'buy' the legal product that is most attractive for them because it best fits their interests and needs and, in most cases, reduces their costs.

Of course, competition and law are not conceptual strangers. The basic connection is that law is a political instrument to set the framework for any kind of competition, much like the rules of a football match or any other game or sport. 'Competition law' states what firms competing with one another in certain markets can and cannot do to gain advantage over their competitors.

A market for law itself, however, with suppliers of law competing for the success of their legal products, is not what traditionally comes to mind when we think of law. This study is about why it is not, discussing some of the reasons why the idea of legal rules as market commodities collides with our understanding of law and its role as a social practice and political instrument.

A candid disclaimer on the limits of the following discussion of regulatory competition and law as a market good is appropriate.

[6] For a discussion of regulatory responses in this 'race to laxity' among OECD member states see ibid 63–4.

The following chapters are concerned with competitive dynamics regarding mandatory law.[7] The exclusion of non-mandatory (or default) legal rules from the focus of this study is one of choice. While supply-side competition with respect to non-mandatory law is not impossible, the grounds on which it might be criticized differ from the arguments against markets that affect mandatory law. This is because of differences in the functions that these types of legal provision are meant to fulfil. Non-mandatory provisions per definition allow for derogation, typically by contractual agreement. Evading their demands thus regularly requires no mobility of either the physical or legal kind. The central purpose of such provisions is to save transaction costs by providing a default arrangement that serves the hypothetical interests of those subject to it.[8] Regulatory competition with respect to non-mandatory legal rules is perfectly imaginable, for example, in the form of suppliers competing with regard to a quick readjustment of their offering of default arrangements when technical progress has given rise to new types of agreements, such as contract law provisions tailored to the specifics of e-commerce.

The restriction of individual autonomy that mandatory legal rules constitute is typically justified by competing interests that such rules are there to serve, and values and ideals they are supposed to help realize. Intuitive examples are the rights of third parties that may not be compromised by a contract, or the general duty of good faith that is to be observed. In light of competing interests that are—from a political perspective—of such central importance, the risk of individual bargaining and contracting around them must be excluded.

In economic terms, mandatory legal rules are justified by market failure that has been shown to realize or must be expected to realize absent provisions that do not depend on party choice for their effectiveness. Such market failure may have various causes,

[7] Hence, in the following, whenever the term 'law' is used without further qualification, it refers to national or supranational legal provisions of mandatory character.

[8] On the nature of non-mandatory/default rules in contract law and their function of 'filling gaps in incomplete contracts' see I Ayres, 'Filling Gaps in Incomplete Contracts: An Economic Theory of Default Rules' (1989) 99 Yale Law Journal 87.

such as an asymmetric dispersal of information and bargaining power among parties to a transaction, externalities, the involvement of public goods, or principal-agent problems. Regulatory intervention in the form of legal rules intends to compensate for these reasons of market failure.

The focus of this study lies in the ways in which regulatory competition loosens legislators' ability to exercise regulatory authority through the use of mandatory law.[9] The key reason for this focus is that the main source of criticism of legislative decisions that are observably influenced by competitive pressure pertains to those instances in which they appear to compromise objectives protected by mandatory law, or—as Hans-Werner Sinn has argued—that reintroduce the threat of market failure that mandatory law was designed to prevent.[10]

THE STRUCTURE OF THE STUDY

Chapter 1 introduces regulatory competition as a theoretical concept as well as a factual phenomenon. The structural preconditions of a law market are discussed, including state suppliers' incentives to compete at all. It closes with a glance at a number of areas in which competitive dynamics among legislators can be found to operate.

[9] See below Chapters 2-5. A case could be made, even, that regulatory competition qua meaning of the term 'regulation' properly refers only to mandatory, or binding legal rules. The interventionist understanding of 'regulation' is found already in JS Mill, *Principles of Political Economy* (S Nathanson ed, first published 1848, Hackett Publishing 2004) Book V Chapter XI, eg 280: 'Scarcely any degree of utility, short of absolute necessity, will justify a prohibitory regulation, unless it can also be made to recommend itself to the general conscience [. . .]'; see also B Orbach, 'What is Regulation?' (2012) 30 Yale Journal on Regulation Online 1-10.6: 'So what does regulation mean? We return to the starting point—the intuitive understanding of the word "regulation": government intervention in the private domain or a legal rule that implements such intervention. The implementing rule is a binding legal norm created by a state organ that intends to shape the conduct of individuals and firms.'

[10] H-W Sinn, 'The Selection Principle and Market Failure in Systems Competition' (1997) 66 Journal of Public Economics 247; H-W Sinn, *The New Systems Competition* (John Wiley & Sons 2003); for a discussion of Sinn's argument see Chapter 2, section B.1.(c).

Chapter 2 presents the economic case for regulatory competition as an approach to law and policy, briefly sketching the positive hopes that have been put forward by its advocates before turning to problems that have been voiced in the law and economics literature on regulatory competition.

The main focus of the study, however, are various kinds of critical approaches to 'law as a product' or regulatory competition as a political strategy to 'improve' law. There are several ways to discuss and criticize a scientific theory.[11] Immanent criticism accepts the axioms and presuppositions a theoretical structure is built upon and points to internal contradictions and inconsistencies, or shows how conclusions drawn from a theory do not in fact follow from its set of assumptions.

Critical arguments of this immanent kind are discussed in the second part of Chapter 2. They revolve mainly around scepticism that regulatory competition can in fact be expected to deliver on the promises it is associated with, such as more efficient law, a 'race to the top' in the quality of legal rules. Forceful arguments have been made to the effect that the assumptions upon which advocates of regulatory competition build their case somehow do not add up to the conclusions they claim to be able to derive from them.

Another strategy can be described as 'external criticism', in the sense that the set of premises of a theory is rejected, at least in part, to the effect that its conclusions lose their axiomatic basis. With this strategy, the challenge is to show why one or more assumptions underlying a theory are wrong or implausible.[12] This

[11] A theory is understood here as a set of axioms, principles, or ideas. Depending on the nature and purpose of the theory in question, its assumptions and the conclusions drawn from them can be meant to explain factual occurrences that we observe empirically (descriptive/explanatory purpose) or to establish reasons for acting in a particular way so as to change or at least influence factual states of affairs (prescriptive/normative purpose). Democracy could be described as a political theory, building on a number of key assumptions such as the principle of majority rule and the idea of citizen equality, giving rise to a number of conclusions about how political systems not only are in fact, but how they should be structured and organized (for a discussion of democracy and regulatory competition, see Chapter 4, section A).

[12] Thinking further down this route leads to developing alternative sets of assumptions and arguing for their comparative advantage over the set that is criticized, as it is sometimes claimed: 'It takes a theory to beat a theory.' For a

can be done, for example, by exposing frictions, contradictions, and incompatibilities between the axiomatic set of a particular theory and other sets of assumptions that we appear to hold and are not willing to give up. Inconsistencies of this kind are not internal to the theory that is criticized, yet they are reasons to rethink its plausibility.

Criticism of this kind is offered in Chapters 3, 4, and 5—highlighting various ways in which the assumptions that regulatory competition builds upon do not fit well into our more comprehensive set of beliefs and convictions about law. Although literature on regulatory competition has become abundant during the last decades, the issue has received surprisingly little attention from the perspectives of legal philosophy, sociology, and political theory.

Chapter 3 traces the utilitarian pedigree of regulatory competition as a normative approach to law creation and reform. The hypothesis is that regulatory competition is promising only if one shares a number of basic premises that are associated with political utilitarianism. The questions that are to be answered are thus:

1. In what way could regulatory competition be interpreted as being linked to utilitarianism?
2. To what extent does the appeal of regulatory competition depend on utilitarian assumptions?

An answer to these questions leads to the conclusion that problems with these utilitarian assumptions translate into criticisms of regulatory competition as a policy approach. Two examples are used to illustrate the connection: first, tax competition and its effects on states' ability to implement redistributive policies; second, the lowering of residual debt discharge periods as an outcome of regulatory competition in insolvency law that exhibits utilitarianism's failure to adequately account for past relationships and commitments.

discussion of the phrase and its implications for legal scholarship see LB Solum, 'Legal Theory Lexicon: It Takes a Theory to Beat a Theory' (2015) <http://lsolum.typepad.com/legaltheory/2015/07/legal-theory-lexicon-it-takes-a-theory-to-beat-a-theory.html> accessed 1 August 2018.

The arguments presented in Chapter 4 spell out the idea that regulatory competition is at odds with how the state, as the primary political entity of our time, works—or should work. It will be argued that regulatory competition runs counter to the normative implications of political concepts such as autonomy, democracy, and authority. These are arguments within the conceptual framework of moral and political philosophy. Their starting point is the way we understand these normative concepts and to what extent a political and legal reality shaped by regulatory competition is consistent with this understanding.

Chapter 5 develops a criticism of regulatory competition based on the commodity status of law that is a consequence of the existence of law markets. Commodification, as a concept and theme, is not new to legal discourse. There has been considerable debate on whether certain goods such as human organs or democratic votes should be excluded—by law—from market exchange. Chapter 5 deals with the increasing commodification of law itself and discusses whether critical considerations regarding other types of goods are applicable here as well. The argument's starting point is that regulatory competition leads to the law being perceived as a commodity that is subject to the market mechanism. It proceeds with the premise that the market mechanism comes with its own kind of valuation, with the price mechanism serving as the primary indicator of value. Criticism of commodification is often based on the perception that market valuation tends to be dominant over other evaluative standards, sometimes 'crowding out' considerations that cannot be directly translated into market vocabulary. Exposure to the market mechanism can thus change the norms and standards according to which a good or a social practice is valued. The norms and standards with which market valuation may clash can be derived from the social meaning that law as a social practice and political instrument has for us, and the functions it is taken to fulfil in society.

Of course, these are not the only concerns that may be brought forward in favour or against a market-oriented perspective on law. They are, however, ones that have been largely neglected in the discussion about the merits and shortcomings of regulatory competition. The point of the critical chapters is, each in a different way, to expose and analyse the 'philosophical externalities' of regulatory competition. If taken seriously as an interpretive framework of law production and reform, regulatory competition commits to an understanding of law and its role in society that is inconsistent with other views that we appear to hold.

What does not follow from these analytical arguments is that regulatory competition is, in any possible scenario, inherently bad. It would be utopian to assume that we could simply undo the structural preconditions that have led to competitive dynamics in several areas of law. One of the reasons for this is that, to a significant extent, regulatory competition is one of the many symptoms of globalization. The global integration of political, legal, and economic spheres in many ways calls into question the role and impact of the state. What you think about regulatory competition, therefore, may not depend so much on the plausibility of a race to the top or to the bottom in legal standards, but on what you think about the purpose and function of the state in a globalized world.

1

REGULATORY COMPETITION

From a legislative perspective, 'regulatory competition' means that with respect to certain fields or issues, regulation is organized and designed according to the demands of a competitive process. Producers of regulation ask themselves what kinds of legal product they should offer in order to gain the favour of consumers: those who may choose to opt for their legal products instead of those offered by other producers.

The purpose of this chapter is, first, to introduce the conceptual framework that surrounds the idea of a market for legal rules and the resulting competition among suppliers of such rules. Prerequisites for law to be the object of a market cycle will be discussed, as well as the incentives that may be responsible for suppliers of legal rules engaging in competition with one another. Second, we will take a fairly brief look at a few real world examples from fields of law where, arguably, regulatory competition takes place and may be a determining factor in legislative decision-making.

A. A COMPETITIVE LAW MARKET

What is a market? Generally speaking, and apart from its obvious spatiotemporal meaning as a venue where things are bought and sold, the term 'market' can be defined as a form of interaction between at least two agents, who engage in the 'action or business of buying and selling',[1] or 'sale as controlled by demand'.[2] Typically, a currency is used in order to facilitate exchange. Logically, markets need not be competitive: two vendors of fruit may offer their produce on a (literal) market to consumers without regard

[1] Oxford English Dictionary Online, 'Market' (June 2018) <http://www.oed.com/view/Entry/114178?rskey=odMicM&result=1&isAdvanced=false> accessed 1 August 2018, Section II.4.a.

[2] Ibid Section II.7.a.

Law for Sale: A Philosophical Critique of Regulatory Competition. Johanna Stark. Published 2019 by Oxford University Press.

to one another's activities, calculating prices based on their costs of production. Competition as a feature of markets is a three-pole concept:[3] at least two parties competing to gain superiority over the other(s) with regard to something else, such as an award, a consumer's choice of product or service, or someone's favour.

What is a law market? The following definition shall suffice as a starting point:

> 'Market', in this instance, does not refer to any particular set of idealized conditions of exchange, but rather simply to buyers demanding a commodity (law) and sellers being willing to provide it for a benefit.[4]

The characteristic of being a market product is not something that is usually associated with law. On the contrary, law is traditionally thought to be an exogenous framework for the market mechanism,[5] an instrument that is used in order to confine and regulate markets according to social and political decisions as to what goods should be traded and how. From this perspective, laws and markets are different forms of social coordination.

How could it nevertheless be analytically useful to speak of law itself as a product traded on markets?[6] A comparative look at the general features of markets, and the 'law market' as it might translate into these categories, should help. Speaking of a competitive market for law is appropriate only if there is a competitive

[3] L Herzog, 'Markets', *The Stanford Encyclopedia of Philosophy* (2018) <https://plato.stanford.edu/archives/fall2017/entries/markets/> accessed 1 August 2018, Section 1: 'Markets are called "competitive" when they have certain structural features that include a large number of buyers and sellers, comparable goods, and the absence of informational asymmetries.'

[4] EA O'Hara and LE Ribstein, *The Law Market* (OUP 2009) 66.

[5] S Vogenauer, 'Regulatory Competition through Choice of Contract Law and Choice of Forum in Europe: Theory and Evidence' (2013) 21 European Review of Private Law 13, 14 on the model of a law market and its departure from our traditional view of law: 'It is said that the days are gone where the law merely set out the regulatory framework for market participants. Instead, the law itself has become a product in its own right.'

[6] In the following, the terms or phrases 'regulatory competition', 'jurisdictional competition', and even 'systems competition' are used without any differentiation as to their exact meaning. In our context, they all refer to the same phenomenon, ie states as suppliers of legal rules competing against one another for the favour of consumers.

element present on either the demand or supply side.[7] In market terminology, states as suppliers of legal rules are competing with each other for consumers' favour. Such competition presupposes choice options on the demand side. Only if law's addressees can choose between different laws does it make sense to speak of legislators competing against one another to offer the legal product that ends up being chosen.[8] In many of the instances of law markets discussed in this chapter, such choice options are expressly provided by private international law.[9]

The debate surrounding regulatory competition has produced the phrase 'law as a product',[10] sometimes with an intended negative connotation.[11] Law is and has always been a product of something. The issue in question here is, a product of what? There are two kinds of answers to this question: (i) what kind of product *is* law and (ii) what kind *should* it be? Obviously, both questions can be answered in countless ways. As to the descriptive question of what kind of product law is, a traditional answer would be that it is the result of a political process (democratically structured, in most countries today, with some kind of parliamentary involvement). Law's existence and form is always influenced by diverse factors. In democratic systems, its making and content is ideally determined by rules that were originally set by its addressees.[12]

The approach to the descriptive question that has been offered by scholars writing about law markets and regulatory competition is that law can be viewed not only as the end point of a political

[7] GJ Stigler, 'Competition' in SN Durlauf and LE Blume (eds), *The New Palgrave Dictionary of Economics* (Palgrave Macmillan 2008) 51 has described competition as a scenario in which 'a rivalry between individuals (or groups or nations) arises whenever two or more parties strive for something that all cannot obtain.'

[8] A conceptual disclaimer should be made here. In the course of the following chapters, the terms 'law market' and 'law as a product' are used in a wider sense than 'regulatory competition'. Whereas law markets refer to the phenomenon of legal rules being the subject of market interaction, 'regulatory competition' refers only to competitive dynamics on the supply side.

[9] See section A.3.(c).

[10] The conceptual origins of 'law as a product' can be found in R Romano, 'Law as a Product: Some Pieces of the Incorporation Puzzle' (1985) 1 Journal of Law, Economics and Organization 225.

[11] On the contestability of the commodity status of law see Chapter 5.

[12] On regulatory competition and democracy see Chapter 4, section A.

activity, such as a parliamentary process, but also as the outcome of a competitive process among different lawmakers addressing the same group of potential addressees. Whether the competitive model of law and the analogy to other products such as washing machines or other consumer goods is informative and plausible at all remains to be seen.[13] The model is to be tested in the same way as other models, that is, mainly for the plausibility of its presuppositions. In the present case of applying the conceptual framework of the market to a new setting (that of law production and distribution), the market model's plausibility depends in part on contextual similarities between regular market settings, for example, for consumer goods, and a law market. How well, then, does law fit into the market metaphor? How much is the situation of a competitive law market comparable and similar to other markets? Wherein does it differ?

1. LAW AS A MARKET GOOD: PRODUCT OR SERVICE, PUBLIC OR PRIVATE?

Economists rely on a variety of parameters to categorize goods, with implications for their most efficient modes of production and distribution. In the context of regulatory competition, law has been described as a product.[14] Does law deserve to be called a product, just as a washing machine is undoubtedly a product as well? Commonly, a distinction is made between tangible, material goods in a narrower sense and non-physical services.[15] Both are goods in the wider sense of satisfying human preferences, thus also having exchange value.

[13] M Rehberg, 'Spezifika des Systemwettbewerbs' in EV Towfigh and others (eds), *Recht und Markt: Wechselbeziehungen zweier Ordnungen* (Nomos 2009) is sceptical of the analogy.

[14] Romano (n 10).

[15] Another subcategory is intangible goods such as information, which only becomes tangible via the use of another medium, for example, a newspaper or a computer screen.

There are a number of reasons for viewing law as a service instead of a product:[16] its lack of materiality (intangibility) and the fact that it does not change ownership during the hypothetical market exchange. Since we are perfectly familiar with markets for genuine services, such as child care or dry cleaning, this is not a limitation of the market metaphor with respect to legal rules. Another characteristic that supports the view that law is to be thought of as a service instead of a product is its adaptability to the specific needs of those who may wish to 'use' it.[17] For the sake of the arguments developed here, however, the differentiation between law as a product and a service is of no relevance in terms of argument, except in serving terminological accuracy. The discussion of law as a contested commodity will therefore refer to law as a product in the wider sense of an economic good subject to the market mechanism.[18]

Of more importance is the common classification of an economic good according to the criteria of exclusivity and rivalry, depending on whether individuals can be effectively excluded from its use (exclusivity) and whether individual use reduces availability of that good to others (rivalry). Goods that are both non-exclusive and non-rivalrous are called 'public goods',[19] such as clean air or national security. Provision of these goods is made on a non-exclusive basis, in that making people pay for use of them would be impossible or at least attainable only at prohibitively high costs.

The reference to high costs associated with maintaining the exclusive provision of a good points to an important aspect of public goods: clean air appears to be a genuine public good in the sense that its provision under condition of exclusivity would be virtually impossible. With most other goods, their being produced and distributed as public goods is less of a logical necessity deriving

[16] F Möslein, 'Regulatory Competition between Public and Private Rules' in H Eidenmüller (ed), *Regulatory Competition in Contract Law and Dispute Resolution* (CH Beck 2013) 147.

[17] This, however, is true particularly of non-mandatory private law that can be customized by its addressees.

[18] See Chapter 5.

[19] RD Cooter and TS Ulen, *Law and Economics, International Edition* (6th edn, Prentice Hall 2012) 40.

from their inherent nature than a contingent political decision.[20] This is the case, for example, with public parks or roads: they can be provided as public goods (non-exclusive), but other schemes of provision are possible and practicable as well, such as fenced-in parks with an entrance fee to be paid or tolls collected for the use of roads.

It is thus not enough to ask whether law is a public good.[21] We must also ask ourselves, in the case that it is currently a public good, should it continue to be one? If it is not, should it become one? In our traditional, intuitive, layman's understanding, law is a public good—a service provided by the state, open for all, in part mandatory for everyone. We need to work with 'hybrid forms' of public and private goods in order to arrive at a meaningful matrix that enables us to discuss the production and distribution of goods that are not necessarily of public or private character alone.[22]

How, then, is the issue of law as a public good related to regulatory competition? Traditionally, our understanding of law is that of a public good, provided on a non-exclusive basis by a state legislator. As we have already seen, however, provision on a public or private basis is in most cases a political decision. This is the case with law as well: there are instances of legal rules provided on an exclusive basis, as evidenced by franchise fees to be paid for the

[20] On the difference between inherent and contingent public goods J Raz, *The Morality of Freedom* (Clarendon Press 1986) 198–203. Raz offers a narrow account of *inherently* public goods, excluding, for example, clean air, since its non-exclusive provision is only necessitated by our lack of technological ability to control air distribution (198–9).

[21] O'Hara and Ribstein (n 4) 223: '[I]t is worth noting that, to some extent, lawmaking is a public good in the sense that it is costly to make those who benefit from laws pay for these benefits.'; G Wagner, 'The Economics of Harmonization: The Case of Contract Law' (2002) 39 Common Market Law Review 995, 1002: 'From the economic standpoint, legislation may be looked at as a public good to be provided by the government.'; L Gerken, 'Institutional Competition: An Orientative Framework' in L Gerken (ed), *Competition among Institutions* (Macmillan 1995) 11: 'It is also generally accepted that one main reason for the evolution of modern states has been that certain goods, due to their non-exclusive character, are not supplied by markets—for example, legislation and social services.'

[22] Heinrich-Böll-Stiftung (ed), *Der Wert öffentlicher Güter* (Heinrich-Böll-Stiftung 2015).

use of Delaware corporate law,[23] or fees to be paid for the use of procedural rules that govern court proceedings. These fees can be compared to tolls payable for the use of roads.

Regulatory competition arguably creates and intensifies incentives for suppliers of law to provide it on a private instead of a public goods basis, in order to achieve a balanced account in terms of costs associated with the production and maintenance of a legal system versus earnings associated with the 'consumption' of the legal rules it has on offer. Thus, even if there is no logical connection between the occurrence of regulatory competition and law being provided on a private basis, competition among lawmakers appears to be a threat to our traditional understanding of law as a public good.

2. THE COMPETITIVE CYCLE: SUPPLY AND DEMAND

As we have seen in section A.1, competition is a three-pole concept. In a market setting, two or more rivals act independently to attain the same goal, such as serving a particular consumer, or buying a particular work of art.

In the case of the law market, who occupies the three poles? On the demand side, we find all potential addressees of legal rules. On the supply side, generally speaking, all kinds of sources of legal rules in a wider sense can theoretically—and do practically—compete with one another. Thus, there are several types of competitors in this game. The paradigmatic case is certainly nation states and their statutory law. Competitive dynamics among them have been termed 'horizontal regulatory competition'.[24] However, they are not alone in a competitive setting that determines the fate of their legal rules.[25] There are other sources of

[23] See section B.2.(a).

[24] See H Eidenmüller, 'The Transnational Law Market, Regulatory Competition, and Transnational Corporations' (2011) 18 Indiana Journal of Global Legal Studies 707, 743; G Bachmann and others, *Regulating the Closed Corporation* (De Gruyter 2014) 221–5.

[25] A Peters, 'The Competition between Legal Orders' (2014) 3 International Law Research 45, 48: 'State and non-State providers: in this "new" competition, the Nation States, more specifically the legislative bodies and the courts, are the providers of the "legal order" as a merchandise. Further providers are the

rules that share certain characteristics of legal rules. The legal status of rules issued by international or supranational organizations, such as the United Nations (UN) or the European Union (EU), is widely accepted. When legal rules of such organizations compete with state law, the scenario is called 'vertical regulatory competition'.[26] Instances of this dimension of regulatory competition have been witnessed particularly in the EU, with the Union starting to offer its own 'legal products' to rival those of national origin, such as the Societas Europaea (SE), as a European alternative to national stock corporations.[27]

Another source from which law markets have increasingly drawn is rules of non-state, private origin, such as trade customs that have been codified into multilaterally recognized bodies of law. Whether these rules should be called 'law', and if so under what circumstances, is contested. There are pressing questions to be asked and answered in this respect.[28] What are the criteria for rules of private origin to be regarded as legal rules? How do, and should, nation states deal with these emerging forms of de facto

constituent units of federal States, regional and local authorities such as municipalities, and international or supranational organizations. National legal systems are in competition not only with one another, but also with "supra"- and "infra"-national systems.'

[26] Generally on the term 'vertical competition' in the context of legal systems, citing the example of the EU JP Trachtman, 'International Regulatory Competition, Externalization, and Jurisdiction' (1993) 34 Harvard International Law Journal 47, 103–4; Eidenmüller (n 24) 743–5; L Klöhn, 'Supranationale Rechtsformen und vertikaler Wettbewerb der Gesetzgeber im europäischen Gesellschaftsrecht' (2012) 76 Rabel Journal of Comparative and International Private Law 276; on the vertical dimension of regulatory competition in US corporate law see MJ Roe, 'Delaware's Competition' (2003) 177 Harvard Law Review 588.

[27] H Eidenmüller, A Engert, and L Hornuf, 'Incorporating under European Law: The Societas Europaea as a Vehicle for Legal Arbitrage' (2009) 10 European Business Organization Law Review 1.

[28] For a critical view of this narrow perspective only on state-made law, leaving aside rules of private origin, see Möslein (n 16). H Collins, 'Regulatory Competition in International Trade: Transnational Regulation through Standard Form Contracts' in H Eidenmüller (ed), *Regulatory Competition in Contract Law and Dispute Resolution* (CH Beck 2013) 121 provides an even more critical view: the role of national jurisdictions is very limited, the real competition lies between 'competing standard forms'.

authoritative rules? What are the drivers of competition within the domain of private rules and accompanying fora of dispute resolution? Do they follow similar patterns as regards competition that exclusively involves state law?[29]

3. STRUCTURAL PRECONDITIONS

In 1956, Charles Tiebout published 'A Pure Theory of Local Expenditures'.[30] The economic model he proposed dealt with local public finance. His point was to examine the conditions under which local jurisdictions would be in perfect competition for the provision of the most attractive bundles of public goods to (taxpaying) consumer voters. The idea was that people would be 'voting with their feet' for the jurisdiction that offered the bundle of public goods that best fit their divergent preferences, leading to an optimal provision and allocation of (bundles of) public goods in exchange for taxes paid in that jurisdiction.[31]

Tiebout's model has been the blueprint for most of the discussion about the merits and limits of regulatory competition,[32] structured by the central premises his model was based upon:[33]

1. Full mobility of taxpayers
2. Perfect information of taxpayers about all bundles on offer
3. A large number of different bundles on offer (matching many possible sets of preferences)

[29] Competitive dynamics between suppliers of state courts and non-state suppliers of alternative dispute resolution are discussed in section B.6.(b).

[30] CM Tiebout, 'A Pure Theory of Local Expenditure' (1956) 64 Journal of Political Economy 416.

[31] Ibid 422: 'Just as the consumer may be visualized as walking to a private market place to buy his goods, the prices of which are set, we place him in the position of walking to a community where the prices (taxes) of community services are set. Both trips take the consumer to market. […] Spatial mobility provides the local public-goods counterpart to the private market's shopping trip.'

[32] For a detailed discussion see Chapter 2.

[33] Tiebout (n 30) 419, with two additional assumptions on the optimal size of a community; for a discussion of these assumptions and their role in the debate about regulatory competition see B Gabor, *Regulatory Competition in the Internal Market* (Edward Elgar Publishing 2013) 2–3.

4. Differences in employment opportunities considered irrelevant
5. No inter-communitarian external effects of provided goods and services

Much criticism of regulatory competition has focused on the assumptions of Tiebout's model being unrealistic.[34] It is worth noting that Tiebout himself never claimed the model's premises to be an adequate description of social and political reality.[35] To the contrary, by juxtaposing his theoretical construct to that reality, he hoped to gain insights on how to deal with the political challenges posed particularly by imperfect mobility, informational inequality, and external effects. More generally, a theoretical model can never be criticized directly for being unrealistic—the point of a model is to show that, granted a number of initial assumptions, certain results can be expected to occur. The connection between a theoretical model and reality is one of explanatory power. The closer a model's assumptions capture real life facts and dynamics, the more we can expect it to explain past and present events as well as potentially predict future developments.

That said, it does not 'contradict' the Tieboutian model to find that its assumptions are rarely or never completely satisfied in practice. It is, instead, worth acknowledging the way in which the model has contributed to a structured discussion about the preconditions and outcomes of regulatory competition. Two of the model's assumptions can be described as preconditions to the very occurrence of regulatory competition. First, a diverse landscape of 'legal bundles' on offer and second, mobility of regulatees in question, in two respects—physically and legally. All three will be discussed in the following sections.

(a) Legal diversity

Choice requires options to choose from. Without legal diversity, there would be no opportunity for consumers of legal products to choose, and no point in speaking of suppliers of those goods

[34] This type of criticism is taken up in Chapter 2, section B.

[35] Tiebout (n 30) 423: 'Consumer-voters do not have perfect knowledge and set preferences, nor are they perfectly mobile.'

being in competition with one another. The third assumption of Tiebout's model would not be met. Think of several street vendors offering bottles of water on a hot summer day. It is safe to assume that their goal is to attract most consumers, thus attracting more business than neighbouring vendors. What should they do in order to be successful? There are numerous things they could and would presumably do to gain a competitive advantage, such as advertising the quality of their water bottles (extra clear, extra cold, larger bottles), at lower prices than their competitors. If they just all stood there, side by side, each offering water bottles of the exact same type at the same price, we would be reluctant to speak of competition among them. Unless there is legal diversity—a plurality of rules or regimes for legal subjects to choose from—the basis of regulatory competition is missing.

Legal diversity as a precondition links regulatory competition to another policy debate, namely that of the best design of federalist systems, or the issue of centralized or harmonized versus decentralized (competitive) rulemaking.[36] Legal diversity is less likely to be found within centralized legal systems than in federalist systems with lawmaking autonomy on different political sublevels. The most prominent example is certainly the United States of America (US), with different legal solutions for a variety of policy issues that initiated scholarly debate about regulatory competition in the first place.

(b) Physical mobility

That there is demand for law to be satisfied by market transactions presupposes people actually being able to choose which of a number of different legal regimes should govern their affairs. The idea that people should be able to choose which law applies to them seems theoretically counter-intuitive with respect to many areas of the law, such as criminal or tax law. By default, so to speak, everyone is bound by the laws of their own jurisdiction, which is usually the jurisdiction they physically reside in. For legal subjects other than natural persons (eg companies and

[36] WW Bratton and JA McCahery, 'The New Economics of Jurisdictional Competition: Devolutionary Federalism in a Second-Best World' (1997) 86 The Georgetown Law Journal 201.

institutions), this may be the centre of their commercial or other activities. According to the 'territoriality principle' (borrowing a phrase from public international law), to avoid being bound by certain legal rules requires physically or geographically moving out of their domain of application.

From a historical perspective, competitive dynamics between political systems originated and were driven by people 'voting with their feet',[37] that is, by physically exiting a polity and moving to another, such as moving from New York to New Jersey, or from the (former) Soviet Union to the US.

Over the past century, production factor mobility has increased dramatically for various reasons.[38] Technological progress such as the advent of affordable transport of both passengers and goods over long distances (via air traffic) has created opportunities for individuals to consider relocating to far removed jurisdictions, even if only temporarily, for example, in order to conclude a marriage under different legal preconditions than in the home jurisdiction. As far as goods and services are concerned, the advent and prospering of e-commerce has done its share to increase the occurrence of cross-border transactions by decreasing their costs. Political changes have been influential as well. One of the central purposes of the EU project has been to enable and increase mobility of both people and capital,[39] as evidenced by the fundamental freedoms.[40] In the Eurozone, the introduction of a common currency has contributed significantly to financial mobility.

[37] Ibid 216.

[38] DM Andrews, 'Capital Mobility and State Autonomy: Toward a Structural Theory of International Monetary Relations' (1994) 38 International Studies Quarterly 193, 199.

[39] Ibid 99–201, with a discussion of capital mobility and integration of capital markets as a source of competitive pressure on nation states; see also PB Musgrave and RA Musgrave, 'Fiscal Coordination and Competition in an International Setting' in CE McLure (ed), *Influence of Tax Differentials on International Competitiveness* (Kluwer Law and Taxation Publishers 1990) 61, 66–8.

[40] Consolidated Version of the Treaty on the Functioning of the European Union [2012] OJ 326/47 (hereafter TFEU); the fundamental freedoms are laid down in Art. 34 TFEU (free movement of goods); Art. 45 TFEU (free movement of workers); Art. 49 TFEU (freedom of establishment); Art. 56 TFEU (freedom to provide services); Art. 63 TFEU (free movement of capital).

Whereas the mobility of capital is hardly a recent phenomenon and the mobility of people is limited by social factors such as familial connections, language, and cultural preferences, it is the mobility of real capital that has emphasized the competitive scenario among nation states. In an international landscape of liberal trade relations and sinking transportation costs, relocation of operations to jurisdictions with comparatively low wages and taxes has become increasingly attractive.[41]

Possibilities of choice of law via choice of residence or at least physical presence have always existed within the limits of emigration and immigration law of the affected states. Secession in terms of public international law, such as claimed recently by the Republic of Kosovo from Serbia, can also be interpreted as a collective choice of law.[42] In the same vein, Brexit can be interpreted as a collective opt-out from the EU law framework.

A recent and intriguing example of choice of law via physical relocation and the role of technological progress in advancing jurisdictional mobility can be found with a group of Silicon Valley entrepreneurs who are working on options to 'secede' from US territory, with the primary intent of escaping US law. Under the ideological heading of 'competitive government', their plan is to enable a new form of regulatory product. So-called 'seasteads', structures in high sea territories that are subject only to minimal regulation, promise to be a 'playground' for entrepreneurial activity unhindered by mandatory law of most kinds.[43]

The reason that financial capital is the most mobile factor of production (compared to people and real capital) is not only that its largely non-physical nature dramatically reduces transportation costs, but also that it is separable from ownership.[44]

[41] H-W Sinn, *The New Systems Competition* (John Wiley & Sons 2003) 2.

[42] Peters (n 25) 50: '[C]ollective emigration of citizens along with their territory through secession, can in the competition paradigm be reconstructed as a choice of law, made by that collective.'

[43] A Giridharadas, 'Silicon Valley Roused by Secession Call' New York Times (28 October 2013) <http://www.nytimes.com/2013/10/29/us/silicon-valley-roused-by-secession-call.html?_r=0>, accessed 1 August 2018; see also Peters (n 25) 50.

[44] Musgrave and Musgrave (n 39) 67.

(c) Legal mobility

However, due to globalization and integration of the international (legal) sphere, choice options that do not necessarily have a physical component have increased significantly.[45] Besides changes in the legal environment, the 'legal mobility' of addressees has also been favoured by technical progress, such as the Internet, which makes it much easier and less costly to gather information on which (foreign) law might be best suited for one's needs.[46]

For a number of reasons,[47] legislators have over the last few decades significantly restricted the application of the territoriality principle. By providing choice of law clauses in their private international law, they have created opportunities of choosing to be bound by foreign law without having to match this choice with a physical exit of the 'home jurisdiction'.[48]

Expansion of choice of law opportunities granted by states to their laws' addressees has changed the landscape of possible reactions to law that is perceived as unfit for one's activities. The first option is built into the democratic design of a polity: if you do not like the law, try to change it via the appropriate democratic mechanisms. This is what Albert Hirschman, in his classical analysis of reactions to perceived deficits in institutional performance,[49] would have called 'voice'. However, it is also a strategy that is in most cases unattractive, because the 'democratic route' is too long, bumpy, and of an uncertain destination. The second option would be to go somewhere else where you like the law better—in Hirschman's terms 'exit'. If you do not like Swedish law, for example, move to Switzerland. This option is unattractive for many as well, particularly for natural persons. Changing one's place of residence often comes at (prohibitively) high costs. Finding a new place to live, a new job for you and possibly your spouse, perhaps having to learn a new language, and leaving your family and friends behind is not what many people would opt for in order to

[45] On the presuppositions of institutional competition W Schön, 'Playing Different Games? Regulatory Competition in Tax and Company Law Compared' (2005) 42 Common Market Law Review 331, 333.

[46] Eidenmüller (n 24) 712. [47] Ibid 707. [48] Ibid 710–11.

[49] AO Hirschman, *Exit, Voice, and Loyalty: Responses to Decline in Firms, Organizations and States* (Harvard University Press 1970).

enjoy a legal system they prefer. The third option introduced by choice of law opportunities in many legal areas seems to offer an attractive midway. Voluntarily subjecting one's affairs to a foreign law of one's liking without having to physically move brings very little additional costs while potentially offering a lot of benefits.

This may be illustrated by an example from company law.[50] If you want to set up a limited liability company in Germany, but are unable or unwilling to put up the minimum capital of €25,000 required for a *Gesellschaft mit beschränkter Haftung* (GmbH), you may consider opting for a limited liability company under English company law instead, with a minimum capital requirement of £1.

Developments such as recent European Court of Justice (ECJ) case law illustrate how the existence of a law market is a 'dialectical phenomenon', in the sense that opportunities of choice on the demand side are themselves consequences of law.[51] In the case of European company law, market pressure resulted from ECJ decisions such as *Centros*[52] stating that the freedom of establishment according to Article 49 TFEU entails the right to set up a company according to another Member State's company law even if this is done only or primarily in order to circumvent the unattractive regulation of one's own Member State (eg minimum capital requirements). The fundamental freedoms that led the ECJ to decide the *Centros* case as it did, however, are themselves the outcome of Member State's sovereign decisions on what provisions to include in EU primary law. If more decisions in favour of choice of law options on the basis of the fundamental freedoms are to be expected, that is not without a preceding and 'enabling' political decision by the Member States themselves.

It should be added that choice of law options granting legal mobility are logically possible only in private law (with good reason, there is no such thing as choice of law in core areas of public or criminal law). The difference between direct choice of law and indirect choice of law (via choice of the territorial environment that determines legal treatment) is, in the end, mainly one of the costs that are incurred. Indirect choice of law, that is, one accompanied

[50] See also section B.2. [51] Eidenmüller (n 24) 730.

[52] *Centros Ltd v Erhvervs-og Selskabsstyrelsen* [1999] ECLI:EU:C:1999:126 (hereafter *Centros*).

by a physical or geographical component, tends to involve higher costs than a mere choice of law 'on paper'. Thus, the lack of direct choice of law opportunities in public law provides no principled objection to a treatment of regulatory competition in both private and public law within a common analytical framework.

Opt-out of a legal regime thus comes in different forms, with significantly differing costs that are associated with such choice. Legislators may employ various strategies to enable or restrict the mobility of legal subjects.

1. Opt-out of dispositive legal rules is most easily done, that is, by an autonomous party decision to deviate from the default solution on offer.
2. Mandatory law is characterized by the fact that contractual or unilateral deviation within the confines of the legal system in question is not available.

   Opt-out may nevertheless be possible in structural similarity to non-mandatory rules when there are choice of law opportunities and a large body of opt-in solutions to choose from. It should be added that private international law recognizes the institution of 'overriding mandatory rules' of a state that serve as intervention standards and cannot be set aside by the application of a law other than that of the forum.[53] More generally, according to the public policy (or ordre public) doctrine, laws expressing the fundamental political principles and values a legal system is built upon are accorded overriding force as well, with the consequence that choice of law resulting in a violation of such norms will not be acknowledged.[54]

[53] Such as stated in Art. 9(1) Council Regulation (EC) 593/2008 on the law applicable to contractual obligations [2008] OJ L 177 (hereafter Rome I Regulation): 'Overriding mandatory provisions are provisions the respect for which is regarded as crucial by a country for safeguarding its political, social or economic organisation, to such an extent that they are applicable to any situation falling within their scope, irrespective of the law otherwise applicable to the contract under this Regulation.'

[54] For an overview of the public policy/ordre public doctrine in private international law see I Thoma, 'Public Policy (Ordre Public)' in J Basedow and others (eds), *European Encyclopedia of Private International Law* (Edward Elgar Publishing (2016) 1453.

3. The barriers for opt-out are set even higher when choice of law opportunities are not granted and opt-out is thus necessarily accompanied by a physical component, such as a change of domicile.
4. States have the opportunity to raise the costs of opt-out even higher by 'bundling' the application of their legal rules, making specific opt-out more difficult, such as tying the applicable law to factors that cannot be moved at all or only at extreme costs (such as citizenship taxation in the US: opt-out is possible only at the price of giving up US citizenship).[55]

4. INCENTIVES

The structural preconditions sketched in the chapter so far are necessary, yet not sufficient for regulatory competition. Competitive cycles require some kind of reaction on the supply side—for example, by law reform, as Ogus argues:

> If, and to the extent that, competition between national legal systems emerges, we can predict that this will impact on the content of law. In response to the demand from market actors, national law makers will compare their own legal products with those available in competing jurisdictions; if the latter better meet the preferences of the actors, they will be motivated to adapt their products.[56]

The focus of research has so far been on the incentives for 'law customers', that is, the reasons why people or firms would choose one legal regime over another. This dimension of the issue has been captured illustratively by the terms 'legal arbitrage' and 'forum shopping' (focusing on jurisdictional aspects, ie finding the most beneficial jurisdiction in which to have your case heard). These dynamics will not be dealt with in much detail here. Without doubt, an adequate understanding of the motivational structure of the demand side is of enormous regulatory importance, as it informs lawmakers on how to be successful in competition with

[55] See section B.1.; on the US practice of citizenship taxation see R Mason, 'Citizenship Taxation' (2016) 89 Southern California Law Review 169.

[56] A Ogus, 'Competition between National Legal Systems: A Contribution of Economic Analysis to Comparative Law' (1999) 48 International and Comparative Law Quarterly 405, 409.

other providers of legal rules. In order to be a good competitor, it is essential to know what customers are looking for and what the reasons are for the decisions they make.

The exercise of choice of law opportunities in the form of legal arbitrage and forum shopping, however, does not deserve to be called 'regulatory competition' when there is no legislative reaction.[57] In many instances, arbitrage will have no effects in terms of law reform. What are the incentives for state suppliers of law to engage in such competition?[58]

(a) Political incentives

Market success of legal products can be interpreted as a viable goal within the motivational framework of the political sphere, as O'Hara and Ribstein observe:

> Politicians care about who buys their state's or country's laws for the same reasons they care about other political issues – because they get campaign contributions and votes.[59]

Whereas campaign contributions may be a strong source of motivation in political systems where electoral success depends highly on campaign funding, competitive success in law markets can also be desired for fairly general and 'intangible rewards', such as increased political prestige and reputation.[60] Governments that are subject to periodical democratic approval have a genuine interest in presenting themselves as suppliers of successful legal products. Domestic opt-out in particular is likely to lead to negative media coverage, which in turn may threaten voter satisfaction.[61]

[57] This distinction is often overlooked, as E-M Kieninger, *Wettbewerb der Privatrechtsordnungen im Europäischen Binnenmarkt* (Mohr Siebeck 2002) 17 observes.

[58] For a detailed analysis of supply side incentives that differentiates explicitly between the incentives of (i) legislators and governments, (ii) independent regulatory agencies, (iii) courts, and (iv) private regulators in an EU context see Gabor (n 33) 30–47.

[59] O'Hara and Ribstein (n 4) 14–15.

[60] R Sacco, 'Legal Formants: A Dynamic Approach to Comparative Law (Installment II of II)' (1991) 39 American Journal of Comparative Law 343; Ogus (n 56) 409; Vogenauer (n 5) 28.

[61] Klöhn (n 26) 296 specifically on the issue of regulatory competition in European company law, admitting that non-economic incentives do play some role, but are hard to pin down exactly (293) and make passive competition more

In some European countries, particularly those with civil law systems such as Germany and France,[62] engaging in regulatory competition has, beyond direct economic consequences, also been perceived as a matter of the protection and advancement of one's own legal culture vis-à-vis Anglo-Saxon common law systems.[63]

(b) Economic incentives

With respect to some fields in some jurisdictions, there are direct financial advantages to be gained from successfully marketing legal wares (and, correspondingly, losses which result from refraining to do so). In the US, for example, there are 'franchise fees' to be paid by companies in the jurisdiction of their incorporation. The market leader Delaware makes around 20 per cent of its annual gross domestic product (GDP) from such franchise fees,[64] which is quite a significant incentive to keep the business of regulatory competition with respect to corporate charters going.

In many other fields and jurisdictions, however, direct financial incentives cannot be discerned. In the EU, for instance, there are no franchise fees for companies. Nevertheless, we see states competing for their corporate forms to be successful on the European market for incorporations. Indirectly, financial or fiscal incentives play an important role as well.[65] A strong market position of a

likely than proactive competition (293–8). On the difference between passive and proactive competition see section A.5.

[62] Vogenauer (n 5) 30–1.

[63] P Häberle, *Europäische Rechtskultur: Versuch einer Annäherung in zwölf Schritten* (Suhrkamp 1997) 9; T Giegerich, 'Wettbewerb von Rechtsordnungen' (2009) 69 Veröffentlichungen der Vereinigung der Deutschen Staatsrechtslehrer 57, 63–5; P Mankowski, 'Rechtskultur' (2009), 64 Juristenzeitung 321; J Kersten, 'Wettbewerb der Rechtsordnungen?' in J Isensee and P Kirchhof (eds), *Handbuch des Staatsrechts, VoL XI* (CF Müller 2013) §233.

[64] Eidenmüller (n 24) 712–13.

[65] Bratton and McCahery (n 36) 266; see also Ogus (n 56) 408: 'Lawmakers will also be motivated, particularly in small countries heavily dependent on international trade, to attract firms from other jurisdictions and multinational corporations since that should entail increased investment, demand for labour and tax revenue.' See also JG Brown, 'Competitive Federalism and Legislative Incentives to Recognize Same-Sex Marriage' in W Bratton and others (eds), *International Regulatory Competition and Coordination* (Clarendon Press 1996) 271; S Woolcock, 'Competition among Rules in the European Market' in W Bratton and others (eds), *International Regulatory Competition and Coordination* (Clarendon Press 1996)

jurisdiction is expected result in higher demand for corresponding legal services, which will in turn lead to the creation of jobs and tax revenue.[66] Around the beginning of the 1990s, in financial centres such as the Cayman Islands and the British Channel Islands, offshore companies accounted for up to 20 per cent of employment, with even higher percentages of GDP linked to activities of offshore companies.[67]

Another reason might be that successfully 'exporting' one's own law makes it easier for home businesses to flourish abroad.[68] This argument can be made with respect to contract law in particular. Transaction costs associated with export business grow with the variations in foreign legal rules and standards that need to be accommodated. In comparison, a situation in which export activities are largely governed by the 'home law' of a business,

289, 305–6; a different position is taken by Peters (n 25) 51 even with regard to the straightforward incentive of generating tax revenue, at least from an 'orthodox tax law perspective': 'From a legal perspective, taxes are by definition not the remuneration for specific services provided in return by the State.'

[66] For the charter competition context (incorporation leading to litigation in the respective state, thereby generating business for local bar) see Romano (n 10) 240–1; LA Bebchuk, 'Federalism and the Corporation: The Desirable Limits on State Competition in Corporate Law' (1992) 105 Harvard Law Review 1435, 1443; see also Klöhn (n 26) 292; Vogenauer (n 5) 17: 'The indirect benefits, such as job creation and overall growth of the economy, may be less predictable, but there is a high probability that they will materialize.' See also ibid 28: 'There has been some informed guesswork based on anecdotal evidence, such as the comment that "those in the know" estimated "the income derived from arbitration by the legal professions, hotels and other services in London alone" to be GBP 1 billion per year', quoting and translating C-D Schumann, 'Plan eines zentralen Gerichtshofs für die Anerkennung von Schiedssprüchen – Was ist daraus geworden?' (1993) 39 Recht der internationalen Wirtschaft 701; taking this 'informed guesswork' as accurate regarding the year of 1993, adjusted numbers would of course be significantly higher today; for the general claim of local benefits see also G Wagner, 'The Dispute Resolution Market' (2014) 62 Buffalo Law Review 1085, 1132: 'The well-being and growth of the legal industry […] has positive spill-over effects for other local suppliers such as restaurants and hotels, but also for sellers of real estate and office space'; J Dammann and H Hansmann, 'Globalizing Commercial Litigation' (2008) 94 Cornell Law Review 1, 57 expect that the incentive to procure business for the local bar and suppliers of other services (ie restaurants and hotels) is at work in New York as well; Kieninger (n 57) 190, however, is sceptical of the significance of such positive spillover effects.

[67] Murphy (n 81) 101.

[68] Eidenmüller (n 24) 713.

accompanied by a corresponding forum clause, economies of scale will play out favourably in terms of familiarity, competent legal advice at hand, and lower travel costs.[69]

Even though it is plausible that non-economic incentives do act as motivating factors for legislators when it comes to competing for 'legal business' or not, they are difficult to quantify and therefore hard to pin down in their effect on legislative decisions. The upshot of this diagnosis is that the intensity of regulatory competition, and the increase of legal innovation and efficiency that it promises,[70] can be expected to be strongest in those fields in which the rewards to be gained directly or indirectly from competing successfully are measurable in principle, or at least roughly assessable in practice.[71]

Absent direct or significant indirect financial incentives, one might also ask why states open up their jurisdictions for regulatory competition in the first place. Why do they increasingly grant opportunities for choice of law at all, if that will result in competitive pressure to be successful on the resulting law market? Would sticking to the territoriality principle not make things easier?

One answer lies in the options of the addressees of law that Hirschman[72] has outlined: those who are unhappy with legal rules could move away entirely ('exit'), which in the case of taxpaying companies would hurt efforts to survive in standard regional competition (for workplaces, investments, taxes, etc.). Giving them an opportunity to deselect part of the legal bundle of a jurisdiction and select another regime for certain issues instead might keep them in their physical taxpaying place after all. From a strategic perspective, competing for non-opt-out with respect to particular legal issues (such as taxation) may be easier than competing to retain companies with a whole 'bundle' that cannot be separated into parts by choice of law.[73]

[69] S Vogenauer, 'Regulatory Competition through Choice of Contract Law and Choice of Forum in Europe: Theory and Evidence' in H Eidenmüller (ed), *Regulatory Competition on Contract Law and Dispute Resolution* (CH Beck 2013) 227, 234, 238.

[70] See Chapter 2, section A.

[71] Such as is arguably the case in tax and company law, see sections B.1 and B.2.

[72] Hirschman (n 49).

[73] On the issue of 'bundling' see Chapter 2, section B.3.

Another answer is that, beyond enabling regulatory competition, there are other reasons for including choice of law clauses in private international law. This is particularly so in complex transactions that span multiple jurisdictions; legal certainty as to which law applies to which issues would, without such clauses, be almost impossible to attain.[74]

5. DIMENSIONS OF REGULATORY COMPETITION: PROACTIVE VERSUS PASSIVE

Regulatory competition has different dimensions, to be differentiated according to the goals regulators aim to achieve. Those who engage in 'proactive' regulatory competition seek to win 'market share' from other jurisdictions, whereas 'passive' or 'defensive' regulatory competition is aimed at preventing opt-out of domestic subjects in favour of other legal regimes. Some have argued that defensive competition is more plausible in light of the utility function of the individuals involved in law creation and reform.[75] These individuals are risk and loss averse, having a preference for leisure time or other career goals.

It should be noted, however, that the fact that governments enact or have enacted legislation that is obviously attractive for foreign subjects to opt into does not necessarily have to be based on an expressed desire to attract additional 'consumers'. The fact that same-sex marriages are legal in the Netherlands, for example, or that it is possible to receive IVF via the help of an anonymous sperm donor, may be instead an expression of liberal political views on these issues, a conviction that marriage and reproductive chances should be granted to these groups. There is no evidence that Dutch law on these issues may be significantly

[74] O'Hara & Ribstein (n 4) 8: '[C]hoice of law decisions are messy, and in many cases it is unclear what law applies without a choice-of-law-clause. Choice-of-law-clauses reduce uncertainty about the parties' legal rights and obligations and enable firms to operate in many places without being subject to multiple states' laws.'

[75] DJ Cumming and JG MacIntosh, 'The Role of Interjurisdictional Competition in Shaping Canadian Corporate Law' (2000) 20 International Review of Law and Economics 141, 144–6; similarly Klöhn (n 26) 293–8.

motivated by a desire to generate revenue from people coming to the Netherlands because of its more liberal laws.

So, if this is how we can theoretically make most sense of the idea of regulatory competition, we can hardly escape the question of whether dynamics of this kind can actually be witnessed in reality. That we do in fact see instances of regulatory competition, and where and to what extent, will be discussed in section B.

B. REGULATORY COMPETITION AS A REAL WORLD PHENOMENON

Literature on regulatory competition with respect to particular areas of law has come to be abundant during the last decades.[76] Contributions to this debate that are critical of regulatory competition can roughly be divided into two categories: (i) those who warn that regulatory competition has detrimental effects or at least is unable to deliver on its promises, and (ii) those who doubt or deny that the conceptual paradigm of the market and competition has any analytical use as it does not adequately capture what is in fact happening—in other words, regulatory competition does not exist.

That we do in fact see states engaging in regulatory competition has, however, been empirically demonstrated and discussed with respect to various fields, such as corporate, contract, family, and insolvency law.[77] In some cases, states have even actively and expressly taken to 'marketing' their legal wares to potential demanders. In 2007, the Law Society of England and Wales published a document with the promising title 'England and Wales: The Jurisdiction of Choice', enthusiastically advertising the advantages of the English legal system.[78] Not long thereafter, a German brochure of similar content entitled 'Law Made in

[76] See, for instance, K Kocaoglu, *A Comparative Bibliography: Regulatory Competition on Corporate Law* (Georgetown University Law Center 2008), a 90-page bibliography on regulatory competition in corporate law and related fields alone.

[77] For an extensive discussion of examples from these fields, albeit from a decidedly US-American perspective, see O'Hara & Ribstein (n 4).

[78] The Law Society of England and Wales, 'England and Wales: The Jurisdiction of Choice' (2007) <http://www.eversheds.com/global/de/what/publications/books.page> accessed 1 August 2018.

Germany' appeared, comparing the German law and court system to the known qualities of German engineering. The German version has seen a third edition in 2014,[79] the English brochure was updated in 2016 and is now titled 'England & Wales: Global Legal Centre'.[80]

Even though the 'battle of the brochures' should not be overstated in its importance and effects on the behaviour of regulatees, it does tell us something about how lawmakers have come to perceive the products of their work, as Vogenauer concludes:

> [P]olicymakers from all political quarters in the three major European jurisdictions and some senior judges seem to have subscribed to the idea of a law market and […] and more particularly to the notion that attracting legal business […] is beneficial and should receive political support.[81]

Authors of other studies on actual occurrences of competition among lawmakers agree that instances of such dynamics are likely to increase both in terms of the affected fields of law and of their intensity:

> [I]nter-jurisdictional competition […] is likely to increase. Virtually all economic activity is regulated, with wide variation among countries' regulatory schemes. Increased trade, and the increasing role of non-state actors, is likely to put more and more regulatory issues on the agenda.[82]

79 Bundesnotarkammer and others (eds), 'Law Made in Germany: Global, Effective, Cost-Efficient' (2014) <https://www.lawmadeingermany.de/Law-Made_in_Germany_EN.pdf> accessed 1 August 2018; besides English and German, the brochure is also available in French, Arabic, Chinese, Russian, and Vietnamese languages. For an extensive discussion of marketing initiatives and brochures that were set up both in the United Kingdom (UK) and continental Europe see Vogenauer (n 5) 30–5; Faria (2015), 108 reports that particularly the initiatives in Germany and France were in part motivated by an impression that the 'quality' of their respective legal systems had been underrepresented in the World Bank's Doing Business Reports.

80 The Law Society of England and Wales, 'England & Wales: Global Legal Centre' (2016) <https://www.lawsociety.org.uk/policy-campaigns/documents/global-legal-centre-leaflet/> accessed 1 August 2018.

81 Vogenauer (n 5) 35, however, focusing only on contract law and dispute resolution.

82 DD Murphy, *The Structure of Regulatory Competition: Corporations and Public Policies in a Global Economy* (OUP 2006) 250–1.

A critique of regulatory competition and law markets would make little sense if the object of the critique does not in fact exist, or only to the extent of an inconsequential niche phenomenon. The purpose of this section is thus not to give an extensive overview of all that has been said pro and contra regulatory competition in all sorts of areas of law, but to offer a small number of examples that lend credence, plausibility, and analytical appeal to regulatory competition as a conceptual framework.

Suffice it to show therefore that there is regulatory competition, at least in some fields and with regard to some matters. For even if we do not see regulatory competition in many fields today—if there are plans to advance it and increasingly use it as a regulatory tool (for a variety of reasons), we do well to be clear about the consequences this development may entail in the long run.

As the focus of this study is on regulatory competition specifically as the supply side dimension of law markets in a more general sense, we will look briefly at a few examples of scenarios in which there is empirical evidence that suppliers of law actually adapt to competitive pressure. The fields that will not be at the centre of attention are those in which we see very lively arbitrage dynamics mainly on the demand side, but less or no corresponding activity on the supply side, such as in family law with the occurrence of marriage and divorce tourism.[83] The same goes for developments that could be interpreted as 'negative competition',

[83] JG Brown, 'Competitive Federalism and Legislative Incentives to Recognize Same-Sex Marriage' in W Bratton and others (eds), *International Regulatory Competition and Coordination* (Clarendon Press 1996) 271 has tried to pin down the economic incentives of legislators to recognize same-sex marriage (based on the average amount spent on weddings, increased retail revenue generated by tourism etc.); O'Hara and Ribstein (n 4) 171–5 describe a historical instance of regulatory competition regarding the legal preconditions of divorce among US states in the twentieth century, which has led to a prevalence of 'no-fault divorce' laws in most states. In recent times, however, the market for divorce laws has seen the advent of so-called 'covenant marriages', which can be dissolved only under strict conditions such as adultery, crime, abuse, or other specified criteria, see A Stewart, 'Covenant Marriage: Legislating Family Values' (1999) 32 Indiana Law Review 509; K White, 'Covenant Marriage: An Unnecessary Second Attempt at Fault-Based Divorce' (2010) 61 Alabama Law Review 869; see also Chapter 5, section E.2.(b).

that is, states using legal rules in order to fend off external opt-in, for example, by tightening asylum law and the conditions for residence and work permits.

1. TAX LAW

Tax law offers perhaps the oldest and most paradigmatic example for competition involving legal rules. There is a vast amount of literature on the issue of tax competition, from the perspective of both economic and legal scholarship.[84]

Tax competition differs from other instances of regulatory competition in an important respect. Whereas in company law regulatory competition is fiercely advocated by its proponents pointing to its promises in terms of welfare increases, tax competition has always been met with a fair amount of scepticism. It is rarely marketed as a promising policy. It is instead perceived as an undeniable and, just as importantly, unchangeable fact, as well as a problem.[85]

How have states responded to competitive pressure from mobile taxpayers? Several strategies are, in principle, on offer:[86]

1. Giving in to pressure by competing, for example, incentives for taxpayers to opt out into jurisdictions with lower taxes by cutting tax rates or restricting tax bases themselves.

2. Limiting taxpayers' legal mobility by tax system design, such as a shift in tax policy from direct to indirect taxation, from

[84] See from a pool of many RS Avi-Yonah, 'Globalization, Tax Competition, and the Fiscal Crisis of the Welfare State' (2000) 113 Harvard Law Review 1573; W Schön, 'Playing Different Games? Regulatory Competition in Tax and Company Law Compared' (2005) 42 Common Market Law Review 331; see also GDA MacDougall, 'The Benefits and Costs of Private Investment from Abroad: A Theoretical Approach' (1960) 22 Bulletin of the Oxford University Institute of Economics and Statistics 189; PB Richman, *Taxation of Foreign Investment Income: An Economic Analysis* (John Hopkins Press 1963); A Easson, 'Taxing International Income', in RE Krever (ed), *Tax Conversations: A Guide to the Key Issues in the Tax Reform Debate: Essays in Honour of John G Head* (Kluwer Law International 1997) 415.

[85] The main reasons for this assessment are discussed in Chapter 3, section C.1.

[86] Peters (n 25) 54; both strategies also have implication for the ability of states to implement redistributive policies that depend on fiscal resources. We will return to these implications in Chapter 3, section C.1.

mobile factors such as capital to immobile factors such as labour, or even by introducing a system of citizenship taxation as is practiced in the US.[87]

Tying people's liability to pay income tax to their citizen status instead of habitual residence dramatically increases the costs of relocating outside of the Internal Revenue Service's reach. In the wake of reports of several high volume individuals having given up US citizenship,[88] presumably motivated by tax reasons, an even more drastic regulatory response in terms of mobility costs followed. Since 2008, individuals above certain thresholds are liable to pay an 'exit tax' of 15 per cent, calculated on the basis of the fair market value of their assets (reliefs not considered) upon giving up citizenship.[89]

Recent studies point to the conclusion that smaller countries such as Ireland, Estonia, and Luxembourg in particular have engaged in practices deemed as harmfully aggressive. Smaller countries have greater chances of profiting from tax competition through lower tax rates and are consequently more readily willing to employ aggressive policies in this respect. The best explanation for this phenomenon is that they lose little domestic tax base while potentially gaining a lot of revenue from foreign tax inflow.

Under the auspices of the Organisation for Economic Co-Operation and Development (OECD), considerable attempts have been made to define 'harmful tax competition'[90] and to

[87] On the peculiarities and problems of the US citizenship taxation system R Mason, 'Citizenship Taxation' (2016) 89 Southern California Law Review 169.

[88] One of them being Eduardo Saverin, co-founder of Facebook, who became a citizen of Singapore shortly before Facebook's IPO, saving an estimated up to $700 million in taxes (based on financial filings); see L Saunders, 'So How Much Did He Really Save?' Wall Street Journal (New York, 18 May 2012) <http://www.wsj.com/articles/SB10001424052702303360504577410571011995562> accessed 1 August 2018.

[89] Internal Revenue Code 1986, 26 US Code §877A on the tax responsibilities associated with expatriation.

[90] OECD, Harmful Tax Competition: An Emerging Global Issue (OECD Publications 1998) <https://www.oecd-ilibrary.org/taxation/harmful-tax-competition_9789264162945-en> accessed 1 August 2018; see also Peters (n 25) 61, who adds a cautionary note regarding the link between taxation and state sovereignty: 'Taxation policies reflect different, culturally conditioned views. Against

implement political measures to prevent its most common forms. In 1997, in line with the report of the OECD group, the EU Council of Economics and Finance Ministers adopted a 'Code of Conduct' for business taxation in order to ensure that Member States cooperate and refrain from particular practices that are branded as unfair.[91] In 2015, the so-called 'Base Erosion and Profit Shifting' (BEPS) Project initiated by the OECD/G20 saw a final report including a total of 15 Actions that were meant to serve as a coordinating framework for national tax policies in order to prevent strategies of corporate tax planning that shift profits from high-tax to low-tax jurisdictions, thereby leading to an 'erosion' of developed countries' tax bases.[92]

Interestingly, the focus and main 'culprits' thus have shifted vis-à-vis the aforementioned 'harmful tax competition' debate: from states who present themselves as 'tax havens', thereby withdrawing fiscal revenue from other states, to corporations who evade taxation by aggressive arbitrage.[93] Prima facie, this seems to be an easy way out of political conflict over how to allocate taxation rights internationally. When the issue can be solved by enlarging the fiscal cake, that is, increasing tax revenue from sources that have until now entirely evaded the global tax radar altogether, distributional conflicts appear not as pressing. In the end, however, competitive dynamics among states seeking to secure as large a slice of that cake as possible will likely return via the regulatory back door of enabling tax planning strategies to an extent that does not violate commitments made on an international or supranational level.

this background it is difficult to define the point at which the legitimate exercise of taxation sovereignty turns into unfair "poaching" on foreign tax territory.'

[91] Economic and Financial Affairs Council, 'Conclusions of the ECOFIN Concil Meeting on 1 December 1997 concerning taxation policy' (Information) 98/C 2/01.

[92] Organization for Economic Co-Operation and Development, *Addressing the Tax Challenges of the Digital Economy, Action 1 – 2015 Final Report* (OECD Publications 2015) <http://www.oecd.org/tax/addressing-the-tax-challenges-of-the-digital-economy-action-1-2015-final-report-9789264241046-en.htm> accessed 1 August 2018.

[93] W Schön, 'Leichter auf die Anklagebank' (2014) 02 EY TAX & LAW Magazine <https://www.tax.mpg.de/fileadmin/TAX/docs/TL/WS/EY_BEPS.pdf> accessed 1 August 2018.

Regardless of the degree to which political initiatives such as the BEPS Project will in fact be able to fulfil governmental hopes that have been associated with the agreed measures, the fact that such responses are in fact being implemented in order to preserve fiscal resources under conditions of tax competition can be inferred from a number of empirical resources. Since the 1980s, the average corporation tax rate among OECD countries has fallen from almost 50 per cent to an average of under 24 per cent in 2018.[94] A similar development can be read from data on the comparative development of tax rates on capital gains versus personal income, a less mobile factor: a shift of the tax burden from mobile capital to less mobile personal income.[95]

2. CORPORATE LAW

State competition for corporate charters is another straightforward example of how regulatory dynamics can be interpreted as exhibiting the features of a competitive market. The starting point of the debate was the opposition of centralized versus state level regulation in American corporate law.

(a) Origins of the debate: charter competition in the US

One of the most vigorous debates in American corporate law scholarship during recent decades has concerned the merits of decentralized regulation regarding corporate charters. US corporations are able to 'shop around' for an incorporation law of their liking, with a vast majority domiciling in the state of Delaware, the market leader accounting for over 40 per cent of corporations whose stock is traded on the New York Stock Exchange.[96]

94 OECD Tax Database, Table II.1 Corporate Income Tax Rates (2018) <https://stats.oecd.org/index.aspx?DataSetCode=TABLE_II1> accessed 1 August 2018; P Genschel et al, 'Accelerating Downhill: How the EU Shapes Corporate Tax Competition in the Single Market' (2011) 49 Journal of Common Market Studies 585, 591; MP Devereux, B Lockwood, and M Redoano, 'Do Countries Compete over Corporate Tax Rates?' (2008) 92 Journal of Public Economics 1210 argue for this dynamic to be the result of tax competition.

95 See Chapter 3, section C.1.

96 Wagner (n 21) 1003; for a historical account of the 'incorporation market' in the US see D Charny, 'Competition among Jurisdictions in Formulating Corporate Law Rules: An American Perspective on the Race to the Bottom in the European Communities' (1991) 32 Harvard International Law Journal 423.

Critical discussion about the merits of states competing for incorporations (leading to franchise tax collection and other sources of revenue) was set off particularly by William Cary in 1974, who claimed that such regulatory competition would lead to a 'race to the bottom' instead of enhancing the quality of legal rules.[97] The dominant position in US corporate law scholarship, however, seems to have been more on the 'race to the top' side of the debate, citing shareholder benefits in particular and increased efficiency and positive welfare effects in general as reasons for a system of decentralized charter competition.[98] Recent empirical findings paint a more ambiguous picture, with some arguing that at present no race can clearly be made out from available data.[99]

(b) The race to Europe: Limited, GmbH, and UG

The debate around regulatory competition made its way to the EU in the late 1990s in the aftermath of factual developments that demanded rethinking the division of legislative authority between the EU and its Member States. A series of ECJ judgments[100]

[97] WL Cary, 'Federalism and Corporate Law: Reflections Upon Delaware' (1974) 83 Yale Law Journal 663, arguing for a 'race to the bottom'; LA Bebchuk, 'Federalism and the Corporation: The Desirable Limits on State Competition in Corporate Law' (1992) 105 Harvard Law Review 1435, arguing that regulatory competition leads to rules biased in favour of management.

[98] See, eg, RK Winter, 'State Law, Shareholder Protection, and the Theory of the Corporation' (1977) 6 Journal of Legal Studies 251; D Fischel, 'The "Race to the Bottom" Revisited: Reflections on Recent Developments in Delaware's Corporation Law' (1982) 76 Northwestern University Law Review 913; Romano (n 10), with empirical evidence for a race to the top; R Romano, *The Genius of American Corporate Law* (The AEI Press 1993); R Daines, 'Does Delaware Law Improve Firm Value?' (2001) 62 Journal of Financial Economics 525 with empirical evidence that incorporation choices account for significant differences in companies' valuations.

[99] See M Kahan and E Kamar 'The Myth of State Competition in Corporate Law' (2002) 55 Stanford Law Review 679, 684: 'Other than Delaware, no state is engaged in significant efforts to attract incorporations of public companies' (with numerous references on scholarship doubtful of the 'race' diagnosis); they acknowledge, however, that competition 'may well have existed in the past' (685), eg before network effects had cemented Delaware's position as market leader.

[100] Most notably the judgments *Centros* (n 52); *Überseering BV vs Nordic Construction Company Baumanagement GmbH (NCC)* [2002] ECLI:EU:C:2002:632; *Kamer van Koophandel en Fabrieken voor Amsterdam v Inspire Art Ltd.* [2003] ECLI:EU:C:2003:512.

on the freedom of establishment of companies and their being governed by the corporate law of the place of their incorporation (instead of their real seat, as some Member States had previously insisted) opened up de facto arbitrage opportunities for firms and founders regarding the corporate law that should govern their affairs.[101] The opinion of the Advocate General in the *Centros* case even stated explicitly that 'in the absence of harmonization, competition among rules must be allowed free play in corporate matters'.[102] This newfound mobility has led to a competition among the corporate laws of Member States, although differences to the US scenario should not be underestimated,[103] with regard to both shareholder and stakeholder structure.[104]

In a seminal study, Becht, Mayer, and Wagner showed that the number of UK Limiteds founded by Germans rose considerably in the aftermath of the *Centros* judgment, mainly driven by drastic divergences in setup costs and minimum capital requirements.[105] As a consequence, apparently unattractive features of corporate law regimes that were affected by opt-out came under

[101] Although details are at this point fundamentally unclear, what appears to be clear is that corporate mobility between the UK and other (remaining) Member States will be affected by Brexit, as both the inbound and outbound dimension of such mobility will cease to be covered by Art. 49 TFEU (freedom of establishment); on Brexit's impact on regulatory competition in European private law, including corporate law see H Eidenmüller, 'Collateral Damage: Brexit's Negative Effects on Regulatory Competition and Legal Innovation in Private Law' (2018) ECGI Working Paper 403/2018 <https://ssrn.com/abstract=3171973> accessed 1 August 2018.

[102] *Centros* (n 52), Opinion of AG La Pergola, ECLI:EU:C:1998:380, para 20 n 48.

[103] See, eg, L Enriques, 'EC Company Law and the Fears of a European Delaware' (2004) 15 European Business Law Review 1259; M Gelter, 'The Structure of Regulatory Competition in European Corporate Law' (2005) 5 Journal of Corporate Law Studies 247.

[104] Gabor (n 33) 56–8, stressing that corporate financial structure in continental Europe tends to be more bank-based as opposed to a market-based model predominant in the UK and US.

[105] B Becht, C Mayer, and HF Wagner, 'Where Do Firms Incorporate? Deregulation and the Cost of Entry' (2008) 14 Journal of Corporate Finance 241; R Braun and others, 'Does Charter Competition Foster Entrepreneurship? A Difference-in-Difference Approach to European Company Law Reforms' (2013) 51 Journal of Common Market Studies 399.

visible pressure, such as minimum capital requirements for closed corporations.[106]

Contrary to initial hopes (and fears, respectively),[107] no European Delaware has emerged. The developments following the boom of 'German Limiteds' (ie UK Limited companies founded exclusively by directors living in Germany) in the early 2000s provide a telling story. A few years into their corporate lives, large numbers of these Limiteds had already disappeared, exhibiting significantly higher rates of early mortality than traditional closed corporations set up by individuals in their home jurisdictions. Several explanations for this phenomenon have been offered, the most plausible one being that entrepreneurs had drastically underestimated the long-term costs associated with administering such 'foreign companies'.[108] Evidence of the existence of regulatory competition among Member States, however, can be

[106] Ibid; arguing against minimum capital requirements as an inappropriate regulatory tool for creditor protection J Armour, 'Share Capital and Creditor Protection: Efficient Rules for a Modern Company Law' (2000) 63 Modern Law Review 355; L Enriques and JR Macey, 'Creditors Versus Capital Formation: The Case against the European Legal Capital Rules' (2001) 86 Cornell Law Review 1165; P Mülbert and M Birke, 'Legal Capital – Is There a Case Against the European Legal Capital Rules?' (2002) 3 EBOR 695; M Kahan, 'Legal Capital Rules and the Structure of Corporate Law: Some Observations on the Difference Between European and U.S Approaches' in K Hopt and E Wymeersch, *Capital Markets and Company Law* (OUP 2003) 145.

[107] For an extensive discussion of the problems and merits of legal capital from a European perspective see the contributions in M Lutter (ed), *Legal Capital in Europe, ECFR Special Volume 1* (De Gruyter 2006a), with an overview of various pro and contra arguments by M Lutter, 'Legal Capital of Public Companies in Europe – Executive Summary of Considerations by the Expert Group on "Legal Capital in Europe"' in M Lutter (ed), *Legal Capital in Europe, ECFR Special Volume 1* (De Gruyter 2006a) 1, 2–6; for *minimum* legal capital requirements see H Eidenmüller, B Grunewald, and U Noack, 'Minimum Capital in the System of Legal Capital' in M Lutter (ed), *Legal Capital in Europe, ECFR Special Volume 1* (De Gruyter 2006a) 17.

[108] Caused, for example, by disclosure obligations, filing of annual accounts and foreign legal advice; see W-G Ringe, 'Corporate Mobility in the European Union – a Flash in the Pan? An Empirical Study in the Success of Lawmaking and Regulatory Competition' (2013) 10 European Company and Financial Law Review 230; on the behavioural dimension of this particular scenario as well as choice of law in general see H Eidenmüller and J Stark, 'Behavioral Economics and Private International Law' in J Basedow and others (eds), *European Encyclopedia of Private International Law* (Edward Elgar Publishing 2017) 171.

found in reform measures that were adopted in various European countries, with the express objective of raising their corporate forms' attractiveness in comparison to European competitors.[109] In 2008, the German *Unternehmergesellschaft* (UG) was introduced, essentially a GmbH with significantly less strict capital requirements.[110] Other European countries have recently adopted similar measures. In France, the *société à résponsabilité limitée* (S.à.r.l.) was stripped of its minimum capital requirement in 2003;[111] the Dutch *besloten vennootschap* (BV) followed in 2012 (becoming a 'Flex BV').[112]

To sum up, while the normative assessment of regulatory competition in corporate law has sparked vigorous debate, its mere existence has come to be an accepted fact not only in the US, but also in European corporate law,[113] illustrated most visibly by pressure on minimum capital requirements for closed corporations.[114]

(c) Corporate governance issues: employee representation

One of the more controversial instances of regulatory competition can be found in the corporate governance issue of employee representation in European stock companies. What is the rationale

[109] L Enriques and M Gelter, 'Regulatory Competition in European Company Law and Creditor Protection' in H Eidenmüller and W Schön, *The Law and Economics of Creditor Protection* (TMC Asser Press 2008) 421, 428: 'The final outcome of this process may be the practical elimination of minimum capital requirements'.

[110] According to §5a(1), 5(2) of the 2008 German Limited Liability Companies Act (*Gesetz betreffend die Gesellschaften mit beschränkter Haftung*, GmbHG), a minimum capital of €1 per shareholder is required, however, subject to additional constraints regarding raising and maintenance of capital, such as a yearly reserve to be accumulated until the level of €25,000 is achieved and the UG converts into a regular GmbH.

[111] Loi n° 2003-721 du 1 août 2003 pour l'initiative économique, 13449.

[112] 2012 Act for Simplification and Flexibilisation of Private Company Law (*Wet Vereenvoudiging en Flexibilisering BV-Recht*) (NL); for an assessment of the Dutch reform activities see C Van der Elst and E Vermeulen, 'The Dutch Private Company: Successfully Relaunched?' (2013) ECGI Law Working Paper No 215/2013 <http://ssrn.com/abstract=2267522> accessed 1 August 2018.

[113] For influential voices from the German perspective see Eidenmüller (n 24); Kieninger (n 57) Part 2; D Zimmer, 'Zwischen Theorie und Empirie: Zur Konkurrenz der Gesetzgeber im Gesellschaftsrecht' in G Bitter and others (eds), *Festschrift für Karsten Schmidt zum 70. Geburtstag* (Dr Otto Schmidt 2009) 1789, 1800: 'Wir haben ihn also unbestreitbar, den Wettbewerb der Gesellschaftsrechte.'

[114] Enriques and Gelter (n 109) 428.

behind mandatory law prescribing co-determination mechanisms? Much of the debate about co-determination has been focused on the question of its merits and problems in economic terms.[115] While some claim that mandatory co-determination cannot be Pareto-optimal and must lead to inefficient organizational structures of companies, others have attested a positive influence of co-determination on overall economic performance and productivity. Various forms of economic arguments in favour of co-determination have been brought forward: from the correction of market failure[116] to the improvement of management-labour relations that increase worker motivation and identification, which in turn are conducive to a cooperative relationship built on social peace that ensures long-term productivity.[117]

Others have stressed non-economic arguments for co-determination, particularly in the German form of parity employee representation on corporate boards. Mandatory co-determination is justified by reference to the realization and protection of values such as distributive justice in a context that is characterized by a structural asymmetry of power.[118] Legislation is thus meant to increase bargaining power on the employee side, informed by their comparative vulnerability in large companies. In Germany, parity employee representation is perceived as 'part of democratic culture', a central part of the German social welfare

[115] FR Fitzroy and K Kraft, 'Co-Determination, Efficiency and Productivity' (2005) 43 British Journal of Industrial Relations 233.

[116] SN Smith, 'On the Economic Rationale for Codetermination Law' (1991) 16 Journal of Economic Behavior and Organization 261.

[117] For an overview see M Gelter, 'Tilting the Balance between Capital and Labor? The Effects of Regulatory Arbitrage in European Corporate Law on Employees' (2010) 33 Fordham International Law Journal 792; a further advantage is seen by some in the expectation that mandatory co-determination 'discourages wasteful behavior such as strikes or lock-outs'; G Bachmann and H Richter, 'Contracting Co-Determination: The SE-Directive as a Model?' in H Eidenmüller (ed), *Regulatory Competition in Contract Law and Dispute Resolution* (CH Beck 2013) 192.

[118] HA Henzler, 'The New Era of Euro capitalism' (1992) 70 Harvard Buisness Review 60: 'Laws on co-determination, combined with a tradition of patriarchal concern, have made European CEOs deeply committed to their employees, treating them more like partners in a long-term enterprise than anonymous factors of production.'

state, and enjoys widespread political support,[119] despite calls for reform such as a departure from its paritarian design.

Two recent changes in European corporate law have led to a considerable increase of arbitrage opportunities. First, the introduction of the SE[120] as a new, hybrid company form, and second, the Cross-Border Mergers Directive that has been merged into the 2017 Directive relating to certain aspects of company law.[121] The new system aims at protecting the co-determination regime that was present in a corporation before conversion into an SE or merger with a foreign corporate entity. However, the bargaining approach taken (negotiations with employee representatives as to the future level of representation are possible) is structured such that, in the long run, protection of the prior regime is ineffective.[122]

Anecdotal evidence points to the conclusion that board representation is in fact one of the aspects contributing significantly to German corporations' decisions to transform into an SE and thus be able to contract with the employee side into a different representation arrangement.[123] So far, Europe has seen no examples of mandatory co-determination regimes crumbling under the pressure of corporations' mass conversion into SEs. The case for factual regulatory competition with clearly identifiable supply reactions thus is currently not terribly strong. 'Yet', one might add, as the SE regime has been on offer for a relatively short time.

[119] Bachmann and Richter (n 117) 187.

[120] Council Regulation (EC) 2157/2001 on the Statute for a European Company (SE) [2001] OJ L294/1; Council Directive (EC) 2001/86 supplementing the Statute for a European Company with regard to the involvement of employees [2001] OJ L294/22.

[121] European Parliament and Council Directive (EC) 2005/56 on cross-border mergers of limited liability companies [2005] OJ L310/1; European Parliament and Council Directive (EU) 2017/1132 relating to certain aspects of company law [2017] OJ L169/46.

[122] Gelter (n 117) 810–18, 852–5, describing strategic moves (such as merging with a foreign corporate entity) that can be employed to evade current representation regimes, at least after a period of two to three years.

[123] Eidenmüller, Engert, and Hornuf (n 27) 25; H Eidenmüller, L Hornuf, and M Reps, 'Contracting Employee Involvement: An Analysis of Bargaining over Employee Involvement Rules for a Societas Europaea' in H Eidenmüller (ed), *Regulatory Competition in Contract Law and Dispute Resolution* (CH Beck 2013) 155, 156, 160–1; a discussion of these studies is provided by Bachmann and Richter (n 117).

Mid- and long-term effects remain to be seen, with prominent voices expecting that the new situation will lead to an 'erosion of co-determination',[124] at least from the German perspective.

3. CONTRACT LAW

The case for the existence of regulatory competition in contract law is not as straightforward. As far as the preconditions of competition are concerned, contract law is a probable candidate. First, there is legal diversity in the form of differing contract law regimes on offer both on a national and supranational level;[125] and, second, mobility regarding the applicable contract law comes to a large extent without the costs of a physical component. In contract law, choice of law enjoys widespread recognition.[126]

Regulatory competition in contract law is disputed, however, on the grounds of lacking incentives to engage in market behaviour both on the demand and on the supply side.[127] Both business and consumer 'customers' of contract law, it has been argued, are rationally disinterested in the substantive characteristics of the contract law applicable to a transaction and that choice of

[124] Gelter (n 117) 852–5; M Habersack, 'Grundsatzfragen der Mitbestimmung in SE und SCE sowie bei grenzüberschreitender Verschmelzung' (2007) 171 Zeitschrift für das gesamte Handels- und Wirtschaftsrecht 613, 643; C Teichmann, 'Verhandelte Mitbestimmung für Auslandsgesellschaften' (2009) 30 Zeitschrift für Wirtschaftsrecht 1787.

[125] Such legal diversity pertains not only to inevitable formal details, but can be found on a more abstract and general level, as comparisons between English and German contract law have found: see H Koetz, 'The Jurisdiction of Choice: England and Wales or Germany?' (2010) 6 European Review of Private Law 1243, 1248: '[W]hat does emanate from English law is a certain commercial flavour and a particular belief that, at least in some cases, it is better—in the words of Roy Goode – "that the law should be certain than that in every case it should be just".'; P Legrand, 'Pre-Contractual Disclosure and Information: English and French Law Compared' (1986) 6 Oxford Journal of Legal Studies 322, 349.

[126] G Rühl, 'Choice of Law by the Parties' in J Basedow, K J Hopt, and R Zimmermann (eds), *Max Planck Encyclopedia of European Private Law* (OUP 2012) 190; many legal regimes restrict choice of law opportunities in B2C transactions, such as Art. 6(2) Rome I Regulation regarding cross-border consumer contracts in the EU.

[127] Among those who deny that there is regulatory competition in contract law are Kieninger (n 57) 275–332; Wagner (n 21); Vogenauer (n 5); Vogenauer (n 69).

law is primarily driven by other factors, such as familiarity and language.[128] On the supply side, critics see a lack of incentives to compete,[129] absent direct advantages such as revenues from franchise taxes to be gained.

Others have stressed that there are signs of competitive dynamics among suppliers of contract law on an EU as well as a global level,[130] as illustrated by the aforementioned 'battle of the brochures'. Characteristics of legal rules need not be the only factor determining choice of law in order to feed competition among suppliers: their relevance for choice may suffice.[131] With respect to the European context, there is evidence that states do in fact respond to competitive pressure on their contract law by implementing law reforms, such as seen in Germany and the Netherlands as well as in a number of Eastern European countries (ie Estonia, Hungary, Lithuania, Poland, and Romania).[132]

One of the more specific issues arguably driving arbitrage in European contract law is judicial review of standard terms in B2B contracts according to standards of fairness, as practiced notably in Germany, [133] contrary to English[134] or Swiss law. Different approaches to such terms are particularly relevant when the validity

[128] H Eidenmüller, 'What Can Be Wrong with an Option? An Optional Common European Sales Law as a Regulatory Tool' (2013) 50 Common Market Law Review 69, 74 and Kieninger (n 57) 311–14 for B2C contracts; Vogenauer (n 5) 48, 51–2, 59, 71–3; Wagner (n 21) 1006–13.

[129] Kieninger (n 57) 286–94.

[130] Eidenmüller (n 24) 719–22; R Van den Bergh, 'Subsidiarity as an Economic Demarcation Principle and the Emergence of European Private Law' (1998) 5 Maastricht Journal of European and Comparative Law 129.

[131] Rühl (n 126) 288.

[132] Ibid 288–9 with detailed references to the respective reform acts.

[133] S Brachert and A Dietzel, 'Editorial: Deutsche AGB – Rechtsprechung und Flucht ins Schweizer Recht' [2005] Zeitschrift für das gesamte Schuldrecht 441; KP Berger, 'Abschied von der Privatautonomie im unternehmerischen Geschäftsverkehr? Zum Differenzierungsgebot im AGB-Recht' [2006] Zeitschrift für Wirtschaftsrecht 2149; J Lischek and V Mahnken, 'Vertragsverhandlungen zwischen Unternehmen und AGB – Anmerkungen aus der Sicht der Praxis' [2007] Zeitschrift für Wirtschaftsrecht 158; Eidenmüller (n 24) 720–2 with reference to the subissue bond conditions in particular, including a reform of the German Bond Act in 2009 that may plausibly interpreted as an answer to perceived competitive pressure.

[134] As with regard to corporate law, the consequences of Brexit in terms of legal mobility, albeit hard to foresee at this point, will likely be substantial: see

of standard clauses that exclude or limit liability is concerned.[135] Recent criticism of the German approach paired with a call for reform thus comes as no surprise.[136]

Even if there are reasons to remain sceptical about the intensity of regulatory competition in contract law, particularly in Europe, there is reason to believe that policy efforts in the EU point towards fostering regulatory competition. One of the signs for these efforts was the proposal of a Common European Sales Law (CESL)[137] that, had it come into existence, would have opened up a vertical dimension of regulatory competition among Member States' respective sales laws and the new European instrument.

4. LABOUR LAW

The debate about regulatory competition in labour law shows parallels to that in tax law. The main issues that cause arbitrage and competitive responses among legislators are labour standards imposing mandatory requirements on employers, for example, in terms of minimum wages, safety protections, arbitrary discharge opportunities, or the protection of collective bargaining.[138] This

C MacMillan, 'Brexit, Business and Trade: The Impact of Brexit upon English Contract Law' (2016) 27 King's Law Journal 420; Eidenmüller (n 101) 19.

[135] For a comparative discussion of the treatment of such clauses on a national as well as supranational level see I Schwenzer and C Whitebread, 'International B2B Contracts – Freedom Unchained?' (2015) 4 Penn State Journal of Law and International Affairs 33.

[136] T Pfeifer, 'Flucht ins schweizerische Recht' in FC Genzow, B Grunewald, and H Schulte-Nölke (eds), *Zwischen Vertragsfreiheit und Verbraucherschutz – Festschrift für Friedrich Graph von Westphalen* (Dr Otto Schmidt 2010) 555; Eidenmüller (n 24) 720–1.

[137] Commission, 'Proposal for a regulation of the European Parliament and of the Council on a Common European Sales Law' COM/2011/0635 final; on the CESL and vertical regulatory competition in European contract law Eidenmüller (n 128).

[138] W Sengenberger, 'Labour Standards: An Institutional Framework for Restructuring and Development' in W Sengenberger and D Campbell (eds), *Creating Economic Opportunities: The Role of Labour Standards in Industrial Restructuring* (International Institute for Labour Studies 1994) 3 distinguishes two meanings of the term 'labour standard': its descriptive meaning refers to the 'actual terms of employment [. . .] at a particular location and point in time', whereas in a normative sense such standards 'specify rights, such as the right to form associations of workers and employers, and the right to bargain collectively; they stipulate

comes as no surprise because such standards can, and often are, interpreted, albeit rather simplistically, as a tax increasing the costs of labour in a given jurisdiction.[139] Standards with a redistributive component (such as minimum wage) are most likely to come under pressure through regulatory competition, that is, jurisdictions relaxing such standards in the hope of reducing cost of labour, thereby attracting mobile investment of capital.[140]

States' efforts to prevent or reign in competitive dynamics with respect to labour standards have a long history, as seen, for example, in the Treaty of Versailles that includes an agreement to establish conventions on certain minimum standards,[141] with the effect of removing legal diversity required for competitive manoeuvres. Recent developments in ECJ case law on employers' arbitrage opportunities show an interestingly straightforward restriction of the principle of territoriality regarding mandatory labour standards.[142] In the path-breaking judgments

normative rules such as minimum wages, or maximum hours per week, or rules of conduct and dispute resolution.'

[139] D Charny, 'Regulatory Competition and Labour Law Standards' in DC Esty and D Geradin (eds), *Regulatory Competition and Economic Integration: Comparative Perspectives* (OUP 2001) 311, 312: 'A natural way to view a labor standard is as a tax on labor; the funds from the tax are used to confer a public good', with a subsequent offering (315–23) of a typology of labour standards that distinguishes between various policy objectives, eg redistribution versus empowerment; in an EU context, the policy objective of common labour standards among Member States is not necessarily strict parity of labour costs across the EU ('level playing field'), but according to S Deakin and F Wilkinson, 'Rights v Efficiency? The Economic Case for Transnational Labor Standards' (1994) 23 Industrial Law Journal 289, 305 instead the 'setting of a minimum floor below which state regulation may not fall, thereby seeking to prevent destructive competition between states'.

[140] Charny (2001), 322, 323: 'It is a familiar lesson from the tax literature that a jurisdiction pursues suboptimal redistributive policies when faced with competition from other jursidictions: those subject to the redistributive exactions leave the jurisdiction, while those who benefit flock to it.'

[141] Treaty of Versailles, signed 28 June 1919 in the Palace of Versailles, France, effective 10 January 1920, Part XIII, Section I, bridge yearbook stating that 'Labor is not a commodity'; upon this agreement, the Internal Labor Organization was founded with the aim of coordinating international labour law by conventions to be adopted by its member states. See also Collins (2013), 121; for an overview of the economic arguments pro and contra transnational labour standards see Deakin and Wilkinson (n 138).

[142] S Deakin, 'Regulatory Competition After Laval' (2007) 10 Cambridge Yearbook of European Legal Studies 581; Z Adams and S Deakin, 'Freedom of

Viking[143] and *Laval*,[144] the Court qualified union action against the exercise of arbitrage opportunities (such as, in the *Viking* case, re-flagging of vessels with the objective of wage reductions possible under the law of the flag state while operating on the territory of another state) as an unjustified restriction of the freedom of establishment (Art. 49 TFEU).

Comparative analyses of recent empirical data on the evolution of labour rights indices that go beyond the EU context have come to the conclusion that, at least considering the last decades of the twentieth century, there is robust evidence of states actively competing for the attraction of foreign direct investment by lowering labour standards.[145] Interestingly, the use of labour standards as a vehicle to attract investment comes in different forms. Whereas in OECD countries competition is driven primarily by changes in the legal rules on labour standards themselves, less developed countries appear to compete by leaving the legal landscape intact and instead relaxing *enforcement* of labour laws.[146]

5. INSOLVENCY LAW

Competitive dynamics on the supply side of insolvency law and its handling in particular proceedings could be witnessed among US states and their bankruptcy courts as well since the early

Establishment and Regulatory Competition' in D Chalmers and A Arnull (eds), *The Oxford Handbook of European Union Law* (OUP 2015) 537, 556: '[T]he effect of that case [ie *Laval* [2005] ECLI:EU:C:2007:809 (hereafter *Laval*)] is to allow a foreign service provider to retain the benefit of the (less regulatory) home state regime when operating on the territory of the (more regulatory) host state. [. . .] This is not *permitting* regulatory arbitrage, so much as *mandating* it.'

143 *Viking* [2007] ECLI:EU:C:2007:772 (hereafter *Viking*); Adams and Deakin (n 141) 556 state that '[I]n Viking, the Court [asserted] that encouraging regulatory arbitrage was the *purpose* of the internal market laws', however without citing a particular section of the *Viking* case.

144 *Laval* [2005] ECLI:EU:C:2007:809.

145 RB Davies and KC Vadlamannati, 'A Race to the Bottom in Labor Standards? An Empirical Investigation' (2013) 103 Journal of Development Economics 1; W Olney, 'A Race to the Bottom? Employment Protection and Foreign Direct Investment' (2013) 91 Journal of International Economics 191.

146 Davies and Vadlamannati (n 144) 12: '[C]ompetition in practices is most evident for non-OECD countries, [while] OECD nations seem to compete in laws.'

1990s.[147] Courts in the state of New York and again Delaware were particularly active in their pursuit of competitive success in the marketplace for 'bankruptcy business'. The means of choice were demonstrated friendliness to the 'case placers', that is, regularly current management of distressed companies and the bankruptcy bar:[148] 'The race to the bottom competition that resulted from unilateral choice of the bankruptcy forum has favoured those courts that adopted a passive attitude, rubber-stamping management's proposals regarding asset sales, critical vendor lists, and pre-packaged plans.'[149]

In Europe, regulatory competition in company insolvency law has received considerable attention in recent years, particularly after the European Insolvency Regulation (EIR)[150] came into force and—against its original intentions—[151] proved to provide a fruitful basis for 'forum shopping' by companies in search of a suitable place for restructuring.[152] Article 3 EIR identifies the jurisdiction of main insolvency proceedings as the 'centre of a debtor's main interests' (COMI), a criterion that has proven to be too ambiguous and open to manipulation.[153] Unsurprisingly, regulatory arbitrage in insolvency law 'has become an everyday

[147] For a critical diagnosis of competition among US states and courts for 'bankruptcy business' see L LoPucki, *Courting Failure – How Competition for Big Cases is Corrupting the Bankruptcy Courts* (University of Michigan Press 2005); against LoPucki's analysis of available data on the above average recidivism of companies after bankruptcy proceedings in Delaware see D Baird and R Rasmussen, 'Beyond Recidivism' (2006) 54 Buffalo Law Review 343, with further references on available empirical data.

[148] LoPucki (n 146) 49–76, 124–8, 137–8; L LoPucki and J Doherty, 'Bankruptcy Fire Sales' (2007) 106 Michigan Law Review 140–41; Wagner (n 66) 1088.

[149] LoPucki (n 146) 137.

[150] Council Regulation (EC) 1346/2000 on insolvency proceedings (EIR) [2000] OJ L160/1.

[151] See Recital 4 of the EIR: '[I]t is necessary for the proper functioning of the internal market to avoid incentives for the parties to transfer assets or judicial proceedings from one Member State to another, seeking to obtain a more favourable legal position (forum shopping)'; see Enriques and Gelter (n 109) 441.

[152] H Eidenmüller, 'Wettbewerb der Insolvenzrechte' (2006) 35 Zeitschrift für Unternehmens- und Gesellschaftsrecht 467, 474–9; Eidenmüller (n 24) 724; Enriques and Gelter (n 109) 440–53.

[153] H Eidenmüller, 'Abuse of Law in the Context of European Insolvency Law' (2009) 6 European Company and Financial Law Review 1.

legal reality'[154] under the EIR. Suitability of a jurisdiction, from a debtor's perspective, is determined by factors such as the length of proceedings (the quicker the better) or the amount of control that remains in the debtor's hands, for example, by being able to choose an insolvency administrator (versus having to accept a court appointed administrator) or to retain prior management. For these reasons, a number of German companies have migrated their COMI to London in the vicinity of insolvency,[155] prompting reform considerations regarding company insolvency law in the German Ministry of Justice that were implemented in the recent past.[156]

Aside from corporate insolvency proceedings, private insolvency matters have been shown to be sensitive to legal arbitrage as well, with the main motivation to 'shop' for a suitable insolvency forum being the availability and minimum length of waiting periods before residual debt discharge can be achieved.[157] Whereas in some jurisdictions discharge was historically unknown, others have been far more liberal. From the perspective of the individual, a difference of one or two years that have to be waited before a 'fresh start' is possible may in many cases be incentive enough to offset the costs incurred by physically moving into the territorial reach of another jurisdiction. Whereas in Germany discharge is regularly granted six years after the opening of insolvency proceedings (three years under additional conditions after a reform in 2014),[158] France offers significantly quicker discharge opportunities of a few months in some cases.[159]

[154] Eidenmüller (n 24) 724, giving examples of German companies (Schefenacker, Deutsche Nickel) that were transformed into English companies with a COMI in London before entering restructuring proceedings there.

[155] Ibid.

[156] See the 2012 German Act on Further Facilitating the Restructuring of Distressed Companies (*Gesetz zur weiteren Erleichterung der Sanierung von Unternehmen*, ESUG).

[157] Eidenmüller (n 24) 725 with the example of Germans who have 'recently begun to navigate their private insolvency matters to France'.

[158] §287(2) 2014 German Insolvency Code (*Insolvenzordnung*, InsO); since July 2014, §300(1) Nr. 2 InsO allows for discharge after three years under the condition that the proceedings' costs and 35 per cent of debts have been settled; §300 (1) Nr. 3 InsO permits the court to grant discharge after five years, if the proceedings' costs have been paid.

[159] Eidenmüller (n 152); Eidenmüller (n 24) 725.

A comparative picture of the supply side with respect to discharge periods in Europe shows a tendency towards lower barriers, with a period of three years as an emerging minimum standard.[160] The Republic of Ireland has taken radical steps towards liberalizing the conditions for debt discharge in 2012, when a twelve-year period was replaced by, in the regular case, three years.[161]

6. DISPUTE RESOLUTION

On the first page of their seminal 1979 paper titled 'Adjudication as a Private Good', Elizabeth Landes and Richard Posner observe that '[e]ven economists who assign a highly limited role to government consider the provision of judicial services an indisputably apt function of government'.[162] Notwithstanding this traditional conception of adjudication, that is, in the picture of a state versus market divide an activity that falls into the proper confines of the former, forum competition between venues and their structural conditions of dispute resolution is very much happening. Gerhard Wagner has distinguished two dimensions of such competition in the market for adjudication: 'In reaction to challenges from arbitral institutions and from jurisdictions overseas, states have reformed their judicial systems in order to make them more attractive to litigants'.[163] Not only is there forum competition between national courts, but also between suppliers of

[160] B O'Neill, 'A Minimum Standard for Debt Discharge in Europe?' [2014] The Commercial Law Practicioner 156, 163.

[161] Ibid 156.

[162] EM Landes and RA Posner, 'Adjudication as a Private Good' (1979) 8 The Journal of Legal Studies 235, citing Adam Smith as one of those economists, see A Smith, *An Inquiry into the Nature and Causes of the Wealth of Nations* (RH Campbell and AS Skinner eds, first published 1776, OUP 1979); anthropological studies on dispute resolution in primitive societies show that rule-based adjudication as a social practice precedes even the existence of a state in its wider modern understanding, see Landes and Posner (n 161) 242–5 with further references.

[163] G Wagner, 'Dispute Resolution as a Product: Competition between Civil Justice Systems' in H Eidenmüller (ed), *Regulatory Competition in Contract Law and Dispute Resolution* (Beck 2013) 347, 348; see also the revised version in Wagner (n 66) 1097, stressing the often 'virtual' nature of choice: 'The choice of a particular court or other dispute resolution mechanism does not force citizens to physically leave their jurisdiction in order to relocate elsewhere. Instead, similar to the case of choice of law, firms and consumers may make "virtual" choices, ie opt in favour

state adjudication and non-state arbitration, mediation, and other forms of dispute resolution.[164]

(a) Judicial services

The locational dimension of regulatory competition among state courts as venues for dispute resolution cuts across several fields of law. Disputes are mobile in the sense that there is more than one adjudicative forum with (potential) jurisdiction. The exercise of such mobility may occur shortly before the adjudicative process, or further in advance, such as in the form of a contractual choice of law and accompanying forum clause.[165] There is a case to be made that court competition for cases is problematic particularly when forum shopping is driven by one side of the dispute to be settled.[166] In some fields more than others, when plaintiffs are those who decide where to file a case given a choice between several venues,[167] courts appear to 'outperform each other in becoming ever more plaintiff-friendly'.[168]

In patent litigation, for example, this dynamic is observable: courts in several US states are vying for the status as so-called 'rocket dockets', for being known for speedy disposition of cases and, as it appears, for having a tendency to favour plaintiffs'

of a mechanism of dispute resolution without changing their permanent affiliation with a particular jurisdiction and its system of civil justice'.

[164] In the course of this study, only arbitration will be given a closer look, as it is the 'prime contender' of all methods of alternative dispute resolution; see N Blackaby and others (eds), *Redfern and Hunter on International Arbitration* (6th ed. OUP 2015) para 1.01: 'International Arbitration has become the principal method of resolving disputes between States, individuals, and corporations in almost every aspect of international trade, commerce, and investment.'

[165] An empirical study of the frequency of such clauses and their content in contracts of publicly-held companies in the US is provided by T Eisenberg and GP Miller, 'The Flight to New York: An Empirical Study of Choice of Law and Choice of Forum Clauses in Publicly-Held Companies' Contracts' (2009) 30 Cardozo Law Review 1475.

[166] Wagner (n 66) 1089: '[U]nilateral choice, inevitable as it may be, is something the legal system needs to worry about and should take care to limit and rein in.'

[167] Landes and Posner (n 161) 254.

[168] Wagner (n 66) 1087.

interests, or a perceived 'pro-patentee bias', as in the case of Eastern District of Texas courts.[169]

When forum selection is exercised 'bilaterally' in the form of a contractual agreement, however, supply side incentives to provide an attractive offer to all involved in the choice make one-sided bias less likely,[170] at least absent information asymmetries and significant discrepancies in bargaining power at the time of choice, a qualification that is met in practice less often than one would hope for.[171] The problem is familiar from the context of consumers' consent to standard form contracts that they neither read nor understand.[172] Legislative solutions include a far-reaching ban of choice of forum clauses in consumer contracts, or judicial review of such clauses as to their unfairness towards the consumer.[173]

(b) Adjudication versus alternative dispute resolution

One of the factors that drive arbitrage regarding the method and forum of dispute resolution is the cross-border enforceability of binding judgments. In this respect, arbitration has its advantages, as arbitral awards are internationally enforceable under the New York Convention[174] that has—so far—been signed by 159[175] countries.[176] Other reasons for 'opting out' of dispute resolution

[169] S Vishnubhakat, 'Reconceiving the Patent Rocket Docket: An Empirical Study of Infringement Litigation 1985–2010' (2011) 11 The John Marshall Review of Intellectual Property Law 58, 69.

[170] Wagner (n 66) 1089; Dammann and Hansmann (n 66) have argued for competition among jurisdictions for commercial cases, and with the suggestion of permitting differentiated court fees to strengthen incentives for jurisdictions to offer attractive judicial services. They, too, restrict their argument to bilateral choice of forum (15).

[171] EA O'Hara and LE Ribstein, 'From Politics to Efficiency in the Choice of Law' (2000) 67 University of Chicago Law Review 1151, 1186.

[172] See §38 of the 2005 German Code of Civil Procedure (*Zivilprozessordnung*, ZPO).

[173] See US case law, eg *Carnival Cruise Lines v Shute* [1991] 499 US 585, 593–4; *Caspi v Microsoft Network* [1999] 732 A.2d 528, 531 (NJ Super Ct).

[174] New York Convention on the Recognition and Enforcement of Foreign Arbitral Awards (1958).

[175] The current number can be found at <http://www.newyorkconvention.org/list+of+contracting+states> accessed 1 August 2018.

[176] EA O'Hara O'Connor, 'Jurisdictional Competition for Dispute Resolution: Courts versus Arbitration' in H Eidenmüller (ed), *Regulatory*

before state courts into private venues, particularly in the US legal system, are 'features that private parties condemn, including extensive discovery, jury trials, potential class actions, and punitive damages remedies'.[177] Another factor is language: when the working language in a relationship among international partners is English, settling disputes in any other language is unattractive as it creates additional costs (for interpretation, translation, etc) as well as insecurity.

The language issue provides an illustrative example of legislators' reform activities that are openly motivated by reasons of competitive success vis-à-vis both foreign state courts and arbitration (which is susceptible to parties' choice of language). In Germany, after experimenting with English as a courtroom language in several regional courts,[178] a proposal to generally amend the German Code of Civil Procedure that would allow courts to establish special 'Chambers for International Commercial Matters' (*Kammern für internationale Handelssachen*) has been introduced into the parliamentary process.[179] The proposal has drawn extensive debate. Some emphasize the positive effects that a departure from the current 'The courtroom language is German'[180] would entail for Germany as a jurisdiction of choice,[181] whereas sceptics[182] argue that the courtroom language is part of national and cultural identity and thus should not be amended for reasons

Competition in Contract Law and Dispute Resolution (CH Beck 2009) 428; Wagner (n 66) 1137.

177 O'Hara O'Connor (n 175) 430.

178 M von Pommern-Peglow, 'Deutsche Zivilgerichte im internationalen Wettbewerb' [2015] Zeitschrift für Rechtspolitik 178.

179 See Bundesrat Drucksache 53/18 of 2 March 2018, <https://www.bundesrat.de/drs.html?id=53-18> accessed 1 August 2018.

180 §184 of the 2006 German Judicial Systems Act (*Gerichtsverfassungsgesetz*, G VG).

181 C Armbrüster, 'Englischsprachige Zivilprozesse vor deutschen Gerichten?' (2011) 44 Zeitschrift für Rechtspolitik 102;

182 See A Flessner, 'Deutscher Zivilprozess auf Englisch – Der Gesetzentwurf des Bundesrats im Lichte von Staatsrecht, Grundrechten und Europarecht' (2011) Neue Juristische Online Zeitschrift 1913 with an overview of arguments, including systematic and constitutional frictions.

of competitive success in a global marketplace for high volume commercial disputes.[183]

C. CONCLUSION

There is considerable debate about whether particular instances of developments in specific fields are properly interpreted as regulatory competition or under the heading of a different paradigm.[184] All in all, however, there is convincing evidence of competitive dynamics among lawmakers to support the claim that law markets have come into existence and continue to develop in a growing number of fields, with overall increasing intensity.

The factual instances of regulatory competition that have been discussed in this chapter provide an overview of possible reactions and strategies that suppliers of legal rules can in theory and do in practice employ in order to deal with regulatory competition. First, regulatory competition may be prevented or restricted by removing or at least reducing its structural preconditions (diversity and mobility). Second, a competitive scenario may be taken as given and be either ignored or adapted to. Such adaptation comes in two forms: (i) imitation of successful players and their legal products, or (ii) legal innovation with the goal of an even more attractive product than those currently on offer. Third (and possibly in addition to adaptive strategies), political efforts may be put into increasing arbitrage opportunities and low-cost mobility on a national, international, or supranational level.

In the end, regulatory competition, when it occurs, appears to be one instance of locational competition and to follow its

[183] Flessner (n 181) 1924: 'Der Staat scheint selbst auf einem zentralen Funktionsbereich zu erwägen, teils sogar bereit zu sein, seine eigene Sprache – neben dem Territorium sein festestes Identitätsmerkmal – für erhoffte Wettbewerbsvorteile und Zusatzeinnahmen der Disposition privater Parteien preiszugeben – die Sprache des deutschen Staates wird von diesem selbst für verhandelbar erklärt auf dem Markt.' See also von Pommern-Peglow (n 177) 178 with reference to similar debates in Israel.

[184] A large body of literature deals with this question based on empirical data, mostly with regard to the de facto evolution of (US and European) company law, see section B.2.

patterns.[185] The above-mentioned 'battle of the brochures' can be seen as one aspect of the larger phenomenon of 'political marketing', the key figures of which have discovered legal rules as a potentially powerful instrument to attract capital and labour,[186] as Hugh Collins has put it in rather sharp words:

> Unfortunately, regulatory competition may equally prove to be one weapon in the armoury of imperial states, by assisting their aim to preserve and enhance their prosperity and power through the acquisition and subjugation of territory, raw materials, and populations of cheap labour.[187]

The examples of regulatory competition that offer the most compelling evidence of legislative orientation towards the demands of a real or perceived law market are best understood as instances of defensive competition.[188] The objective of attracting foreign opt-in appears to be comparatively weaker than a strong motivation to keep domestic legal subjects from exercising opt-out possibilities.

Nevertheless, what we have seen is that regulatory competition, as a theoretical framework within which the creation and evolution of legal rules can be analysed, is more than a negligible niche phenomenon. The law market perspective allows an analysis of the law that takes into account the fact that we live in an increasingly globalized world, with interconnections on many levels, such as the political, legal, economic, and cultural sphere. In the following chapters, we will therefore consider the arguments that have been presented both in favour of and against regulatory competition as a policy approach.

[185] To this effect H Collins, 'Regulatory Competition in International Trade: Transnational Regulation through Standard Form Contracts' in H Eidenmüller (ed), *Regulatory Competition in Contract Law and Dispute Resolution* (CH Beck 2013) 121; Ogus (n 56); Peters (n 25) 51.

[186] J Kersten and U Battis, *Standortmarketing im Bundesstaat* (Duncker and Humblot 2008); J Kersten, 'Standortmarketing für die Bundesrepublik - verfassungsrechtliche Rahmenbedingungen und verwaltungsrechtliche Steuerung der Werbung für den Investitions- und Wirtschaftsstandort Deutschland' [2008] Verwaltungsarchiv 30.

[187] Collins (n 186) 121.

[188] A theoretical explanation with regard to European company law is given by Klöhn (n 26) 293–8.

2

THE ECONOMIC CASE FOR REGULATORY COMPETITION

The purpose of this chapter is to give a brief overview of the theoretical case for regulatory competition as it has been discussed among economically inclined legal scholars. What are its advantages? What kinds of positive effects does it promise to lead to, from a theoretical perspective?[1] Before assuming a critical perspective on regulatory competition, the arguments of its proponents should be heard (section A). In the second part of the chapter, we will then look at points of criticism that have been discussed within law and economics discourse (section B).

A. PROMISES OF REGULATORY COMPETITION

The advantages that have been associated with regulatory competition are, unsurprisingly, closely linked to the advantages of competitive markets in general, among them the satisfaction of diverse preferences, preservation of individual freedom, and the taming of the Leviathan state that would over-regulate and overtax if unrestrained. Competition, welfare economists argue almost unanimously, is the structural element of choice when it comes to building a framework that promotes progress:

> It is generally accepted by economists that competition is an essential precondition for the increase of welfare in that it induces individuals to develop, for a specific problem, different solutions among which, in the course of time, inadequate solutions will be substituted by more efficient ones. Simultaneously, competition prevents the stabilization of

[1] Questions as to how to interpret *empirical* evidence on legal arbitrage and supply side reaction, whether we see competitive dynamics at all, and, if so, whether they show a race to the bottom or the top, are discussed in Chapter 1, section B.

accumulated power and thus enhances the preservation of individual freedom.[2]

1. DISCOVERY OF EFFICIENT LEGISLATIVE SOLUTIONS

In federalist systems characterized by decentralized regulatory authorities and a certain degree of mobility among regulatees, diverse legislative products offered will enjoy differing degrees of success. Diversity and experimentation are promoted.[3] Market interaction, the argument continues, will further enable suppliers of law to identify potential for improvement.[4]

Competition has been characterized as a discovery procedure for efficient legislative solutions under conditions of dispersed and undisclosed knowledge.[5] Market settings do a better job of revealing people's actual preferences and translating them into adequate supply (via the price mechanism and competitive pressure on suppliers) than a top-down approach ever could. The epistemic argument for competitive markets is closely tied to a subjectivist conception of welfare.[6] Within the theoretical framework of

[2] L Gerken, 'Introduction' in L Gerken (ed), *Competition among Institutions* (Macmillan 1995) x.

[3] S Deakin, 'Legal Diversity and Regulatory Competition: Which Model for Europe?' (2006) 12 European Law Journal 440, 441.

[4] Ibid 441–2: '[B]y providing mechanisms for the preferences of the different users of laws to be expressed and for alternative solutions to common problems to be compared, it enhances the flow of information on what works in practice.'

[5] The idea of competition as a discovery procedure goes back to the writings of Friedrich von Hayek. In his seminal paper 'Competition as a Discovery Procedure', however, not much is to be found in terms of explanation as to how exactly competition can foster epistemological progress, see FA Hayek, 'Competition as a Discovery Procedure' (MS Snow tr, first published 1968, 2002) 5 Quarterly Journal of Austrian Economics 9; a slightly more detailed account is given in 'The Use of Knowledge in Society', see FA Hayek, 'The Use of Knowledge in Society' (1945) 35 The American Economic Review 519. For a critical discussion of Hayek's argument see J O'Neill, *The Market: Ethics, Knowledge and Politics* (Routledge 1998) 129–42.

[6] L Gerken, 'Institutional Competition: An Orientative Framework' in L Gerken (ed), Competition among Institutions (Macmillan 1995) 1: 'In economics, it is generally agreed that competition discloses knowledge, enhances efficiency and restrains power'; G Wagner, 'The Economics of Harmonization: The Case of Contract Law' (2002) 39 Common Market Law Review 995, 999: '[T]he whole

welfare economics, allocative efficiency is realized by an optimal satisfaction of individual preferences.[7]

The main advantage of regulatory competition compared to other structural approaches to lawmaking, such as centralization of competences (reducing the number of suppliers) and harmonization of legal rules (reducing supply diversity), is that it leads to efficient regulatory outcomes:[8] 'Regulatory competition matches individual preferences and legal results because actors have the opportunity to exit cheaply from an unsatisfactory jurisdiction.'[9] When exit is possible and sends a negative signal, law that is flawed in that it fails to promote overall welfare is more likely to be amended in a process of 'creative destruction'.[10]

From a philosophical perspective, preference satisfaction is no end in itself, but closely linked to personal liberty and autonomy. If market settings enable regulatory preferences to be revealed and aggregated into a political signal, welfare-enhancing solutions can be found without having to rely on a conception of the good that is not universally shared, leading to measures that are paternalistic vis-à-vis at least some of those whom they bind.

That progress resulting from regulatory competition—apt to be characterized as a 'race to the top'—leads us to the temporal dimension of regulatory competition. Not only will a market scenario allow comparisons between what works in practice and

field of economics as a social science rests on the assumption that individuals know best what is good for them.'

[7] RD Cooter and TS Ulen, *Law and Economics, International Edition* (6th edn, Prentice Hall 2012) 14, refer only to Pareto efficiency; on the more sophisticated and more widely used Kaldor-Hicks criterion for allocative efficiency see N Kaldor, 'Welfare Propositions of Economics and Interpersonal Comparisons of Utility' (1939) 49 The Economic Journal 549; JR Hicks, 'The Foundations of Welfare Economics' (1939) 49 The Economic Journal 696; for its use in law and economics see R Posner, *Economic Analysis of Law* (first published 1973, 9th edn, Wolters Kluwer Law and Business 2014) Section 1.2.

[8] On this 'normative economic' argument in favour of regulatory competition in the European context J-M Sun and J Pelkmans, 'Regulatory Competition in the Single Market' (1995) 33 Journal of Common Market Studies 67, 70.

[9] WW Bratton and JA McCahery, 'Regulatory Competition, Regulatory Capture and Corporate Self-Regulation' (1995) 73 North Carolina Law Review 1861, 1884.

[10] J Schumpeter, *Capitalism, Socialism and Democracy* (Harper 1975) 82–5.

what does not; competitive pressure will also help to speed up the evolution of law towards greater efficiency.

2. ACCELERATION OF LAW REFORM

The Hayekian idea of competition as a discovery procedure should be complemented by a temporal aspect. Competition serves as an accelerator of such discovery compared to other processes, such as mono-serial trial and error.

Regulatory competition may thus be an acceleration mechanism for law reform, in the sense that legislatures will be motivated to react promptly to market signals, particularly negative signals in the form of significant opt-out. Overdue reforms may not only be identified by looking at the products of more successful competitors, but once discovered may also be faster implemented, for fear of market disadvantages.

O'Hara and Ribstein have alluded to this temporal dimension that otherwise has received little attention:

> We have shown how this market can discipline lawmaking by forcing states to compete with each other. Moreover, contractual choice of law better enables states to experiment with alternative solutions to difficult policy problems. Enforcing choice of law clauses will help legal improvements to evolve more quickly and effectively.[11]

Competitive pressure as an accelerator of reform and change is a general feature of markets, one that has often been welcomed as a useful political device; for example, in order to justify 'hard choices', such as spending cuts or tax increases, vis-à-vis the democratic sovereign.[12] Compared to lengthy arguments about the need for reform and the course it should take, 'competitive images are exciting, and thrills sell tickets'.[13]

The reform of German company law that gave rise to a company form named the 'Unternehmergesellschaft', that is, essentially, a

[11] EA O'Hara and LE Ribstein, *The Law Market* (OUP 2009) 217.

[12] P Krugman, 'Competitiveness: A Dangerous Obsession' (1994) 73 Foreign Affairs 28, 40, adding that 'overblown fear of the Soviet Union was used in the 1950s to justify the building of the interstate highway system and the expansion of math and science education' (41) in the US.

[13] Ibid 39.

Gesellschaft mit beschränkter Haftung (GmbH) without the minimum capital requirement of €25,000, was clearly motivated by a mass opt-out of German founders in favour of UK company law and the Limited company option it had on offer.[14] Minimum capital requirements had long been controversially debated among legal scholars in Germany and elsewhere. Nevertheless, it appeared that competitive pressure exerted by demand exit and the fear of continuing to lose out in the incorporation market played a significant role in the reform considerations.

3. TAMING OF THE LEVIATHAN STATE

Another argument in favour of competition in general, as well as regulatory competition in particular, draws on Hobbes' characterization of the state as a fictitious 'Leviathan'[15] that—if not properly constrained—will encroach upon citizens' freedom by spending and taxing excessively.[16] A scenario of regulatory competition has been credited with the effect of supplying proper constraints on the interventionist powers of government, reducing the probability of citizen exploitation. One of the deficiencies is an asymmetric allocation of information and influence. Governments necessarily have limited information as to what would be the optimal way to proceed in terms of overall welfare consequences, and particular interest groups may gain disproportionate influence on the legislative process and thus 'manipulate' its outcome according to their preferences.[17]

By opting into another legal regime, a quick and effective signal of disapproval can be sent when the balance of goods and services offered versus the price (ie taxes and other disadvantages) to be paid should fall out of balance.[18] Thus, the hope is that 'jurisdictional competition will discipline government producers for the benefit of taxpaying citizens just as price competition

[14] See Chapter 1, section B.2(b).

[15] T Hobbes, *Leviathan* (first published 1651, Penguin 1985).

[16] G Brennan and JM Buchanan, *The Power to Tax: Analytic Foundations of a Fiscal Constitution* (CUP 1980).

[17] M Olson, *The Logic of Collective Action* (Harvard University Press 2009).

[18] S Sinn, 'The Taming of Leviathan: Competition among Governments' (1992) 3 Constitutional Political Economy 177.

disciplines producers of private goods for the benefit of consumers'.[19] Regulatory competition is thus seen, more generally, as a cure for deficits of the political process, particularly in democratic systems.[20] When legislation is negatively affected by public choice failures, opt-outs will create pressure for swift reform.[21]

B. DYSFUNCTIONAL REGULATORY COMPETITION

For all the positive attention that regulatory competition has achieved, critical voices have also not been hard to find. The first group of objections identifies reasons why regulatory competition is prevented from *emerging* in the real world versus a Tieboutian paradise,[22] such as a lack or high costs of mobility and insufficient information on the demand side, or a dearth of incentives to compete on the supply side.[23] In effect, the impetus of these objections is descriptive. They make the case that the Tieboutian model of competitive lawmaking with its extremely demanding preconditions is too far removed from reality as to be able to provide us with any insights of practical relevance.[24]

[19] WW Bratton and JA McCahery, 'The New Economics of Jurisdictional Competition: Devolutionary Federalism in a Second-Best World' (1997) 86 The Georgetown Law Journal 201, 204, proceeding to attack the robustness of the economic models backing the analogy of competitive government behaviour to regular product markets.

[20] Sinn (n 18); R Van den Bergh, 'Subsidiarity as an Economic Demarcation Principle and the Emergence of European Private Law' (1998) 5 Maastricht Journal of European and Comparative Law 129, 131.

[21] H Eidenmüller, 'The Transnational Law Market, Regulatory Competition, and Transnational Corporations' (2011) 18 Indiana Journal of Global Legal Studies 707, 732: 'Regulatory competition gives citizens the means to counteract public choice failures in the legislative process in their own country; "bad law" is not chosen.'

[22] CM Tiebout, 'A Pure Theory of Local Expenditure' (1956) 64 Journal of Political Economy 416.

[23] Bratton and McCahery (n 19) 233–5; with respect to contract law Wagner (n 6) 1006–13, concluding that 'it is very doubtful how many of the virtues competition among lawmakers promises in theory might be obtained in practice' (1011).

[24] For a discussion of the model and its premises see Chapter 1, section A.3; Wagner (n 6) 1006–10.

The second group of objections points to problems associated with regulatory competition under the assumption that it is a descriptively adequate conceptual framework for legal developments that we observe. In other words, if we take regulatory competition to be existent in the sense that empirical reality is adequately captured by the model, how it could nevertheless be that the beneficial effects its proponents have put forth will not materialize.[25] These objections are normative in the sense that they accept the Tieboutian model insofar as it yields an explanation of legal dynamics as determined by competitive interaction of lawmakers, but reject the associated claim that such dynamics would lead to beneficial results in terms of overall welfare.

1. MARKET FAILURE AND EXTERNALITIES

There is a lot to be said about the problems that a law market presents, in all kinds of contexts. The most prominent line of critique is that regulatory competition brought about by a law market leads to a 'race to the bottom' in the quality of legal rules, such as a 'race to laxity' in the mandatory standards designed to prevent negative externalities and spillover effects of a transaction, that is, harm to third parties.

(a) The 'race to the bottom'

Consider again the example of 'flags of convenience'. The convenience of such flags derives from the fact that labour and safety regulations on board vessels are comparatively low.[26] Lowering of protective standards has occurred in a number of fields affected

[25] A third kind of normative argument builds upon principled objections that remain even if all Tieboutian premises are assumed to be fulfilled. These are objections that do not share basic assumptions of the perspective of welfare economists on law, policy, and regulatory competition—such as a subjectivist conception of welfare, or changes in the social meaning of goods once they become market commodities. Objections of this kind are the subject of Chapters 3, 4, and 5.

[26] Competitive pressure on high standards in labour and safety regulations is not the only factor that prompts legislative reaction; from the supply perspective, tax implication are highly relevant, which is illustrated by states efforts to induce 'reflagging' by granting tax reliefs to ship owners, see A Peters, 'The Competition between Legal Orders' (2014) 3 International Law Research 45, 56.

by regulatory competition.[27] It has been most widely discussed in corporate law, with respect to the protection of external and involuntary creditors (such as tort victims), and disclosure regulation.[28] Justice Brandeis observed, in 1933, that '[c]ompanies were early formed to provide charters for corporations in states where the cost was lowest and the laws least restrictive. The states joined in advertising their wares. The race was one not of diligence but of laxity.'[29]

Many have seen the lowering of protective standards, tellingly referred to by the metaphor 'race to the bottom',[30] as the main problem associated with the emergence of law markets: 'Only the most Panglossian or willfully unobservant would deny that this problem exists; the controversy relates to how serious it is, and whether harmonization at the federal level is the best way to deal with it.'[31]

That the dynamic towards a lowering of standards is described not only as a tendency but as a 'race', points to the temporal dimension of competition already discussed. While proponents may claim that such competition accelerates legal evolution towards a higher level of efficiency, critics fear an 'escalation'[32] in the opposite direction.

27 See DD Murphy, *The Structure of Regulatory Competition: Corporations and Public Policies in a Global Economy* (OUP 2006) 45–71 for the example of flags of convenience and 72–112 for the example of offshore finance, observing that the '*raison d'être* of offshore finance is regulatory laxity' (72).

28 See, eg, LA Bebchuk, 'Federalism and the Corporation: The Desirable Limits on State Competition in Corporate Law' (1992) 105 Harvard Law Review 1435.

29 *Louis K. Liggett Co. V. Lee* [1933] 288 US 517, 558–9.

30 WL Cary, 'Federalism and Corporate Law: Reflections Upon Delaware' (1974) 83 Yale Law Journal 663, 705: 'A civilizing jurisdiction should import lifting standards; certainly there is no justification for permitting them to deteriorate. The absurdity of this race for the bottom […] should arrest the conscience of the American bar when its current reputation is in low estate.' See also S Schram, *After Welfare: The Culture of Postindustrial Social Policy* (NYU Press 2000) 91 on the metaphor 'race to the bottom' and its negative connotation, as opposed to the more positive alternative 'laboratories of democracy' discussed by JD Donahue, *Disunited States* (Basic Books 1997) 13.

31 Deakin (n 3) 443.

32 J Kersten, 'Wettbewerb der Rechtsordnungen?' in J Isensee and P Kirchhof (eds), *Handbuch des Staatsrechts, VoL XI* (CF Müller 2013) §233 para 9.

(b) Externalities

A criticism closely related to the 'race to the bottom' metaphor points to external effects that a scenario of regulatory competition can be expected to produce.[33] Absent externalities, all costs and benefits of a market transaction are divided among the parties to that transaction, who have been able to influence its outcome.[34] In reality, however, costs (and benefits) at times 'spill over' the boundaries of a transaction, imposing costs (or benefits) on third parties who often have had no prior chance of adjusting their position to the risk of bearing these costs or of influencing the outcome of the transaction.

Under conditions of regulatory competition, the argument relating to externalities can be made with respect to two different levels. First, those who are able to exercise legal mobility within a given legal framework may not be identical to those who are affected by the choice that is made, potentially imposing costs on these third parties.[35] This is a point relating primarily to the appropriateness of choice of law opportunities. It can also be framed as a problem of democratic legitimacy: '[T]he (mandatory) provisions of the British Companies Act are democratically legitimated, but not by those who are confronted with the Ltd. outside Great Britain.' [36]

On another level, the costs that are associated with law *reform* or creation of a certain form will often be external in the sense that they are partly borne by those who were not able to exert decisive competitive pressure on legislatures, thus failing to shape legislation according to their interests. Corporate mobility that exhibits a preference for jurisdictions with a comparatively low level of environmental protection may, for example, lead to a situation in which governments attract capital by lowering their pollution standards, while the costs of higher pollution are felt in neighbouring territories subject to higher standards as well.

[33] For the field of corporate law see Bebchuk (n 28) 1485–95.

[34] See, eg, Cooter and Ulen (n 7) 39.

[35] Eidenmüller (n 21) 735.

[36] Bachmann G and others, *Regulating the Closed Corporation* (De Gruyter 2014) 224; for a more detailed discussion of the issue democratic legitimacy see Chapter 4, section A.1.

In the logic of the competition paradigm, to the extent that negative externalities present a risk of market failure they also offer a justification for regulatory intervention.[37] Eliminating transactions that produce external effects would at the same time mean a restriction of regulatory competition (that is, based on these transactions).

(c) The selection principle

The debate among economists concerning 'systems competition', a phenomenon closely related to regulatory competition,[38] has produced a criticism that has become known by the term 'selection principle':

> The selection principle says that governments have taken over all those activities which the private market has proved to be unable to carry out. Because the state is a stopgap which fills the empty market niches and corrects the failures of existing markets, it cannot be expected that the reintroduction of the market by the back door of systems competition will lead to a reasonable allocation result. Instead, it must be feared that the failures that originally caused the government to take action will show up again at the higher level of government competition.[39]

This is an argument from market failure as well, albeit on a meta-level; translated into the conceptual framework of regulatory competition, the idea is the following:

1. The purpose and primary justification of *mandatory* law is to prevent market failure of various kinds in terms of a 'reasonable allocation' of goods.[40]

[37] DC Esty and D Geradin (eds), *Regulatory Competition and Economic Integration: Comparative Perspectives* (OUP 2001) xxii: 'From a theoretical perspective, where the issue to be addressed involves interjurisdictional spillovers or externalities, the case for governmental intervention at an overarching level is strong [...]. More broadly, whenever there exists a risk of market failure, governmental intervention at a scale that is sufficient to address the market failure may be welfare-enhancing.'

[38] Systems competition is a broader term than regulatory competition; for the purposes of this study, however, no distinction is made.

[39] H-W Sinn, *The New Systems Competition* (John Wiley & Sons 2003) 6.

[40] Sinn (n 39) 8: 'Despite all its weaknesses and problems, the state must be seen as an instrument for meeting the collective responsibilities which the private market cannot fulfill.'

2. Regulatory competition enables individuals to evade mandatory law by opting out and into another legal regime with different legal products on offer.
3. Regulatory competition will replicate market failure that mandatory law was designed to prevent.

In the context of regulatory competition, the argument, of course, applies only to instances of mandatory law that is justified by the fact that it prevents market failure. As the argument departs from the function and justification of governmental market intervention by mandatory law, it shows how the debate about the economic case for or against regulatory competition is linked to the discussion about the proper confines of mandatory law. Against this background, it has been argued that the debate about regulatory competition and its positive or negative consequences should be more adequately framed in terms of the proper confines of mandatory law.[41]

2. ASYMMETRICAL INFLUENCE OF INTEREST GROUPS

The hope that regulatory competition would serve as a cure for deficits of the democratic process and serve to restrain the Leviathan state has been countered with a related criticism. When such deficits are seen in the fact that powerful interest groups would—absent competition—'capture' legislators in order to gain priority vis-à-vis other groups, it is by no means clear that regulatory competition would in fact ameliorate the situation. For influence on the legislature may, in a competitive scenario, still be highly asymmetric, as it depends on the comparative credibility of an exit threat combined with a legislature's interest in preventing that exit.[42]

[41] M Rehberg, 'Spezifika des Systemwettbewerbs' in EV Towfighand et al (eds), *Recht und Markt: Wechselbeziehungen zweier Ordnungen* (Nomos 2009).

[42] Monopolkommission, *Sondergutachten Systemwettbewerb* (Nomos 1998); Peters (n 26) 53; Sinn (n 39) 60 with a diagnosis on how differences in mobility will play out: 'Capital, except possibly, for corporate capital trapped by divided taxes, will be the big winner of systems competition.'

3. BUNDLING AND THE PRICE MECHANISM

Another problem from an economic perspective is that the signalling mechanism of the market (higher prices for better products) does not work with respect to legal rules due to 'bundling effects'. In most decisional settings, legal rules are only one among many factors influencing locational decisions.[43] Thus, when such decisions are made, an interpretation of them as statements about the perceived quality or value of the legal rules affected is often unwarranted. Bundling effects make it extremely difficult to isolate reasons why people demonstrate a preference for this or that location. Is it the weather? Is it family members living there already? Is it the language? Or, in case of financial capital, is it high-quality living conditions for the managers of said capital? These are all factors that do not have much to do with legal rules in particular.

When parties specify that English contract law should govern their transaction, for example, this might be due to a number of reasons that do not bear directly on the substantive characteristics of English law:.that the parties' 'lowest common denominator' in terms of language is English, for example, or that the legal teams involved have, for reasons of familiarity, a strong preference for English law, or that London is an attractive venue to carry out negotiations and resolve disputes.[44] Thus, to say that locational decisions of people or firms are decisively determined by the legal rules associated with a particular jurisdiction is, for some, a hasty conclusion not warranted by robust data. Some studies have shown that the law does in fact play a role as one factor among others with regard to some fields,; while others have not been able to verify the hypothesis, or have claimed to find that it is

[43] See E-M Kieninger, *Wettbewerb der Privatrechtsordnungen im Europäischen Binnenmarkt* (Mohr Siebeck 2002) 62 with the example of an entrepreneurial decision to relocate factories to Middle and Eastern European countries.

[44] S Vogenauer, 'Regulatory Competition through Choice of Contract Law and Choice of Form in Europe: Theory and Evidence' (2013) 21 European Review of Private Law 13; S Vogenauer and C Hodges, *Civil Justice Systems in Europe* (Hart 2016).

certainly not one of the most important reasons for one or the other place.[45]

The bundling argument has another, arguably even more problematic, dimension. Whereas 'bundling' may prevent competitive dynamics from unfolding—because suppliers cannot read the price signals sent by en bloc locational decisions properly—'unbundling', when it is possible, invites a different criticism. 'Unbundling' appears when an isolated choice of law is possible, leading to pure legal mobility. However, '[t]his kind of "cherry-picking" is bound to lead to inefficiencies where legal institutions that complement each other are unbundled.'[46] When a complementary set of legal rules that are meant to 'cooperate in order to achieve an efficient result—like a clockwork'[47] is taken apart by partial opt-out, the result may be straightforwardly inefficient, for example due to externalities.

C. CONCLUSION

In the end, the economic cases both for and against regulatory competition so far are inconclusive. There are plausible considerations recommending a competitive scenario vis-à-vis centralization and harmonization. However, a *tout court* judgment in favour of regulatory competition appears unwarranted in face of structural differences among legal fields: some are closer to the Tieboutian thought experiment; others are so far removed that the model's sufficient approximation of real conditions must be questioned.

The first part of this chapter laid out the considerations that have led economically inclined authors to argue in favour of competition among suppliers of legal rules. The first strand of arguments refers to the merits of competition in general, mainly in terms of identifying and establishing efficient legislative solutions.

The second type of argument builds upon the premise that regulatory competition serves as a restraining factor against the Leviathan state. Competitive structures based on credible exit

[45] Vogenauer (n 44). [46] Eidenmüller (n 21) 739.

[47] W Schön, 'Playing Different Games? Regulatory Competition in Tax and Company Law Compared' (2005) 42 Common Market Law Review 331, 353.

threats by the addressees of law could force governments to consider the interests of legal customers instead of, for example, taxing excessively.

The second part of the chapter dealt with arguments that have questioned the promise of regulatory competition from an economic perspective. The most prominent criticism is that regulatory competition brought about by a law market leads to a 'race to the bottom' in the quality of legal rules, such as a 'race to laxity' in the case of mandatory standards designed to prevent negative externalities of a transaction. The idea is that, under market pressure, legislatures are forced to give way to the pressure of groups of demanders threatening to withdraw business from the polity unless law is amended according to their interests, thereby imposing costs on third parties.

These arguments boil down to the claim that, if there are markets for law with competitive dynamics on the supply side, in many cases they must be expected to be dysfunctional, in the economic sense of market failure. Thus Hans-Werner Sinn's conclusion: 'Regulatory competition is bad when government intervention is good.'[48]

Having discussed the purported advantages and two kinds of objections, we will now turn our attention towards a third group of criticisms: those that do not share the axiomatic framework of the 'competition paradigm'.

[48] Sinn (n 39) 270.

3

REGULATORY COMPETITION AND UTILITARIANISM

A. REGULATORY COMPETITION AS AN IMPERATIVE OF UTILITARIAN POLITICS

The hypothesis of this chapter is that regulatory competition is promising only if one shares a number of basic premises that are associated with political utilitarianism. The questions that are to be answered are thus:

In what way could regulatory competition be interpreted as being linked to utilitarianism?
How does the attractiveness of regulatory competition as a political strategy depend on utilitarian assumptions?

An answer to these questions leads to the conclusion that problems with these utilitarian assumptions translate into criticisms of regulatory competition as a policy approach. Two particular instances of regulatory competition will be used to illustrate the problematic inheritance of utilitarian weaknesses: tax competition and a corporate governance issue, namely the involvement of employees in corporate decision-making.

The utilitarian argument for regulatory competition may roughly be set out as follows:

1. Subjectivist conception of welfare: people know best what is good for them.
2. People communicate their legal preferences inter alia via physical relocation and via choice of law.
3. Meeting people's expressed preferences regarding legal rules maximizes utility, understood as overall welfare.
4. Regulatory competition pressures states to offer law that answers to these individual preferences.

Law for Sale: A Philosophical Critique of Regulatory Competition. Johanna Stark. Published 2019 by Oxford University Press.

5. Regulatory competition leads to legal rules that maximize utility, understood as overall welfare.

Each of the premises of the argument may be criticized on various grounds.

1. SUBJECTIVIST WELFARE

There are essentially two ways to answer the question at the heart of all moral theories: what ought to be done and how is the good life to be achieved? These two ways also make for the fundamental divide between, in a broad sense, utilitarian and deontological approaches to ethical issues. The subjectivist approach, shared by utilitarian philosophers, welfare economists, and others,[1] holds that what is good or right in the end rests on a subjective foundation. The subjectivist claim is typically accompanied by an epistemic component: absent reasons to believe otherwise, people know best what is good for them (premise 1), and what makes their lives worth living. They have certain preferences and are able to communicate them (premise 2).[2] Satisfying these preferences, the utilitarian assumption goes, will lead to a state of the world in which overall welfare is maximized (premise 3).

[1] On the relationship between utilitarianism and welfare economics JL Coleman, 'Efficiency, Utility, and Wealth Maximization' (1979) 8 Hofstra Law Review 509; R Posner, 'Utilitarism, Economics and Legal Theory' (1979) 8 The Journal of Legal Studies 103; AC Pigou, *The Economics of Welfare* (first published 1920, Palgrave Macmillan 2013) Part I; L Kaplow and S Shavell, *Fairness Versus Welfare* (Harvard University Press 2002) Part I.

[2] Difficulties with premise 2 with respect to the present context have been discussed in Chapter 2: there are scholars who doubt that the Tieboutian analysis of people's behaviour has much analytical benefit, as the assumptions it rests on are too far removed from reality. Another problem associated with individual preference aggregation is known as the 'voting paradox' or Arrow's theorem, as it was first developed by KJ Arrow, *Social Choice and Individual Value* (2nd edn, Yale University Press 1963). Under the constraints of few and simple restrictions regarding procedural fairness, rationality of individuals, and stability of preferences, there is no aggregation system that can create a complete and transitive ranking of these preferences. For an overview of the theorem and its implications for theories of social choice see M Morreau, 'Arrow's Theorem', *The Stanford Encyclopedia of Philosophy* (2016) <https://plato.stanford.edu/archives/win2016/entries/arrows-theorem/> accessed 1 August 2018.

Objectivists counter that utilitarianism confuses the relationship central to morality: what is good cannot be derived from conformity with human preferences. The valuable human life derives its status not from being desired or preferred by human beings.[3] There is such a thing as the objectively valuable life that may be realized to a greater or lesser extent in the actual practice of living human beings. In the ideal case, we come to develop preferences for what is good and right. However, from an epistemic perspective, there are good reasons to believe that there are things that make for a good human life but that people do not recognize as such.

People may think they know best what is good for them, and in many cases that is true. In an important respect, it might, however, be false. People may err about their own good, perhaps due to limited knowledge about what will make their life a good one. Or they may not err about their own good, but may be instrumentally irrational about how best to achieve it, that is, which specific preferences they should have and express in their behaviour in order to achieve what they think is good for them.[4]

Research in cognitive psychology and, building on that, in behavioural economics, has shown us that people's behaviour in many situations does not match their true preferences. Take the example of retirement savings: asked what they think is good for them and what their actual preferences are, people confess to wanting to save adequately for their retirement, but then fail to actually do so.[5] This behaviour has been attributed to a cognitive tendency termed 'hyperbolic discounting': the further away an event is, the higher the discount rate (positive or negative) by

[3] The ethical theory of GE Moore may be interpreted as an instance of such objectivism, see GE Moore, *Principia Ethica* (first published 1903, CUP 1993); see also Chapter 5, section B.1.

[4] For an attempt to answer this criticism from the perspective of welfare economics see Kaplow and Shavell (n 1) 410–13.

[5] RH Thaler and S Benartzi, 'Save More Tomorrow™: Using Behavioral Economics to Increase Employee Saving' (2004) 112 Journal of Political Economy 164.

which we calculate its relevance compared to benefits or disadvantages that are temporarily closer at hand.[6]

Trust in the market paradigm and in the competitive process as a mechanism for the selection of legal rules makes sense only on the assumption that it is legitimate to take individuals' subjectively determined preferences as a reliable indicator of what course of action will lead to a welfare-filled life both individually and socially. Psychological research of the kind sketched here that has highlighted the distortive mechanisms involved in the process of preference formation casts doubt on purely subjectivist accounts of human welfare.

2. LEGAL UTILITARIANISM

Premise 3 is important because it captures the utilitarian conviction that satisfaction of individual preferences will in the end maximize utility, understood as overall welfare.[7] Whether this is plausible has been discussed intensely among philosophers;[8] the reasons for being sceptical here also apply to the argument in favour of regulatory competition. The critical force of these objections may even be stronger regarding our argument here. This is an argument about state law, being an instrument of social ordering that is, inter alia, meant to overcome situations in which collective action problems would hinder welfare maximization via individual preference satisfaction. There are situations in which aggregating expressed preferences by individuals (granted that this is even adequately possible) is distorted by collective action mechanisms that overall do not lead to welfare maximization at all: think of prisoner's dilemmas.

[6] For an explanation of the phenomenon and an overview of empirical data see S Frederick, G Loewenstein, and T O'Donoghue, 'Time Discounting and Time Preference: A Critical Review' (2002) 40 Journal of Economic Literature 351.

[7] On the difference between a traditional utilitarian understanding of the overall happiness as the good to be maximized and economists' focus on welfare see Posner (n 1); there is also a strong tradition of economists who see themselves as applying the utilitarian approach to real world problems, see IMD Little, *A Critique of Welfare Economics* (Clarendon Press 1957); Pigou (n 1).

[8] For an overview of the philosophical debate see W Kymlicka, *Contemporary Political Philosophy: An Introduction* (OUP 2002) 10–52.

One reason why individual preference aggregation produces problems particularly in the political and legal sphere is that they are individual preferences directed at everyone's own good. They leave no room for other-regarding considerations. The social common good is no category for individual welfare maximizers. The good of close family and friends may be incorporated via its relationship to someone's own good, but further than that, establishing a link becomes difficult.

Whether this really is a severe problem depends on the concept of 'overall welfare'. Is this kind of welfare simply defined as the aggregation of individual preferences and nothing else? Then the utilitarian position is perfectly coherent. It is backed up by the Smithian conception of the 'invisible hand'.[9] By pursuing their own good, people promote the public interest much better than if they aimed directly at pursing this public interest, whatever it may be.[10]

The utilitarian conception of overall welfare has been sharply criticized, as it appears to leave little or no room at all for values and value-based principles that are difficult to extract from expressed preferences, such as justice, equality, or cultural achievements. One of the purposes of law is to structure social life. According to many constitutions, it also communicates and expresses a commitment to realize certain values.[11] Within this broader political picture, many have argued,[12] welfare must be understood differently. Overall welfare is an ideal state in which not only individual preferences are respected and satisfied to the greatest extent possible (that too, of course), but also in which the values that are the basis of social life are visible in its everyday workings.

[9] A Smith, *An Inquiry into the Nature and Causes of the Wealth of Nations* (RH Campbell and AS Skinner eds, first published 1776, OUP 1979) Book IV Ch. II paragraph IX.

[10] Arrow (n 2); A Peters, 'The Competition between Legal Orders' (2014) 3 International Law Research 45, 56.

[11] See Chapter 5 section 2.

[12] See the papers collected in M Nussbaum and A Sen (eds), *The Quality of Life* (Clarendon Press 1993).

3. REGULATORY COMPETITION AS A MEANS TO PREFERENCE SATISFACTION

Premise 4 is a reference to what has been discussed in Chapter 2. Arguably, regulatory competition, where it unfolds beyond a negligible niche phenomenon, is an expression of pressure on state legislators to offer products that have good chances of market success. Analogously to markets for other products, the communication of preferences is expected to advance the quality of products on offer.

It would be short-sighted to think that preferences of all potential addressees of a body of law would be essentially the same. On the contrary, policy debate is exactly about finding the adequate balance of which preferences and interests of those affected should be satisfied, which should be frustrated, and to what degree.

Where governments respond to the preferences of demanders, the right balance between competing preferences does not materialize automatically. In the traditional picture of a deliberative democracy, it is a competitive dialectic between government and conflicting interest groups that determines the legislative outcome.[13] Those with the loudest voice, to borrow terminology from Albert O. Hirschman,[14] have the greatest chance of being heard. Under conditions of regulatory competition, the loudness of people's voice is determined largely by the credibility of their exit threat, which depends on their mobility costs, and its seriousness in terms of the value of what is threatened to be withdrawn.

Taking this thought further yields the conclusion that the more consequential the exit threat, the higher the chances of having one's preferences reflected in policy decisions. From a utilitarian perspective, giving priority to those with the lowest mobility costs may be perfectly consistent, even morally required. If it yields

[13] With regard to the context of economic activities, E Kane, 'Interaction of Finanical and Regulatory Innovation' (1988) 78 The American Economic Review 328, 332 has coined the term 'regulatory dialectic': 'The tandem nature of regulation and avoidance is featured in a conceptual framework designed to dramatize the process of financial and regulatory innovation: the regulatory dialectic.'

[14] AO Hirschman, 'Exit, Voice and the State' (1978) 31 World Politics 90.

the highest outcome in utility units to be maximized (in contemporary terms 'social welfare'), it is the right way to proceed.

The problem, however, is that mobility must not be equated with legitimacy—which leads us to the problems that utilitarian theories have been confronted with.

B. PHILOSOPHICAL ARGUMENTS AGAINST POLITICAL UTILITARIANISM

Utilitarianism as a moral theory has been highly influential, but equally controversial, particularly as an approach to political matters.[15] In the following, we will take a look at some general critical arguments against utilitarianism that have been advanced by philosophers. Some of these will then be shown to inform the problems arguably associated with particular instances of regulatory competition.

1. ILLEGITIMATE PREFERENCES AND INDIVIDUAL RIGHTS

The subjectivist conception of welfare underlying utilitarian theories leads to problems when it uncritically incorporates preferences that we think are somehow illegitimate. We think that satisfying these preferences is in some form not right and therefore should not be included in a consequentialist calculation of what ought to be done. The subjectivist commitment of utilitarianism does not, in principle, permit a differentiation between preferences more or less worthy of satisfaction.[16] Consider the example of a 'happy sadist',[17] who claims to have a strong preference for

[15] For an introductory overview see Kymlicka (n 8) 10–53.

[16] MJ Sandel, *What Money Can't Buy: The Moral Limits of Markets* (Palgrave Macmillan 2012) 89: '[W]hen market reasoning travels beyond the domain of material goods, it must "traffic in morality," unless it wants blindly to maximize social utility without regard for the moral worth of the preferences it satisfies.'

[17] JC Harsanyi, 'Individual Utilities and Utilitarian Ethics' in A Diekmann and P Mitter (eds), *Paradoxical Effects of Social Behavior* (Physica-Verlag 1986) 1; RM Hare, 'Ethical Theory and Utilitarianism' in A Sen (ed), *Utilitarianism and Beyond* (CUP 1982) 23, 30; the original idea of the 'utility monster' goes back to

seeing others being tortured. True, the utilitarian assessment of the individual's preferences would incorporate the negative utility of those he or she would see suffering as well. Nevertheless, the outcome of this assessment would depend on the final aggregate of utility on all sides, not on a principled objection on the basis of human dignity or individual rights not to be tortured. It would, for example, also depend on the number of sadists claiming to gain utility from seeing a single person being tortured. To many of us, this is strongly counterintuitive. The happy sadist example also points to a kind of situation in which the purpose of law as a social practice appears to be to establish rules for social life that are known to be immune to utilitarian reasoning. The purpose of individual rights such as the right not to be tortured are meant to ensure the safety of everyone from such practices, regardless of the advantages they would produce for others. It is difficult, however, to incorporate individual rights of this type into the theoretical architecture of utilitarianism.

Rule utilitarians might say that utility is maximized by a rule that certain individual liberties and rights must be respected even if this comes with a short-term loss of utility created by the performed actions. The rule itself, however, is still subject to utilitarian scrutiny. That is, should it be the case that a society that is not built upon human dignity and bodily integrity as an inalienable right would produce more utility, for example, by a system of slavery that enslaves some for the great benefit of all others? Utilitarians have a hard time avoiding having to bite the counterintuitive bullet that, in the end, their calculus may require overriding values such as human dignity and individual rights to be protected from severe forms of harm by others.

R Nozick, *Anarchy, State, and Utopia* (Basic Books 1974) 41: 'Utilitarian theory is embarrassed by the possibility of utility monsters who get enormously greater gains in utility from any sacrifice of others than these others lose'; on the fate of illegitimate preferences to see others suffer in welfare economics, compared to utilitarianism, arguing that in a market system, the happy sadist would at least be constrained both by his or her budget as well as by a set of rights protecting potential victims, see R Posner, 'Utilitarism, Economics and Legal Theory' (1979) 8 The Journal of Legal Studies 103, 131–2; contrary to rights, budgetary limits unsurprisingly do little to convince critics of the moral merits of welfare economics compared to act utilitarianism.

2. INSENSITIVITY TO DISTRIBUTIVE JUSTICE

A point that has figured prominently in critical discussions of utilitarianism is its blindness to matters of distributive justice. The utilitarian calculus does not discriminate between the utility of different people. It is indifferent to distributive issues. Put bluntly, for the utilitarian it does not matter much where utility comes from or by whom it is enjoyed, it matters only how much utility is generated overall.

The priority that is assigned to the highest possible sum of overall utility over distributive concerns gives rise to a problem exemplified by Table 3.1.[18]

Table 3.1 Utility comparisons and distributive concerns

	State A	**State B**	**State C**
Member x	10	20	30
Member y	10	5	1
Member z	10	5	0
Total units of utility	30	30	31

The objection is that from a utilitarian perspective, state A and state B would be equally desirable, with an advantage for state C of one unit of utility over both, despite its radically inegalitarian distribution of utility. Why does this amount to an objection to utilitarianism? Values such as fairness or an equal distribution of utility units that may be represented, for example, by resources such as money, do not figure at all in the traditional utilitarian calculus. There is no evaluative basis on which utilitarians could justify a preference for state B instead of state A, as there is likewise no basis on which to argue that, despite a deficit of one utility unit, state A would nevertheless be preferable to state C.

Utilitarians have given various kinds of answers to these charges. The most promising one is the assumption of declining

[18] For illustrative reasons, Table 3.1 suggests a utilitarian calculus based on cardinal comparability of states of affairs (ie concrete values utility-units assignable to each state), a strong and contested assumption. Contemporary utilitarian theory relies on the less demanding assumption ordinal comparability.

marginal utility.[19] Rather plausibly, it is argued that utility functions for people are seldom linear: the more one already has of some good, the less utility is derived from having extra units compared to someone who has less. Think of the dollar that is worth practically nothing to the millionaire, but much more to the beggar.

Does the assumption of declining marginal utility indeed do the trick? By insisting on declining marginal utility, utilitarians have tried to show that the utility maximizing distribution will, in most situations, be one that displays egalitarian features, given that the utility curves of most people are of a similar shape.

There are two main problems with this answer. The first is that if the principle of declining marginal utility is practically applied in a thorough manner, utilitarianism becomes extremely demanding in that the morally right thing to do would be to distribute resources so as to gain a maximum of utility according to marginally declining curves. Radically redistributive imperatives would follow regarding almost all known contemporary societies, a consequence only very few utilitarians would be ready to accept.[20]

The second problem is that—absent an argument that declining marginal utility must logically progress at the same rate for everyone—the assumption does not change the fact that utility maximization is, in the end, the prioritarian goal. Contingently, it may happen that in most cases radically inegalitarian distributions of resources would not yield the maximal aggregate, but if it happened to be so, as in Table 3.1, utilitarians would have to be prepared to bite that bullet.

A third problem is that the assumption of declining marginal utility at a general rate for everyone does not combine well at all with the commitment to a subjectivist approach to human welfare as a function of preference satisfaction. Anyone whose personal utility function does not have the concave shape assumed by

[19] Going back to HH Gossen, *The Laws of Human Relations and the Rules of Human Action Derived Therefrom* (first published 1845, MIT Press 1983).

[20] Utilitarians who apply declining marginal utility to the extreme have been called radical egalitarians, such as K Nielsen, *Equality and Liberty: A Defense of Radical Egalitarianism* (Rowman and Littlefield Publishers 1984).

the declining marginal utility principle will be treated as though his or her preferences do not count.

3. LACK OF REGARD FOR SPECIAL RELATIONSHIPS AND PAST COMMITMENTS

One of the advantages of utilitarianism is that it does not discriminate between different bearers of utility. The consequences of an action in terms of aggregate utility are calculated by considering each person's utility with equal weight. The egalitarian design of the utilitarian calculus has been confronted with the criticism that it leads to an inability to account for special relationships and obligations that characterize our psychological predispositions.[21] In its most radical form, utilitarianism requires us to consider the utility of others (eg the global poor) in the same way as our own, or that of our family and friends. This seems counterintuitive, as we do appear to have a privileged relationship and obligations both towards ourselves and those who are in some way socially connected to us.

Obligations and entitlements that arise from some past circumstance or interaction with others present a related problem: 'Utilitarian reasoning disregards such backward-looking entitlements, for it says that only forward-looking consequences matter'.[22] Again, this does not account for our intuition that past circumstances may create differential entitlements and obligations.[23] When A lends money to B, A is entitled to receive that money back from B, regardless of whether more aggregate utility could be achieved by, for instance, donating the money to charity.[24] Following utilitarian reasoning thus would often mean

[21] Kymlicka (n 8) 22–6. [22] Ibid 23. [23] Nozick (n 17) 155.

[24] Utilitarians would, of course, be able to defend themselves by insisting that the negative consequences of broken promises and other commitments (disappointment and avoidance of future cooperation) are in fact included in the calculation of aggregate utility. This defense has been countered by an insistence that it still gets the relationship between negative attitudes and moral wrongness backwards. Breaking promises is not wrong because people are disappointed; instead, people are disappointed because it is wrong, see B Williams, 'A Critique of Utilitarianism' in JJC Smart and B Williams (eds), *Utilitarianism: For and Against* (CUP 1973) 75, 143.

neglecting past commitments that we have made to others and that contribute to the meaning of our lives: for this reason, utilitarianism has been accused of demanding 'alienation' of the agent from him or herself and others.

In the context of legal scholarship, a variant of this problem has been discussed as the theory of 'efficient breach' in contract law, first stated in 1970: 'Repudiation of obligations should be encouraged where the promisor is able to profit from his default after placing his promisee in as good a position as he would have occupied had performance been rendered.'[25] From the 'moralist' counterposition, it has been argued that, even absent any negative consequences to be reasonably expected from a breach, the parties still are under an obligation to honour the contract.[26] In some legal traditions more than others, contracts have even been credited with a form of sanctity, as it is captured by the maxim *pacta sunt servanda*.[27]

The previous sections have shown that utilitarianism faces a number of challenges. The purpose of this discussion was to lay the ground for a subsequent analysis of two instances of regulatory competition along the lines of these challenges.

C. ARGUMENTS AGAINST PARTICULAR INSTANCES OF REGULATORY COMPETITION

If regulatory competition, as has been claimed here, is closely linked to utilitarian assumptions, we should expect instances of competitive dynamics to exhibit features that may be interpreted

[25] RL Birmingham, 'Breach of Contract, Damage Measures, and Economic Efficiency' (1970) 24 Rutgers Law Review 273, 284; the term 'efficient breach' goes back to CJ Goetz and RE Scott, 'Liquidated Damages, Penalties and the Just Compensation Principle: Some Notes on an Enforcement Model and a Theory of Efficient Breach' (1977) 77 Columbia Law Review 554; forceful arguments in favour of efficient breach have been made by R Posner, *Economic Analysis of Law* (first published 1973, 9th edn, Wolters Kluwer Law and Business 2014).

[26] C Fried, *Contract as Promise: A Theory of Contractual Obligation* (first published 1935, 2nd edn, OUP 2015).

[27] On the history and meaning of *pacta sunt servanda* see H Wehberg, 'Pacta Sunt Servanda' (1959) 53 The American Journal of International Law 775.

as symptoms of weaknesses of utilitarianism. Two examples will be used to illustrate how regulatory competition inherits utilitarian problems. First, tax competition, one of the most established and intensely debated forms of regulatory competition. Second, a recent issue in European insolvency law—residual debt discharge mechanisms that appear to have been adopted or introduced in some countries so as to prevent debtors from emigrating to other jurisdictions.

1. TAX COMPETITION AND REDISTRIBUTION

In economic terms, the purpose of taxation is to ensure that the state can produce public goods for the use of the taxpaying community. Their character as public goods means that they are both non-exclusive and non-rivalrous;[28] private production would be inefficient. Among these goods are protection of public order and safety, education, healthcare (arguably), and culture.[29] Taxation then ensures sufficient funding for various kinds of state expenditures and to distribute responsibility for these costs fairly among the members of a polity. Using the instrument of tax law, the state calls everyone to account for their fair contribution to infrastructure.[30]

Tax competition has led to significant pressure on the (re-)distributive function of national law in general and of tax law in particular. [31] People and firms successfully use their physical and legal mobility to pressure states to comply with their interests in a competitive bid for the retention and attraction of capital

[28] See Chapter 1, section A.1.

[29] See W Schön, 'Der "Wettbewerb" der europäischen Steuerordnungen als Rechtsproblem' in J Pelka (ed), *Europa- und verfassungsrechtliche Grenzen der Unternehmensbesteuerung* (Dr Otto Schmidt 2000) 191, 198; K Vogel, *Taxation of Cross-Border Income, Harmonization, and Tax Neutrality under European Community Law* (Kluwer Law and Taxation Publishing 1994) 25–30.

[30] This is the reason why 'ability to pay', which serves as one of the main criteria according to which individuals' tax responsibilities are determined, may plausibly be interpreted as an imperative of social solidarity.

[31] Schön (n 29); H-W Sinn, *The New Systems Competition* (John Wiley & Sons 2003) 258–9.

of various sorts, such as direct and indirect investment or highly skilled labour. People and firms typically express a preference for paying fewer taxes rather than more.[32] Competitive pressure will thus be directed at lowering taxes, resulting in a dilemma. Citizens and companies also have strong preferences for the existence and ability to use a well-planned, executed, and maintained public infrastructure (ie roads, schools, and well-trained employees); yet the resources to finance this infrastructure must come from somewhere. Given external preferences on all sides to shoulder as little responsibility as possible and instead shift costs to others, universal preference satisfaction would lead ad absurdum.

Tax systems thus reflect political decisions on how to distribute financial responsibility, particularly for the provision of infrastructure and public goods, such as national defence, roads, or public schools. Without a sanction-based tax system, the non-exclusive character of such goods would invite some to free ride on the willingness of others to undertake the costs of their provision. Tax competition is a telling example of how difficult it can be to maintain and enforce mechanisms of collectively shared responsibility. The easier it is for capital to be moved to a different jurisdiction, the more credible exit threats from those in control of that capital are, giving a bargaining advantage to those who bear lower mobility costs than others. The result is a gross disadvantage of immobile capital, particularly labour, over mobile capital.[33]

An important strategy in tax-relevant behaviour of people and firms is the separation of tax addressee and use of infrastructure. Paying your taxes in a country where you are not dependent on

[32] See already JS Mill, 'Considerations on Representative Government' in JM Robson (ed), *Essays on Politics and Society, Collected Works of John Stuart Mill, VoL XIX* (first published 1861, University of Toronto Press/Routledge and Kegan Paul 1977) 371, 441: 'The interest of the government is to tax heavily: that of the community is, to be as little taxed as the necessary expenses of good government permit.'

[33] Among the reasons for this divide are the 'social restraints' of people, see Schön (n 29) 202, 220; for the shift of tax burden from mobile to immobile factors see also A Easson, 'Taxing International Income', in RE Krever (ed), *Tax Conversations: A Guide to the Key Issues in the Tax Reform Debate: Essays in Honour of John G Head* (Kluwer Law International 1997) 415, 419–29.

infrastructure (such as so-called 'tax havens'), while using infrastructure in a country where you are not contributing to its costs. In effect, you are free riding on the residence state's offer of public goods.[34] As a result, inter country equity is compromised.[35] Separation of taxation and use of infrastructure creates a free rider problem of the sort that it allows for the enjoyment of social services and public goods of which one does not share the costs.[36]

A second strategy is using the pressure of influential 'preference groups' to have their preferences accorded priority, by shifting tax burden to those who cannot exert as much pressure on legislatures, mostly because they are less mobile. The shift of tax burden from capital towards (less mobile) labour can be interpreted as a legislative reaction to such pressure.

These developments have been discussed in the context of individual tax justice, which would require that various sources of income be taxed similarly.[37] Tax competition, however, has led to a highly unequal treatment of mobile financial capital versus relatively immobile capital in the form of skilled labour.[38] The reason is that people are not as mobile as capital. Their lives are

[34] Organization for Economic Co-Operation and Development, Harmful Tax Competition: An Emerging Global Issue (OECD Publications 1998) <https://www.oecd-ilibrary.org/taxation/harmful-tax-competition_9789264162945-en> accessed 1 August 2018, para 24; PB Musgrave and RA Musgrave, 'Fiscal Coordination and Competition in an International Setting' in CE McLure (ed), *Influence of Tax Differentials on International Competitiveness* (Kluwer Law and Taxation Publishers 1990) 61, 68–9.

[35] RJ Jeffery *The Impact of State Sovereignty on Global Trade and International Taxation* (Kluwer 1999), 11; Schön (n 29) 201.

[36] Musgrave and Musgrave (n 34) 67 on differential mobility: 'Capital is not only the most mobile factor of production but it is separable from its ownership. […] This feature potentially allows individuals or corporations to avail themselves of public services in their country of residence (incorporation), but to avoid payment of taxes therein.'

[37] Schön (n 29) 202.

[38] RS Avi-Yonah, 'Globalization, Tax Competition, and the Fiscal Crisis of the Welfare State' (2000) 113 Harvard Law Review 1573; V Curzon-Price, 'Fiscal Competition and the Optimization of Tax Revenues for Higher Growth' in A Bergh and R Höijer (eds), *Institutional Competition* (Edward Elgar Publishing 2008) 155; Peters (n 10) 55; W Schön, 'Playing Different Games? Regulatory Competition in Tax and Company Law Compared' (2005) 42 Common Market Law Review 331, 350–2.

characterized by a multiplicity of social bonds that are not as easily dissolved. Changing the place of residence is costly, both financially as well as emotionally and socially. Besides, the political conditions of the contemporary world do not allow anyone to freely choose their place of living.

How do these points of unequal treatment relate to utilitarianism and its problems that were sketched earlier? Utilitarianism is largely insensitive to any problems or issues arising out of inequality. This is one of the main reasons for its appeal to many, and at the same time one of the central grounds for criticism. In the same way that utilitarianism is insensitive to inequality as a value in general, tax competition is insensitive to the unequal treatment it creates in the form of higher taxation of skilled labour compared to mobile capital.

Preferences of mobile individuals to shoulder less of the tax burden as would be imposed upon them absent credible exit threats can, with a view to the demands of tax justice, be interpreted as 'illegitimate preferences' in the sense illustrated here. The utilitarian calculus is again not sensitive to these kinds of legitimacy concerns. The issue of illegitimate preferences is closely connected to distributive issues. When public infrastructure goods are involved, self-interested preferences of some may well be of a form that their satisfaction would result in costs being shifted to others. Due to the insensitivity of utilitarianism for distributive concerns, cost-shifting with overall utility levels untouched cannot be criticized on utilitarian grounds directly.

Under conditions of regulatory competition for mobile taxpayers, redistributive policies can hardly be sustained at all.[39] Their redistributive character requires that some contribute more to the funding of a policy than their interest in tax-based state services is worth.[40]

[39] Peters (n 10) 54: 'In addition, competition does not allow for any, or only a small degree of, social redistribution. This is particularly obvious in tax competition. In order to remove the incentive for wealthy taxpayers to migrate to low-tax jurisdictions, States are inclined to cut taxes, as a result of which the finances available for redistribution shrink. The policy-shift from direct to indirect taxation – which has taken place in response to the risk of emigration – also reduces options for redistribution.'

[40] Schön (n 29) 201; Musgrave and Musgrave (n 34) 70: '[I]t is evident that 'forces of competition' cannot secure an orderly—efficient and equitable—arrangement

The problems that tax competition leads to, particularly from the perspective of individual nation states in need of resources to fund the provision of public goods, can be interpreted as stemming from the fact that such competition is an instance of utilitarian politics. The severity of the problem, of course, depends on the extent of infrastructure responsibility. Fully fledged welfare states should feel competitive pressure more directly than minimal states in which citizens' expectations in terms of high-quality public schools, freely accessible cultural offerings, or general maintenance of transportation infrastructure are rather low.

2. RESIDUAL DEBT DISCHARGE IN INSOLVENCY LAW

Private insolvency proceedings have exhibited mobility as well, motivated mainly by differences in the conditions under which residual debt discharge is granted.[41] A shortening of discharge periods, as it has occurred in several European countries in the past, may, from a utilitarian perspective, make perfect sense, if the utility gains caused by a focus on individual rehabilitation opportunities are greater than negative consequences with respect to creditor protection.

The rationale behind the utilitarian position is that adhering to prior commitments makes no sense if the fulfilment of these commitments has become objectively or subjectively impossible. In the case of someone who will for the rest of his or her life most likely be unable to cope with the pile of debt he or she has accumulated, a weighing of that person's strong interest in a 'fresh start' against the relatively little compensation his or her creditors can expect to ever be able to claim strongly speaks for the possibility of residual debt discharge. Whether the departure from *pacta sunt servanda* that debt discharge invariably constitutes appears justified thus depends on the conditions that must be fulfilled in order to grant discharge, among them typically waiting periods of various length and a requirement of 'good

of public finances in the international setting. The analogy to competition in the private sector is an optical illusion.'

[41] See Chapter 1, section B.5.

conduct'.[42] After all, the availability of discharge opportunities and their restrictions are (at least in theory) known to those who might profit from them in the future. Short waiting periods therefore could lead to less diligence among debtors knowing that, at worst, the price to be paid in order to relieve themselves of financial commitments they have made to others would be bearably small.

It must be granted that even if there is a strong utilitarian case for residual debt discharge (within the constraints of proper restrictions), this is not the only justification one could think of. Human dignity, respect for every citizen as an individual, and social solidarity as (often constitutionally grounded) principles have been invoked as reasons for the possibility of discharge.[43] Imperatives of Christian ethics may be relied upon as well, as in 'and forgive us our debts, as we also have forgiven our debtors'.[44]

From a deontological perspective, however, residual debt discharge appears as a form of socially accepted, yet problematic 'efficient breach'. The objective of granting insolvent individuals a 'fresh start' cannot compensate for neglecting prior commitments vis-à-vis others. This is the case particularly when competitive dynamics have put pressure on the conditions under which discharge is granted, eventually leading to shorter waiting periods and lower demands on good conduct that must be demonstrated during that time. In Kantian terms, the maxim of a legislator easing restrictions on debt discharge in view of competitive advantages it could bring (typically of the defensive kind, ie with the intention of keeping citizens to begin insolvency proceedings in jurisdictions offering 'cheaper' discharge overall) does not pass the categorical imperative in its first formulation: 'Act only in accordance with that through which you can at the same time will

[42] For a comparative overview of good conduct and other preconditions of discharge in the US versus several European countries see M Gerhardt, 'Consumer Bankrupty Regimes in the US and Europe: Further Effects and Implications of the Crisis' (2009) CEPS Working Paper No 318 http://ssrn.com/abstract=1438511, accessed 1 August 2018, particularly 17–18 (table).

[43] See A Bruns, *Haftungsbeschränkung und Mindesthaftung* (Mohr Siebeck 2003) 161, from a German perspective.

[44] Matthew 6:12.

that it become a universal law.'[45] The downward spiral resulting from reform activities of the kind that lowers the restrictions on debt discharge would, having become a universal law, lead to a dissolution of *pacta sunt servanda* altogether.

D. CONCLUSION

Unrestricted regulatory competition leads to results that face the same objections that have been brought forward against utilitarianism in general. It is no surprise that regulatory competition, with its links to utilitarian premises, should lead to such results. By exposing the utilitarian character of regulatory competition, we can see more clearly why it is that many people are worried about such competition being at work in particular fields.

One of the main issues with regulatory competition is that it undermines states' abilities to enforce redistributive policies, as is evidenced by the example of tax competition. This conclusion can be interpreted as an instance of a general criticism of utilitarian approaches: their insensitivity to distributive concerns, resulting in an inability to justify distributive policies based on utilitarian foundations.

Utility is a highly contested concept among political theorists, particularly its reliance on interpersonal comparability.[46] With individual preferences it is similar: what they are, how they are formed and under which influences, and how they should consequently be treated in the political domain is highly controversial among political theorists.[47] If there is at best shaky common ground regarding these fundamental issues, it should come as no surprise that the idea of regulatory competition does not fit well into the conceptual landscape of political theory and philosophy.

We have seen in this chapter that critical perspectives on regulatory competition are plausibly framed as directed primarily at

[45] I Kant, *Groundwork for the Metaphysics of Morals* (Allen Wood ed and tr, first published 1785, Yale University Press 2002) G 4:421.

[46] For a presentation of the debate see Kymlicka (n 8) 13–32.

[47] SO Hansson and T Grüne-Yanoff, 'Preferences', *The Stanford Encyclopedia of Philosophy* (2018) <https://plato.stanford.edu/archives/sum2018/entries/preferences/> accessed 1 August 2018.

the utilitarian commitments that come with the attractiveness of the competitive paradigm. Against this background, regulatory competition as an imperative of utilitarian politics appears to face variants of the problems that utilitarian accounts face in general.

4

POLITICAL VALUES UNDER COMPETITIVE PRESSURE

The arguments presented in this chapter spell out the idea that regulatory competition is at odds with how the state, as the primary political entity of our time, works—or should work. There is reason to worry, it will be argued, that regulatory competition may eventually compromise values that we expect to be realized in a political system. These are arguments within the conceptual framework of analytical political philosophy and jurisprudence. Their starting point is the way we understand certain political concepts—democracy, autonomy, authority, and legitimacy—and the question of whether regulatory competition creates or contributes to tension between these ideas and our political and legal reality.

A. REGULATORY COMPETITION AND DEMOCRACY

When thinking about regulatory competition and the influence it has on how political processes work, what spontaneously comes to mind is that the idea of legislatures competing for the favour of customers of their legal products is in conflict with our understanding of democracy. A commitment to representative democracy, however, is one of the key structural components of most contemporary Western polities. A number of authors have voiced this kind of concern about regulatory competition, referencing a conflict with democratic principles.[1]

[1] G Bachmann, *Vertikaler Regulierungswettbewerb im europäischen Gesellschaftsrecht* (Dr Otto Schmidt 2012) 26–7; A Peters, 'The Competition between Legal Orders' (2014) 3 International Law Research 45, 53–4; R Michaels, 'Make or Buy – a Public Market for Legal Transplants?' in H Eidenmüller (ed), *Regulatory Competition in Contract Law and Dispute Resolution* (CH Beck 2013) 27, 28: 'If we subject law to

Law for Sale: A Philosophical Critique of Regulatory Competition. Johanna Stark. Published 2019 by Oxford University Press.

Democracy is a term used in various disciplines, with slightly different meaning in each context. In the following, it will refer to a type of political organization with two key characteristics. First, a method of group decision-making according to majority rule in all its specific forms, such as unanimity, qualified, or simple majority. Second, a commitment to the idea that human beings are equally worthy of respect and that this should be reflected in the way political decisions affecting them are made.[2] As will be shown, both these characteristics of democracy are potentially affected by regulatory competition.

1. DEMAND RULE VERSUS MAJORITY RULE

At its core, democracy is a method for collective decision-making according to the principle of majority rule. There are countless versions and practices of this method that cannot at this point be discussed in detail. Suffice it to say that it is a way of arriving at common decisions within a large social group and enforcing adherence to these decisions, including by those who do not agree with them.

The political appeal of democratic decision-making on the basis of some form of majority rule has several sources, two of which shall be briefly mentioned here. The first is a kind of pragmatic appeal: the principle of majority rule enables us to decide collectively, in large groups, in situations of conflict and disagreement over what would be the best thing to do.[3] Norberto Bobbio asked, in 1987: 'What's democracy if not a set of rules (the so-called rules of the game) for the solution of conflicts without bloodshed?'[4]

market pressures, do we not undermine democratic values by empowering those actors with enough bargaining power to influence lawmaking processes?'

[2] T Christiano, 'Democracy', *The Stanford Encyclopedia of Philosophy* (2015) <http://plato.stanford.edu/entries/democracy/> accessed 1 August 2018, Section 1, defines the term democracy as 'a method of group decision-making characterized by a kind of equality among the participants at an essential stage of the collective decision-making'.

[3] Ibid Section 2.2.1.

[4] N Bobbio, *The Future of Democracy* (Polity Press 1987) 193.

Without relying on a simple and straightforward principle such as majority rule, compromise would often be unattainable or at least be very time-consuming to achieve. The second source of democracy's appeal is its evaluative neutrality: majority rule is neutral towards the alternatives in any particular decision scenario. Majority rule does not presuppose any particular shared conception of the (common) good, human flourishing, or any other common evaluative standard that in political reality is hardly ever found.

How could regulatory competition pose a problem in light of the principle of majority rule? The concerns that have been articulated particularly in continental European literature are mostly versions of the idea that regulatory competition would somehow intercept or distort the democratic process. Groups of demanders that are particularly influential could 'threaten' to opt into another regime, using their influence to put pressure on governments to enact regulation to their advantage. The effectiveness of such threats depends essentially on two factors. First, their relevance from a supply perspective, stemming, for example, from the amount of capital controlled by those making the threats. Second, the degree of mobility of those who threaten to opt into another regime; the higher it is, the more credible an exit threat is as well. As we have seen, mobility costs tend to be lower for capital than for people. Regulatory competition could thus increase the influence of capital holders on the legislative process, as it will be difficult for government to withstand credible exit threats from suppliers of capital that is needed for the maintenance of growth rates, employment opportunities, and tax revenue.

A dynamic of this kind, however, is not how we perceive democratic decision-making, according to which law is the result of a deliberative process that is structured according to certain procedural commitments, such as periodic and secret ballots in which each person has the same number of votes. Regulatory competition, so the argument often goes, would allow individuals or groups of individuals to illegitimately put their interests above those of all others. Instead of being determined by majority rule, legislative outcomes would be dependent on mobile demand. Some frame the issue as a problem of parliamentary power, highlighting the role of parliament as the political forum in which majority rule is exercised.[5] Others have diagnosed a 'democratic deficit' caused by the fact that national governments have to some extent lost control over economic activities affecting their territories.[6]

Apart from the general problem of asymmetric influence on the process of political decision-making that is, arguably, increased by regulatory competition in the respective field of law, we will discuss three scenarios that describe types of potential conflict between regulatory competition and the core procedural components of democratic state organization.

(a) Open conflict between market demands and majority view

First, the outcome of the majority's view on an issue may be in conflict with what government holds to be required by a successful law market competitor. In light of competitive pressure exerted by a law market and unwanted consequences of unsuccessful or denied participation, government may be tempted to disrespect the electorate's view and nevertheless conform to the (perceived) demands of regulatory competition. In effect, legislative priority would be given to the interests of a minority that happens to be able to exert strong pressure on the legislator via the support of a market structure.

Think of a fictitious European legislator (not the UK) who holds the correct conviction that the respective state's law would have a much greater chance of success in an international law market, say, in charter competition, if it were written in the English language.[7] Now, the legislator is not naïve: he also knows that any proposition to transform national law into an English

[5] Peters (n 1) 42: 'Far from viewing competition as an asset to democracy, some critics of the competition paradigm even argue that competition between legal systems damages democracy because it undermines the power of parliament.'

[6] W Bratton and others, 'Introduction: Regulatory Competition and Institutional Evolution' in W Bratton and others (eds), *International Regulatory Competition and Coordination* (Clarendon Press 1996) 1, 2.

[7] Competitive success would require the binding legal text to be written in English, instead of official translations of legal texts whose binding versions remain in other languages, such as offered by the German Federal Ministry of Justice and Consumer Protection: <http://www.gesetze-im-internet.de/Teilliste_translations.html> accessed 1 August 2018.

text would have no chance of majority support among the general population. Depending on the parliamentary situation, government might nevertheless be able to implement such a decision in favour of a competitive English language company law. After public debate, the popular will to the contrary may be well documented in polls and media coverage. The political price to be paid for deciding against the popular will, for example, in the form of declining approval rates in subsequent elections, is a different story. The demands of regulatory competition will then stand in open contrast to popular majority will.

Does this scenario present a severe problem? A strong conception of democratic legitimacy would require perfect congruency between government action and electorate conviction at all times. However, that is too strong a requirement. Just as it is some milder form of majority instead of unanimity that is required in most kinds of elections, it would be utopian to expect perfect congruency between legislative action and popular will. If, in a representative system with fixed electoral cycles, government respects the limits of its discretionary powers and employs them so as to be or become successful in regulatory competition, there is not much to say from the perspective of democratic requirements. The idea of representative systems, with all its practical advantages, brings with it the cost of imperfect agreement between governmental activity and electoral views at particular times between elections.

A variant of this scenario would be that it is not only the relevant majority's view that is disrespected, but an actual vote against taking the legislative steps required for law market success that has already been cast. The result is an open conflict between competing demands on the legislator. The risk that government would openly neglect principles and outcomes of democratic decision-making by giving priority to competitive strategies is, however, quite small, given the political sanctions and costs that would have to be paid later on.

(b) Indirect erosion of majority rule

A second and more realistic scenario that could be interpreted as a conflict between regulatory competition and democracy builds not upon an open conflict between demands of both commitments, but on the prior question of which substantive issues are and should be subject to majority rule.

The discussion about the proper design and structure of the internal market established by European Union (EU) law can be read against this background. From an economic perspective, the main purpose of the EU is increasing efficiency.[8] The main instrument towards reaching this goal is the internal market as structured by EU primary law, particularly by the fundamental freedoms laid down in the Treaty on the Functioning of the European Union (TFEU).[9] While the motivation behind the legal basis of the internal market may not have been regulatory competition as such, one of the main objectives clearly has been to create an environment characterized by cross-border mobility among nation states that are part of the EU enterprise,[10] as Zoe Adams and Simon Deakin observe: 'The goal of regulatory competition is not an aim of the Union, but is an unavoidable consequence of rules designed to promote cross-border economic mobility.'[11] Thus, in a wider sense, the legal norms underpinning the internal market, primarily those such as the fundamental freedoms ensuring mobility of capital and people, can be interpreted as creating the preconditions of regulatory competition. In European company

[8] See B Gabor, *Regulatory Competition in the Internal Market* (Edward Elgar Publishing 2013) 276: 'In economic literature, the European Union is often examined as a tool for achieving efficiency without much consideration being given to what the legal and political foundations of the Union are.' On the relation between the internal market as a policy goal and regulatory competition E-M Kieninger, *Wettbewerb Der Privatrechtsordnungen Im Europäischen Binnenmarkt* (Mohr Siebeck 2002) 333–79; Z Adams and S Deakin, 'Freedom of Establishment and Regulatory Competition' in D Chalmers and A Arnull (eds), *The Oxford Handbook of European Union Law* (OUP 2015) 537; without doubt, from other perspectives, other goals are equally relevant as well, as the political objective of maintaining lasting peace among European nation states.

[9] Consolidated Version of the Treaty on the Functioning of the European Union [2012] OJ 326/47 (hereafter TFEU); the fundamental freedoms are laid down in Art. 34 TFEU (free movement of goods); Art. 45 TFEU (free movement of workers); Art. 49 TFEU (freedom of establishment); Art. 56 TFEU (freedom to provide services); Art. 63 TFEU (free movement of capital).

[10] On regulatory competition as a by-product of the European single market see Bratton and others (n 6) 35–43.

[11] Adams and Deakin (n 8) 560, discussing the role of freedom of establishment and corresponding ECJ case law.

law, this function has been illustrated by the behaviour of market participants both on the demand and supply side, and ensuing European Court of Justice (ECJ) as well as national case law.[12]

Yet Member States' ability to autonomously create the preconditions for regulatory competition is, in most instances, subject to constitutional constraints. In 2009, the German Constitutional Court delivered its decision on whether the Treaty of Lisbon was consistent with the German Constitution.[13] One of the central questions was whether the treaty leads to a conferral of powers on the EU that is prohibited by unalterable clauses of the German Constitution. The goal of the Treaty of Lisbon was certainly not to foster regulatory competition per se. However, the development of the EU and its primary law as recorded in the central treaties is certainly one towards a competitive internal market, with few barriers for cross-border mobility of people and goods. The hope has been that efficient solutions would be found via a form of 'competitive federalism'.[14] It is in this vein that the fundamental freedoms make economic sense. Therefore, one could say that, in a wider sense, what we have seen here is a deliberation about the proper entailments of democratic commitments. Does the democratic structure of the German Federal Republic preclude a conferral of powers, in part in the form of choice of law opportunities, because this would lead to an erosion of parliamentary control over substantive issues in Germany? The court concluded that the Lisbon Treaty did not cross the line drawn by the German Constitution, but that any further integrative projects would have to be 'compensated' by appropriate measures to ensure EU-level democratic legitimation and that national parliaments would have to have a 'last say' on a core minimum of substantive issues.

[12] See Chapter 1, section B.2.(b).

[13] Bundesverfassungsgericht, Judgment of 30.06.2009, 2 BE 2/08, ECLI:DE:BVerfG:2009:es20090630.2bve000208.

[14] C Barnard, 'Regulating Competitive Federalism in the European Union? The Case of EU Social Policy' in J Shaw (ed), *Social Law and Policy in an Evolving European Union* (Hart Publishing 2000) 49; J-M Sun and J Pelkmans, 'Regulatory Competition in the Single Market' (1995) 33 Journal of Common Market Studies 67, 70–2 with an account of how regulatory competition in the EU has been an intended effect of regulatory strategy at least since 1992.

The example of the internal market shows that national parliaments have been willing to transfer competences in favour of a supranational framework that has led to a significant increase of mobility in Europe, thus restricting the domain of majority rule nationally defined. With regard to trade liberalization agreements (that arguably perform a similar function), Brian Langille has framed his criticism as an issue of 'democratic control and accountability':

> [A] common instinct and part of the standard political reaction to trade and investment liberalization policies, has been that they limit the ability of people to govern their own affairs. Policies are now set, to some increased extent, in the international marketplace of regulatory competition. This is a change and, on a common view, a loss. More precisely it is a loss of democratic control and accountability.[15]

Democratic organization of a polity in practice certainly does not mean that each and every question must be decided by some sort of majority vote. If legislative decisions that are influenced by regulatory competition do not overlap with those in the proper domain of majority rule, a scenario of the first type discussed earlier cannot even arise. Also, it is important to remember that, from a formal perspective, regulatory competition does not touch the 'primacy of politics'.[16] Competitive market dynamics are possible only to the extent that there have been political decisions to create appropriate legal conditions, such as most importantly choice of law opportunities that reduce mobility costs. From this perspective alone, a conflict between the demands of democratic principles and developing law markets would be logically impossible. Whatever form of regulatory competition may be observed, it is dependent on prior democratic approval regarding its structural preconditions.

[15] B Langille, 'Competing Conceptions of Regulatory Competition in Debates on Trade Liberalization and Labour Standards' in W Bratton and others (eds), *International Regulatory Competition and Coordination* (Clarendon Press 1996) 479, 490.

[16] H Eidenmüller, 'The Transnational Law Market, Regulatory Competition, and Transnational Corporations' (2011) 18 Indiana Journal of Global Legal Studies 707, 730; see also Peters (n 1) 42: 'The democratic law-maker remains free to set its political priorities. Nothing compels national parliaments to strive to attain a top rank in the legal systems competition.'

(c) Devolutionary erosion of majority rule

A third perspective from which regulatory competition appears to be in conflict with the principle of majority rule is a dynamic one. The primacy argument discussed in section A.1.(b) implicitly relies on the assumption that either popular will regarding regulatory competition will not change substantially, or that such changes could be implemented in due time according to the set mechanism of majority rule. The reality of competition as it results from enabling political decisions in the past could then, in principle and granted that there are periods of delayed adjustment, for example, between ballots, at all times be assumed to be consistent with present popular will.

Setting the ground for regulatory competition, mostly by creating or enabling mobility, however, is not easily undone. Two strategies are feasible in principle: reducing mobility, and reducing diversity.[17] Raising the costs of mobility for individuals and firms is an instrument that has been employed by legislatures refusing to compete by altering their legal products on offer according to mobile demand. In many contexts, however, it is not straightforwardly possible or promising. In the frequent case that mobility has been granted and increased not by a single state, but as part of a supranational arrangement, such as the EU with its aformentioned establishment of the single market, restricting mobility with respect to certain issues that have shown to set off now unwanted arbitrage dynamics and competitive pressure often would come at a much higher price of withdrawal from the whole supranational architecture.

More promising, particularly in a context of supranational integration, is the route via a reduction of legal diversity in order to calm down competitive pressure. Such coordination may come in the form of multilateral agreements on particular issues, or measures provided for by an existing framework, such as harmonization through EU-level legislation. The detrimental effect of transnational coordination as a 'lesser evil'—compared to unrestricted competition—on the democratic legitimacy of the legislative outcome has been laid out by David Charny:

[17] See Chapter 1, section C. for an overview of states' response options.

> It is now well understood, though, that the practical sacrifices of sovereignty involved in transnational coordination may prevent the more complete erosion that is caused by naked jurisdictional competition [. . .]. Nonetheless, there is an evident tradeoff between the democratic advantages of centralized and decentralized modes of resolving these issues. It is much easier to design institutions that are locally democratic than globally democratic, particularly in terms of responsiveness to the 'cultural' aspects of what counts as democratic decision making.[18]

Coined in 1979 by David Marquand with respect to the then European Community,[19] the 'democratic deficit' of supranational institutions is a staple in contemporary political theory.[20] The point to be made here is that conferral of powers for the sake of transnational cooperation and coordination, be it with the objective of *increasing* mobility in order to foster arbitrage or in order to enable harmonization of legal rules so as to *reduce* competitive

[18] D Charny, 'Regulatory Competition and Labour Law Standards' in DC Esty and D Geradin (eds), *Regulatory Competition and Economic Integration: Comparative Perspectives* (OUP 2001) 311, 326.

[19] D Marquand, *Parliament for Europe* (Jonathan Cape 1979) 64–6, arguing for a powerful European Parliament in order to ensure democratic responsiveness and legitimacy of the EU.

[20] See T Pogge, 'Creating Supra-National Institutions Democratically: Reflections on the European Union's "Democratic Deficit"' (1997) 5 The Journal of Political Philosophy 163; PL Lindseth, 'Democratic Legitimacy and the Administrative Character of Supranationalism: The Example of the European Community' (1999) 99 Columbia Law Review 628; Y Mény, 'De la démocratie en Europe: Old Concepts and New Challenges' 41 Journal of Common Market Studies 1; D Schleicher, 'What if Europe Held an Election and No One Cared?' (2011) 52 Harvard International Law Journal 109, all focusing on the EU. On the democratic deficit of 'international structures' in general see Bratton and others (n 6) 2: '[T]here is a problem of democratic deficit. This stems from a perception that internalized economic activities are no longer subject to control or facilitation by national governments acting alone, while international structures are institutionally underdeveloped.' On the 'fundamental dilemma' that lies beneath the democratic deficit of international institutions see R Dahl, 'Can International Organizations be Democratic? A Skeptic's View' in I Shapiro and C Hacker-Cordón (eds), *Democracy's Edges* (CUP 1999) 1922: 'A smaller democratic unit provides an ordinary citizen with greater opportunities to participate in governing than a larger unit. But the smaller the unit the more likely that some matters of importance to the citizen are beyond the capacity of the government to deal with effectively.'

pressures on legislatures, tends to reduce the degree of democratic legitimacy that the results will enjoy.

Summing up, potential conflict between regulatory competition and majority rule as one of the basic premises of democratic theory comes in various potential forms. Open conflict (first scenario) is fairly unlikely. Hidden erosion (second scenario) is more likely, but not acute as a result of the 'primacy' argument. Progressive or devolutionary erosion of majority rule facilitated by a tendency to restrict national legislative authority for the sake of international cooperation and coordination has the most critical force.

Majority rule as exercised in parliament has been presupposed here as one of the key features of democratic organization of a polity. As a method of decision-making per se, however, it has no normative content—apart from its pragmatic appeal, there is nothing in the concept of majority rule that tells us why we should use this method for important political decisions. From that it does not follow, however, that there is nothing to say in favour of democracy and its mechanisms from a normative perspective.

2. DEMOCRACY AND EQUALITY

What is the source of deep scepticism voiced by some scholars about regulatory competition intercepting or changing the democratic process? What is it about democratic principles that we find not only practical, but genuinely valuable—what are the reasons why we think that democratic principles should be protected from such competitive influence?

An answer to these questions is to be found in the values that underpin democracy as a form of political organization. The value of democracy has been the subject of endless scholarly debate. Rival accounts may roughly be divided into instrumentalist versus intrinsic accounts.[21]

[21] T Christiano, 'Democracy' in C McKinnon (ed), *Issues in Political Theory* (OUP 2012) 80; D Estlund, 'Debate: On Christiano's the Constitution of Equality' (2009) 17 Journal of Political Philosophy 241, 242.

Proponents of 'democratic instrumentalism'[22] have claimed that the value of democracy as a form of government is grounded in the outcomes of democratic decision-making that are comparatively better than those of other types of political organization. A problem that these accounts face, however, is the fact that for the most part of political reality, there will be no shared understanding of the appropriate criteria to measure the quality of political outcomes.[23] Thus, it is difficult to make a comprehensive argument for the value of democracy on these grounds.

An intrinsic justification of democracy is based on the idea that democracy is a good in itself, that it has or expresses an intrinsic value that does not depend on a comparative advantage in achieving good results by democratic methods.[24] This intrinsic value is often seen in the fact that democracy gives expression to the idea that citizens are equal and should, from a political perspective, be treated as equally worthy of respect.[25] Being so treated means, according to many, that people have an equal say in the making of laws that are binding upon everyone including themselves.[26] The equality argument as presented by Thomas Christiano and others has gained some prominence in the recent debate on the value of democracy, which is why it shall be the basis for our assessment of whether it stands in conflict with the idea of regulatory competition.

[22] As the view is called by R Arneson and E Anderson (2009), 'The Supposed Right to a Democratic Say' in T Christiano and J Christman (eds), *Contemporary Debates in Political Philosophy* (Wiley-Blackwell 2009) 197.

[23] T Christiano, *The Constitution of Equality: Democratic Authority and Its Limits* (OUP 2008) 95, 101.

[24] E Anderson, 'Democracy: Instrumental vs Non-Instrumental Value' in T Christiano and J Christman (eds), *Contemporary Debates in Political Philosophy* (Wiley-Blackwell 2009) 213.

[25] Christiano (n 23) 96: '[D]emocracy is a publicly clear way of recognizing and affirming the equality of citizens.'

[26] Christiano (n 2) Section 2.2.3: 'Many democratic theorists have argued that democracy is a way of treating persons as equals when there is good reason to impose some kind of organization on their shared lives but they disagree about how best to do it. […] In effect, democratic decision-making respects each person's point of view on matters of common concern by giving each an equal say about what to do in cases of disagreement.' See also P Singer, *Democracy and Disobedience* (OUP 1973); J Waldron, *Law and Disagreement* (OUP 1999) Ch. 5.

As shines through in the criticisms of regulatory competition that reference the demands of democracy, the critical point indeed is the commitment to treating people as equals that is embodied in the democratic organization of a polity. The worry is that mobile demanders in possession of capital or other resources that states are keen not to lose as 'customers' of their law have, in effect, stronger votes and thus more influence on the outcome of the democratic process. They are, so to speak, given more than their equal share.

One should keep in mind that absent any form of regulatory competition, asymmetries in influence on political decision-making tend to materialize as well, as Anne Peters has characterized the conflict between democratic equality and the competitive paradigm:

> Overall, the unequal positions of the law-consumers is acceptable in a democratic State only as long as democratic and strictly formally egalitarian procedures still formally govern the law-making process. Competition between legal systems that is governed by the principle of unequal market power is not an alternative process to democratic, general and equal elections and ballots.[27]

It would be short-sighted, of course, to blame regulatory competition alone for deviations from the ideal of citizens being treated as equals. Yet, the sceptical argument need not be presented as stronger than it is meant. Regulatory competition, the argument goes, will exert an influence on the political process that further removes it from the ideal of 'one person, one vote'. That is enough to say that there is a conflict between the commitment to ideal democratic principles and a de facto design of legal spheres along the lines of regulatory competition.

B. REGULATORY COMPETITION AND STATE AUTONOMY

Another case in which one could say that regulatory competition carries us further away from certain political ideals is the issue of state autonomy. Facing competitive pressure exerted by the

[27] Peters (n 1) 54.

existence of various law markets, political representatives may not be able to decide autonomously about the right course of action. Once regulatory competition is in full swing and has become an accepted fact in a particular field, it is argued, affected states will have no choice but to play along, for fear of the consequences associated with losing market shares.

Objections of this kind have been voiced particularly among constitutional and public international law scholars, albeit not in much analytical detail.[28] The structure of the argument is basically as follows:

1. Political autonomy requires that legislative decisions made by a state (or its representatives) are 'its own'.
2. Regulatory competition is a source of external pressure on legislators that demands law reform to be conducive to competitive success on an international law market.
3. Hence, regulatory competition has the potential of curtailing political autonomy.

1. AUTONOMY AS A POLITICAL CONCEPT

At first sight, speaking of 'state autonomy' appears to be a curious conceptual choice.[29] In the sense of *personal* autonomy, the term is used as a qualification primarily of individuals' decisions. Someone acts autonomously if he or she decides on their own, as

[28] P Kirchhof, 'Freiheitlicher Wettbewerb und staatliche Autonomie – Solidarität' (2005) 58 ORDO 39; Peters (n 1) 46.

[29] Among political philosophers, autonomy is commonly used as a concept referring to individual people, not to groups or political entities. This appears to be different for political scientists, who continue to use the term 'autonomy' as a characterization of a political entity, most notably the nation state. Usage of 'autonomy of states' can be found, eg, in PG Cerny, 'Globalization and the Changing Logic of Collective Action' (1995) 49 International Organization 595, 619, 625; G Garrett, 'Global Markets and National Politics: Collision Course or Virtuous Circle?' (1998) 52 International Organization 787 bases his argument on the concept of 'national autonomy' and 'policy autonomy'.

a result of critical reflection upon the options at hand, free from outside coercion or manipulation.[30]

How can our intuitions about personal autonomy be translated into the political context? In what sense do we speak of states or other political entities as autonomous? State autonomy, as it will be used in the following, refers to all kinds of political decisions. In the most basic sense, political autonomy means that political decisions are based on the result of (collective) reflection upon the alternatives at hand, as opposed to being dictated by external forces or pressures by actors such as other states or supranational organizations.

In political discourse on the limitations that determine political decisions, refuge is sometimes taken in the concept of 'state sovereignty', which seems to capture a similar idea: the sovereign state decides for itself and its people.[31] The usage of 'state sovereignty' in public international law discourse, however, points to a slight difference in meaning. State sovereignty refers primarily to a state's fundamental decisions about its structure and its place in the world, the ability to give itself a constitution, to enter into relations with other states and defend itself against external attacks on its territorial integrity.[32] State sovereignty thus being a more specific and narrower concept, we will focus our discussion on the broader notion of state autonomy.

In ancient Greek philosophical literature, autonomy[33] refers to the right of a city-state to manage its own affairs, even if

[30] For an overview of usage of the term 'autonomy' in moral and political philosophy and related problems see J Christman, 'Autonomy in Moral and Political Philosophy', *The Stanford Encyclopedia of Philosophy* (2018) <https://plato.stanford.edu/archives/spr2018/entries/autonomy-moral/> accessed 1 August 2018.

[31] Another conceptual alternative would be the more general term 'independence' of the state, which without further clarification does not help much as it begs the question: independence from what or whom?

[32] See Garrett (n 29) 788, relating 'policy autonomy' to 'de jure sovereignty' and critically discussing both as potential casualties of an 'ever more international scale of markets'. On the conceptual history of 'sovereignty' in general see D Philpott, 'Sovereignty', *The Stanford Encyclopedia of Philosophy* (2014) <https://plato.stanford.edu/archives/sum2016/entries/sovereignty/> accessed 1 August 2018.

[33] Etymologically, the term is a compound of αὐτο- (own, independent) and νόμος (law), literally meaning 'according to one's own law'.

there were a superior mother-city.[34] Interestingly, this idea was translated into the sphere of the individual only as late as the Enlightenment, in the sense of the right to manage one's own affairs within a given political and legal framework.[35] Understood in the original sense of autonomy as political self-rule, the concept may very plausibly be applied to groups or states.

(a) Autonomy as an ideal

In political discourse, autonomy figures both as an ideal and as a matter of degree in practice. It is not all or nothing, in the sense that decisions, states, groups, and individuals can be more or less autonomous, depending on how much they are influenced by outside pressures. The perfectly autonomous decision or state of existence may be impossible to find in reality, both with regard to individuals and to political entities.

Setting the threshold for qualifying states, individuals, and their decisions as autonomous too high would lead to an overly narrow conception of an unattainable ideal with very limited relevance for political practice. Gradable autonomy, however, is perfectly compatible with treating it as a political goal that can be realized to a greater or lesser extent. It would be unrealistic, even utopian, to suppose that most or even any political decision could be perfectly autonomous, in the sense of being based on reasons alone that are not in any way related to limitations that the political landscape presents (such as geostrategic or fiscal considerations). We are working with a conceptual continuum here. A decision can be more or less autonomous. Political decisions are seldom, if ever, based on one or two single isolated reasons. More commonly, they are the product of reflection on a number of considerations that, taken together, ideally point towards a particular course of action. Of course, they may also point in different directions, as political debate usually shows. Depending on which reasons 'win the race', so to speak, and emerge as being

[34] T May, 'The Concept of Autonomy' (1994) 31 American Philosophical Quarterly 133, 139.

[35] For a historical account of the concept of autonomy see JB Schneewind, *The Invention of Autonomy: A History of Modern Moral Philosophy* (CUP 1998) Part 1.

decisive, these reasons can in combination make a decision more or less autonomous.

Similarly, however, an understanding of autonomy that is too wide would yield implausible results of the 'autonomous slave'[36] type, who is in the most basic sense unfree but, by reflecting upon his situation and endorsing it (for whatever reasons) would counterintuitively have to be regarded as autonomous.

(b) Autonomy versus self-sufficiency

Coming back to the ancient meaning of autonomy as being entitled and able to manage one's own affairs, it is not required that there be no external limitations and influences on a legislature's actions at all, in a sense that would be possible under conditions of complete self-sufficiency. No man is an island, and even though some countries are, in today's globalized world, they do well not to behave as one constantly.

Managing one's own affairs, personal as well as political, individually as well as collectively, does not involve being able to do whatever one pleases at any time, without regard for negative consequences. To the contrary, managing one's own affairs wisely may instead mean assessing the options at hand, calculating risks and chances, reflecting on the values that one is committed to, and then making a decision that is based on the process of deliberation. Autonomy is thus far less demanding a concept than self-sufficiency.

2. STATE AUTONOMY UNDER COMPETITIVE PRESSURE

The distinction between deciding autonomously and carelessly doing whatever one pleases at a given time points to a second helpful differentiation between autonomy in a formal and in a substantive sense.

In a *formal* sense, autonomy presupposes the authority of a political entity to set its own laws regarding certain issues, as opposed

[36] See for a discussion of the 'autonomous slave' in JS Mill's writings on paternalism AE Fuchs, 'Autonomy, Slavery, and Mill's Critique of Paternalism' (2001) 4 Ethical Theory and Moral Practice 231.

to being bound to the law of a superior political entity. In a stronger *substantive* sense, autonomy not only requires the entitlement to technical lawmaking, but also refers to the content of the rules that are the result of such lawmaking. Substantive self-rule is a stronger notion insofar as legal rules may be formally autonomous in origin, but substantially influenced by other sources of political authority.

A directive issued by the EU legislature, for example, has according to Article 288 TFEU to be transformed into national law by Member States, who retain 'choice of form and methods' within a set time-frame. Technically therefore, whenever this transformation is being carried out, there is an act of formally autonomous lawmaking involved on the part of complying Member States. However, the substance of these laws is to a large degree prescribed by the content of the respective directive.

Prima facie, regulatory competition does not affect state autonomy directly, certainly not in its formal sense. As has already been discussed, even if law markets establish themselves in some fields, the formal 'primacy of politics'[37] will remain untouched, as the preconditions for these markets will always be based on legislative decisions that will continue to be made by state governments, not by 'the market' itself. One may doubt, however, whether such an optimistic perspective on the role of the state in face of established law markets is justified, as the sections that follow will illustrate.

(a) Choice of law opportunities and formal state autonomy

The increase of arbitrage opportunities as a result of national policy may itself be interpreted as a restriction of formal state autonomy. Authority and entitlement to issue law may remain untouched by such arbitrage. However, if potential addressees of law are granted opportunities to opt into a different regime, they are given the opportunity to remove themselves from the default state's juridical reach. By using choice of law opportunities, they are able to distance themselves from the default jurisdiction, whose autonomous legislative decisions in this respect 'run dry'. State autonomy formally understood as collective, active, and

[37] Eidenmüller (n 16) 730; see also section A.1.(b).

reflective self-rule is thus unaffected by competitive pressure due to legal arbitrage.

(b) Substantive state autonomy under competitive pressure

The reason why the primacy of the political appears to be endangered as a result of regulatory competition has to do with what could also be described as a practical, in contrast to a theoretical, kind of autonomy. It not only matters whether states are theoretically entitled to legislatively manage their own affairs, but also whether they are able to transform this right into political practice as well. As has been illustrated, a state may formally be an autonomous lawmaker, self-ruling in the sense that laws are being issued by national authorities alone. At the same time, however, serious constraints may be present as to the substantive content of the legislative decisions that are made. Examples of limiting factors are the relations to other states that could be compromised by a particular course of action, general geostrategic considerations, and, of course, long-term financial consequences of political decisions.[38]

In this vein, regulatory competition could lead to a scenario in which it would be difficult for states to transform theoretical autonomy into political practice. This could be the case if what a successful competitor would have to do is so clear that, given states' commitment to fare well as competitive suppliers of legal wares, there really was no other choice but to act according to the demands of the law market.

As discussed already, autonomy as self-rule is incompatible with a decision being decisively influenced by exogenous forces or actors. In such instances of 'other-rule', these forces could be political agents such as other states or international and supranational organizations (ie the UN, EU, or OECD). 'The market' with the economic pressures that it exerts on states would—in such clear cases—fall into the category of exogenous determinants of political decisions as well.

Regulatory competition thus introduces a reason for legislative action. Facing competitive dynamics, governments have to choose how to treat the fact that there is competition going on

[38] See Chapter 1, section A.4.

and involving them. They are under pressure to take this fact into account, by reversing the structural preconditions that have led to the existence of market structures and thereby isolating themselves from competition continuing among other suppliers, by imitating successful market participants (as happened with German company law in reaction to the UK Limited's success), or by coming up with new 'law products', in the hope of reaping the rewards of successful legal innovation. Ignoring the existence of a law market for a while is possible as well, but overall not very likely, as it often has financial consequences.

From an autonomy perspective, the central question has been whether the influence of regulatory competition on the political process leads to a situation in which legislative decisions are not 'own' decisions of the respective polity, or are so to a lesser extent.

3. STATE AUTONOMY AND DEMOCRACY

The 'ownness' of a political decision is itself a fairly vague concept. In order to better understand what exactly it means, it might help to see more clearly why it is that regulatory competition does not contribute to it.

A more refined version of the autonomy argument discussed takes into account the way political decisions are made in most states of interest to us:

1. Political autonomy requires that legislative decisions made by a state (or its representatives) are 'its own'.
2. The criteria for autonomy as self-rule originate in the organizational structure of a given political entity, such as—in most cases today—the commitment to democratic decision-making.
3. Regulatory competition figures as a reason for legislative action, without being adequately included in the democratic calculus.
4. Thus, regulatory competition has the potential to curtail political autonomy.

Democratic decision-making describes one way in which these 'own' answers to political questions may be reached. Democracy seems to be a political form that we accept as yielding 'own' decisions.[39] Logically, the conditions for 'ownness' of decisions are built into each polity separately, particularly into the constitution. For those polities with constitutional references to democracy in some form or another, adherence to democratic principles appears to be a key element of political autonomy.[40]

The reasons that must be reflected in legislative decisions in order for them to be autonomous cannot be identified independently from the political entity in question. In democratically organized polities, for example, respect for the principle of democratic decision-making and for the scope of discretionary powers of elected representatives plays a crucial role.

The problem, then, is not that the state would not rule itself any more at all, but that it rules itself according to criteria that we find problematic. The idea is, roughly, that legislative decisions should be determined by the outcomes of the democratic process, however that process may be structured in detail. If they are not, if the democratic vote is given less relative weight compared to other considerations such as competitive success, self-rule is only formal in the sense that it does not decisively determine legal rules' content. Formally, the state still makes its own rules. Substantively, however, these rules are dictated by the demands of regulatory competition. These demands will often be in the form that the successful law of a different polity must be imitated so as to gain back market shares or prevent further losses.

[39] H Spector, 'Autonomy' in G Gaus and R D'Agostina (eds), *The Routledge Companion to Social and Political Philosophy* (Routledge 2013) 573–4: 'Because political autonomy refers to collective self-government, it is generally studied under the heading of democracy, as democracy is the best known form of self-government.'

[40] J Bohman and W Rehg, 'Introduction' in J Bohman and W Rehg (eds), *Deliberative Democracy: Essays on Reason and Politics* (MIT Press 1997) ix: '[D]eliberative democracy refers to the idea that legitimate lawmaking issues from the public deliberation of citizens. As a normative account of legitimacy, deliberative democracy evokes ideals of rational legislation, participatory politics, and civic self-governance. In short, it presents an ideal of political autonomy based on the practical reasoning of citizens.'

The problem with regulatory competition is that it introduces rival demands addressed to political decisions; these demands could eventually intercept the legitimizing link between popular will and governmental activity, particularly in representative systems, which are the majority today. Reconciling regulatory competition and democratic commitments would require that questions of how to respond would somehow be actively included in the democratic calculus. Absent strong elements of basic or direct democracy, however, this is not the case.

One of the reasons why legislative motivations flowing from regulatory competition resist adequate integration into the democratic calculus is related to the mills of political communication. Whereas the electorate is largely uninformed about regulatory competition and its consequences in terms of legislative motivation, government representatives are keenly aware of competitive dynamics. Transparent deliberation about merits and disadvantages of giving in to regulatory competition or creating conditions for it to unfold in more and more areas will not take place. Law markets may thus grow without the electorate being aware of them and, once they have been established, path dependencies cement their existence. Following their demands then appears as a political, and in many cases a fiscal, necessity.

In theory, the problem of regulatory competition and democracy and autonomy could be resolved as follows. As long as they are an expression of genuine self-rule, political decisions cannot be criticized on the grounds of autonomy or the principle of democracy. If people's own decisions are influenced somehow, so be it.

If, in a scenario of direct democratic vote on certain issues, the public places much weight on the demands of a certain kind of market—be it a law market or any other market that demands resources to be distributed in a certain way, or legal rules to be amended in a certain way—that is simply an expression of democracy at work, the demands of regulatory competition have in this case been integrated into the democratic calculus. Why should regulatory competition and the political reasons it yields not be treated like all the other reasons that must be considered, weighed against each other during the democratic process?

Competitive pressure as a determinant of political decision-making is not communicated. It is far beyond what the typical voter would want to occupy themselves with.[41] Unlike issues of distributive justice, or of how to create more jobs, regulatory competition and what it demands of the legislator and whether the legislator should give in to these demands is not something that would possibly be debated in the public arena. There may be exceptions in contexts in which the distributive consequences of legal reform are conspicuous, as tends to be the case with competitively motivated tax reform.[42] In most other fields, we are left with the problem that regulatory competition could come to be a determinant of legislative decisions without the people even being aware of it at all. If that is so, there will not be any democratic critique of regulatory competition in the fields where it occurs, neither by positive confirmation nor by negative vote to the contrary. Issues of regulatory competition will thus not be reflected in democratic vote at all. It would thus be a determining factor that is largely unnoticed by the people. That is something that does not fit well with our understanding of democracy.

Democracy demands a certain kind and amount of transparency.[43] How are the people supposed to vote competently on what should be done, or who should make decisions, if they have no idea how this is done, or what the motivations and reasons of those involved in legislation are. As long as regulatory competition is a purely academic issue of technical juridical nature that arises now and then, here and there, this is not a problem. It resembles many other issues of such technical nature that cannot be simplified enough and explained to every single member of the popular body. That does not make legislative decisions on such issues less legitimate. On the contrary, part of the appeal of representative democratic systems is that it allows a polity to have

[41] On the Hobbesian and public choice line of criticism of democracy that people are too apathetic, thus not informed about politics in order to make democracy work positively, see Christiano (n 2) Section 2.1.2.

[42] On tax competition and its distributive dimension see Chapter 3, section C.1.

[43] This corresponds with the approach to democracy as public justification, as Christiano (n 2) Section 2.2.2 puts it: 'laws and policies are legitimate to the extent that they are publicly justified to the citizens of the community'.

experts deciding on issues they know something about, unlike the people in general.

Should, however, the choice of law opportunities grow and widen, and regulatory competition gain traction in more and more fields, this would come to be a problematic scenario of the kind that has been described here.

Together, these premises give rise to the conclusion that regulatory competition may lead to a loss of state autonomy realized in legislative decisions.

With Chapter 2 in mind, this worry appears to be well founded. We have seen already that legislatures do in fact react to pressure brought about by regulatory competition in ways that appear forced by the threat of losing shares in a market for law they cannot afford to ignore. Demands of regulatory competition may be integrated into the democratic calculus, for example, by figuring as arguments in political debate. The options at hand, as well as how they are communicated in the political arena and to the general public, are influenced severely by the fact that regulatory competition offers sanctions to unsuccessful competitors. Democratic vote thus appears pressured to go along with market demands.

In almost poetic (some might say too poetic) words, Paul Kirchhof, a former judge of the German Federal Constitutional Court, has sharply criticized the application of the market paradigm to political and particularly legislative matters.[44] He argues that the mechanism of competitive interaction and democratically legitimized state rule are, at their core, diverging principles. Their incompatibility is shown in the fact that public authorities are bound by the principle of state autonomy, instead of having a claim to competitive freedom. His conclusion is that the state should not overestimate the relevance of competition as a concept or principle for its own matters.

[44] Kirchhof (n 28) 39: 'Wettbewerb ist Ausdruck individueller Freiheit, also eine Handlungsform der freiheitsberechtigten Gesellschaft, nicht des freiheitsverpflichteten Staates. Der Staat muß als Garant des Rechts aus dem Wettbewerb herausgehalten und von Erwerbsmotiven freigestellt werden.'; see also J Kersten, 'Wettbewerb zwischen Hoheitsträgern' in H Kube and others (eds), *Leitgedanken des Rechts – Paul Kirchhof zum 70. Geburtstag* (CF Müller 2013) 845 for a summary (in German).

The intuition the previous sections have been trying to spell out is that regulatory competition leads to a situation in which we would be inclined to view law as being decisively influenced by sources that we do not accept as belonging to the 'self' of a polity. By the definition put forward here, they cannot then be autonomous. The argument is not intended to advance the strong claim that every scenario of regulatory competition necessarily and entirely precludes autonomy of the legislatures involved. On the contrary, it would be utopian to suppose that legislative decisions could be perfectly autonomous, that there could be instances of genuine self-rule uninfluenced by external limitations.

The weaker claim put forth here is that regulatory competition presents reasons for legislative action, reasons that do not make these decisions more autonomous. Legislative decisions are seldom made for one reason alone. As has been discussed, in the majority of cases there are various reasons, influences, and motivations that play a role in the determination of what is done regarding creation, reform, and design of legal rules. This can include a mix of autonomy-conducive and other reasons. The argument presented here leads to the conclusion that regulatory competition contributes to these other reasons.

Speaking about state autonomy as something that should, in principle, not be jeopardized presupposes a favourable attitude towards the state as a form of political organization, including the restriction of *individual* autonomy that comes with living in any kind of state, although the extent and kind of restrictions vary greatly among different states. Whether state representatives and institutions are justified in restricting individual freedom and autonomy is typically discussed under the conceptual headline of 'political authority', which we will turn to in section C.

C. REGULATORY COMPETITION AND POLITICAL AUTHORITY

Scepticism about regulatory competition may also be informed by a conflict with our understanding of legitimate political authority. Authority as 'the right to command and correlatively the right to be obeyed'[45] is central to the functioning of a political system. As a vehicle and means of communication for the directives of an authority, law is understood to 'have' legitimate authority itself, in the sense that it requires people to act in a certain way precisely or in part because it is law.[46] Accepting another person or institution as an authority thus requires treating them as a source of valid reasons for action, without reference to the content of their orders. With the words of Max Weber, from the perspective of those guided by an authority it is 'as if the ruled had made the content of the command the maxim of their conduct for its very own sake'.[47]

There is some debate as to whether the right to rule of an authority is directly correlated with a corresponding duty to obey on the side of the commands' addressees. This is the issue about the existence and if so, provenance of political obligations. Strong conceptions of authority rely on this correlation.

Whether and how regulatory competition is related to political authority is the issue of the following argument that will be discussed in sections C.1–3:

1. There are several ways of trying to justify political authority as a right to rule: the main routes are perfectionist and procedural accounts.
2. Regulatory competition is not compatible with perfectionist accounts, as it introduces reasons for legislation that are not sufficiently linked to human flourishing or other evaluative standards commonly relied upon in perfectionist theories.

[45] RP Wolff, *The Conflict between Authority and Autonomy* (Basil Blackwell 1990) 20.

[46] For an overview see L Green, 'Legal Obligation and Authority', *The Stanford Encyclopedia of Philosophy* (2012) <http://plato.stanford.edu/archives/win2012/entries/legal-obligation/> accessed 1 August 2018, Section 2; see also L Green, *The Authority of the State* (Clarendon Press 1988); J Raz, *The Authority of Law: Essays on Law and Morality* (Clarendon Press 1979) 233–49; RP Wolff, *In Defense of Anarchism* (University of California Press 1970) 9: 'Obedience is not a matter of doing what someone tells you to do. It is a matter of doing what he tells you to do *because he tells you to do it*.'

[47] M Weber, *Economy and Society: An Outline of Interpretive Sociology, VoL II* (University of California Press 1978) 946.

3. Regulatory competition is not compatible with procedural accounts either, as it is a motivating force behind legislative decisions that cannot be properly incorporated into the democratic calculus and leads to a violation of both the principle of majority rule and the democratic commitment to equality.[48]
4. Therefore, regulatory competition makes it difficult to justify political authority, at least within the theoretical landscape of contemporary political philosophy.

1. THE LEGITIMACY OF POLITICAL AUTHORITY

In the ideal political scenario, the conditions for legitimate authority are fulfilled. State government in its role as the political authority issues commands, in the form of law. Citizens accept these commands as binding and act accordingly.

Why is authority part of the ideal political scenario? Anarchistically inclined authors would strongly oppose that claim. A strong argument in favour of political authority as such, whatever its realization in detail, is consequentialist and practical. Authority makes possible meaningful and complex social life in advanced societies, as it provides the stability and order needed for many instances of self-determination.[49] A simple example of why it makes sense to accept an authority is traffic laws. Adhering to traffic rules makes it possible for everyone to travel efficiently and safely. These rules thus enhance people's freedom to go wherever they want, even though, at first sight, they restrict our personal freedom. We cannot travel on the wrong side of the road, for example, or jump traffic lights, at least not without the risk of being sanctioned by the police.

Another argument in favour of political authority is best explained by reference to a certain kind of authority, that of experts in a particular field. We cannot all be lawyers, doctors, or car mechanics. We need people who specialize in these skills and whom we can trust to be competent in their field of expertise. The case with political authority is different, but similar in key

[48] See section A. [49] May (n 34) 133.

respects. We need political authorities, who provide order and stability, who are experts in establishing a peaceful and stable social order, who know how to communicate decisions in the political arena and media so as to gain acceptance among the general public or at least large groups of people. Governing a society may thus be understood as a form of semi-technical skill, as the art of governing. For this we need experts and we need to trust that what these experts order us to do is the right thing to do overall, even if we do not agree in this or that instance.

Legitimacy is part of the ideal scenario as well, as it is a necessary precondition for the justification of political authority. Without legitimacy, we may have a form of de facto authority, whose 'claim to a right to rule', however, is not supported by adequate justification. Legitimate authority means, then, that there is in fact such a 'right to rule' and, consequently, that a claim to that right is true or well-reasoned.

What are the conditions for legitimate political authority? According to what criteria can we determine whether the practice of a particular instance of authority is legitimate or not? There are two main approaches to the justification of political authority. First, the realization of a perfectionist catalogue of substantive values that are understood to be essential to human flourishing. Second, the procedural and institutional design of a polity, particularly with regard to the principle of democracy. In the following, we will discuss whether these strategies of justifying political authority are compatible with the idea of regulatory competition.

2. PERFECTIONIST AUTHORITY AND REGULATORY COMPETITION

The perfectionist argument for granting a right to rule to some members and institutions of society draws on the necessity of some kind of social order and structure. In order to organize life in a society so that as many people as possible can live well, we need an order that is stabilized by the common understanding that some have a right to rule and that their rules must be obeyed.

Who these rulers are, and what justifies them in their claim to a right to rule, is a different question. There is no contradiction in holding that, while the existence of political authority as such is generally justified by perfectionist considerations (this arrangement being the only or the best way to contribute to a good human life), in political reality, not every single decision—legislative, administrative, adjudicative, or other—can or must be directly conducive to a good life of those directly affected. There may be short-term sacrifices that must be made. There could also be uncertainties as to what is the decision that most contributes to human flourishing in the end.

It would be too strict to require that every single rule, every reason for legislation, every authoritative act must be directly connected with and clearly linked to human flourishing. The perfectionist justification of political authority instead sets a general frame for the actions of said authority, who cannot claim to be justified to be acting in a way that is in direct conflict with the understanding of human flourishing that it is based upon.

There is not one single form or type of perfectionism. There is a group of theories that share a commitment to the idea that there is an *objective* account of the good and that it is the purpose of ethical and political theory to construe social life so as to realize this objective good. There is dispute as to what the objective good consists in, the main contenders being Aristotelian accounts[50] of the good as the development of human nature versus objective list theories[51] that are based upon a catalogue of elements that, if realized, make human life a good one.

Joseph Raz has offered an influential account of when and why political authority should be seen as legitimate. According to his 'service conception of authority',[52] the directives of a legitimate

[50] Influential contemporary versions of Aristotelian perfectionism have been developed by T Hurka, *Perfectionism* (OUP 1993) and P Foot, *Natural Goodness* (OUP 2001).

[51] Objective list theories are found in J Finnis, *Natural Law and Natural Rights* (OUP 2011); J Griffin, *Well-Being: Its Meaning, Measurement, and Moral Importance* (Clarendon Press 1986); R Arneson, 'Perfectionism and Politics' (2000) 111 Ethics 37.

[52] J Raz, *The Morality of Freedom* (Clarendon Press 1986) 53; see also J Raz, 'The Problem of Authority: Revisiting the Service Conception' (2006) 90 Minnesota Law Review 1003 with a treatment of objections that were put forward against the 'service conception' of legitimate authority, particularly the criticism that it fails to capture the requirement of a special connection between authorities and

authority generate pre-emptive reasons for us to act. That is, they substitute our own reasons for action by those of the authority. Raz's justification for this notion of authority is that if these directives are in fact treated as binding, the effect is that 'the alleged subject is likely better to comply with reasons which apply to him'.[53] Raz's conclusion is that authority is legitimate to the extent that it helps us to conform to the right reasons for action, thus ultimately being of service to our own flourishing.

(a) Perfectionist authority versus personal autonomy

The service conception has been criticized as being too strong and paternalistic. It is indeed difficult to uphold the service conception with regard to fields in which personal autonomy appears to be a central concern. This could be said about laws on issues of family life, such as marriage and reproductive decisions. In discussions on laws regulating these issues, the qualification as 'perfectionist' is used as an argument against policy proposals that are held to impose a conception of the good life on people who will then lack the autonomy to shape their lives according to their own preferences.

Despite the conflict with personal autonomy, however, perfectionist approaches are plausible with regard to scenarios that involve collective action problems. In some instances, there is reason to suppose that people's decisions and actions would be influenced or even manipulated by mechanisms of collective choice, such as the temptation to behave as a free rider regarding the consumption of non-exclusive but scarce goods.

These are the issues that are most interesting for the legislator, as they present scenarios that can be resolved by a political authority that underpins generally binding rules. In many cases, law functions as an instrument for a minimal and pragmatic kind of

those who are governed by it. In his answer, Raz argues that this link could be derived from a commitment to or identification with the political community that authority and its objects share.

[53] A Marmor and A Sarch, 'The Nature of Law', *The Stanford Encyclopedia of Philosophy* (2015) <https://plato.stanford.edu/archives/fall2015/entries/lawphil-nature/> accessed 1 August 2018, Section 2, with the example of the legal speed limit for public roads: law makes it easier for us to conform to the reasons that apply to us instead of figuring out the right balance of reasons ourselves directly.

social order.[54] It is, then, a vehicle to communicate authoritative directives, used precisely in cases where completely unrestricted autonomous decisions would—in aggregate—lead to undesirable situations.

Another argument for a perfectionist approach to political authority is that there are situations in which people have demonstrated vulnerability to distortive influences on their decisions. Personal autonomy in times of ever refined research in cognitive psychology has come to mean something different than people deciding absent any outside influence. We are highly perceptive of how information is presented to us; we tend to overestimate advantages or the likelihood of uncertain positive events actually happening.

In light of these findings, robust perfectionism does not seem such a bad alternative.

(b) Diverging conceptions of human flourishing

The conceptual and ethical underpinnings of regulatory competition and a perfectionist justification of political authority are in conflict with respect to their underlying understanding of human well-being.

On one hand, the perfectionist approach, as conceptualized prominently by Joseph Raz in his 'service conception' qualifies perfectionist authority as justified insofar as it helps realize the elements of human flourishing, understood as that which objectively makes a human life good and worth living.

The market paradigm, being committed to a subjectivist conception of human welfare,[55] on the other hand, introduces reasons for legislation that cannot be translated into this kind of perfectionist reasoning. Regulatory competition as a source of reasons for legislation does not logically or necessarily stand in conflict with the perfectionist project. However, it seems that such conflict is at least possible, if not that probable. Regulatory competition leads to a prioritization of reasons that are in no way connected to the perfectionist account of human flourishing.

[54] On law's social functions see Chapter 5, section E.

[55] See Chapter 3, section A.1 and Chapter 6, section C.1.

Now, it would be utopian to require that every single legislative decision must be openly and directly justified by perfectionist reasoning. However, a perfectionist commitment sets boundaries to what a political authority can legitimately do and which concerns make for legitimate reasons for legislation. The reasons that legislation is based upon may not be in open conflict with the perfectionist understanding of human flourishing or a good human life.

Philosophical perfectionists, albeit at odds in detail, base their arguments on conceptions of human flourishing that are much richer—including artistic and cultural experiences, the value of social belonging, of close family ties, and so on—that the welfare economics account of the good human life has difficulties in recognizing.

3. PROCEDURALIST AUTHORITY AND REGULATORY COMPETITION

Even if we still do not find perfectionist theories appealing, as they come with heavy substantivist and objectivist baggage, we do not have to give up on the project of justifying political authority.

Perfectionist accounts are not the only justificatory route towards legitimate political authority that is commonly argued for in contemporary political philosophy. The main alternative is based on proceduralist premises, in a broad sense, most commonly in the form of the principles underpinning democracy.

The idea popular among political liberals is that a right to rule must, in the end, be based on the consent of those that are addressed by the rules in question. A restriction of their liberty has to be grounded ultimately in an act of their own free will. Consent theories of political authority and obligation answer the question of how a right to rule may be assumed to exist under these conditions.

One way to put this idea into political practice is through the democratic organization of political rule. As has been discussed here, however, regulatory competition is in conflict with the principles underpinning democratic state organization.

The problem with regulatory competition is that it introduces and equips with force other objectives an authority may follow when issuing its commands, which are related neither to the procedural preconditions for legitimate authority nor to the realization of substantive values. Frictions may thus appear with regard to both the procedural and the perfectionist approach. In case of such frictions, following the demands of regulatory competition will therefore undermine the basis for an authority's legislative decisions to warrant a claim to legitimacy, because they are openly guided by criteria other than the concept of legitimate authority demands.

Why does the conclusion drawn from the three premises amount to a criticism of regulatory competition? What should be expected when legislative decisions lose their claim to legitimate authority? This would eventually show in people's fading acceptance of issued norms as binding, and in a decline in their readiness to act out of respect for the issuing political authority. Theoretically, it should lead to legal norms being disobeyed more often, thus being less effective as an instrument of social ordering.

Both the autonomy as well as the authority argument draw on the scenario that regulatory competition will influence state representatives' decisions in a way that is not compatible with our conception of how political decision-making should work, particularly in light of the claim to authority that it embodies and the ideal of autonomy that we want to see realized by it.

The force of these arguments depends on whether one shares the fundamental scepticism about the political ethics and integrity of state representatives. Market pressure on them is dangerous only if it is to be feared that they will give into the law market's demands without due deliberation, thereby intentionally or inadvertently neglecting the duties that come with their office.

D. CONCLUSION

This chapter has shown that regulatory competition affects a number of key political concepts. The intention of the arguments presented was not to show that regulatory competition would lead to catastrophic consequences for any state, or that nothing would be as before. However, it is fair to say that we should be clear about how our understanding of democracy, autonomy, and authority would be affected by advancing regulatory competition.

The focus of this chapter has been on divergences between regulatory competition as a political strategy and our conceptualization of values and principles that are relevant in the political arena. These divergences are plausibly interpreted as originating in the utilitarian pedigree of the competitive paradigm. Anne Peters has pointed to the necessity of evaluating regulatory competition according to its compatibility with constitutional principles, suggesting that the focus on personal preferences is responsible for frictions, as these individual preferences may in particular instances significantly diverge from the demands of principles such as freedom and equality.[56] The discussion of central political concepts has shown that this is a recurring pattern. The way in which these ideas are conceptualized in contemporary political theory is not entirely consistent with welfare economists' basic theoretical commitments, particularly those that are to be counted as utilitarian in origin. The tension that lies at the heart of these frictions stems from the utilitarian assumptions that lend the law market its theoretical attractiveness. The stronger our scepticism about the plausibility of these assumptions, the less we will be inclined to accept that law as the most important mechanism of social ordering in contemporary large societies should be structured along the competitive paradigm that derives its appeal from them.

This leaves us with the following diagnosis: the appeal of applying the competitive paradigm to matters of legislation builds on utilitarian grounds. Our conception of political values and principles like democracy, autonomy, and authority does not, at least not entirely. The divergence in philosophical pedigree naturally expresses itself in incompatibilities between the demands that come with a regulatory competition approach versus a non-utilitarian understanding of how the state should be structured, as is expressed, for example, in the constitutions of many Western democracies.

[56] Peters (n 1) 47: 'From a legal perspective, however, the merits (or drawbacks) of regulatory competition must be (also) assessed against the yardstick of constitutional principles. Put differently, the lawyerly examination needs to assess and evaluate the benefits of that competition process with a view at legal criteria which do not necessarily coincide with personal preferences of individuals, such as capacity of the competition process to secure respect of legal (and even constitutional) principles, namely security, freedom, and equality.'

5

LAW AS A CONTESTED COMMODITY

In 1978, Elisabeth Landes and Richard Posner published a widely debated article entitled 'The Economics of the Baby Shortage'.[1] The central claim of their paper was a call for the introduction of a 'full-fledged baby market' in order to better align demand and supply of babies for adoption.[2]

Babies are the prototypical example for a contested commodity—a good that can theoretically be bought and sold, but arguably should not be treated as a commodity that may be exchanged according to market standards.[3] There are some things with respect to which most people think that the price mechanism is inappropriate, because it is somehow not fitting for the kind of good they are. Most people think that these things cannot or should not be bought and sold for money, like babies or human organs or Nobel Prizes.[4] The intuition that there are things that should not be traded on markets deserves a closer look, as the assumptions it embodies might also provide a line of argument against treating legal rules more generally as a market product.

The argument of this chapter proceeds along the following lines:

1. Regulatory competition leads to law being understood as a market commodity.
2. There are 'contested commodities' that should not be subject to the market mechanism, for various reasons.

[1] EM Landes and RA Posner, 'The Economics of the Baby Shortage' (2002) 7 The Journal of Legal Studies 323.

[2] Ibid 347.

[3] The term 'market' can be broadly defined as a mechanism by which buyers and sellers exchange things or services, with prices being determined by the laws of demand and supply. See Chapter 1, section A.

[4] A helpful collection of classical texts, introductory remarks, and further analyses of various types of 'contested commodities' is provided by MM Ertman and JC Williams (eds), *Rethinking Commodification: Cases and Readings in Law and Culture* (NYU Press 2005).

3. Law is a contested commodity insofar as its commodity status conflicts with the societal functions we expect it to perform.
4. Insofar as we are unwilling to revise our functional understanding of (mandatory) legal rules, law should not be made a commodity as a result of regulatory competition.

The starting point is the hypothesis that regulatory competition leads to the law not only being treated as a commodity, but as a commodity subject to the market mechanism (section A). The argument proceeds with the claim that not everything should be treated as a market commodity (sections B and C). This is the commodification debate that has seen some prominence in the social sciences, mostly with regard to socially sensitive goods such as human babies, body parts, organs, or sexual services. The legal implications of this debate have traditionally revolved around the question of whether markets in such goods should be legally prohibited and whether that would effectively ban commodification or merely lead to the creation of black markets in these goods and services.

Sections D and E deal with reasons for intuitive scepticism about law itself as a commodity subject to the market mechanism. Why should legal rules not be treated as market goods, granted that regulatory competition does in fact lead to such a perspective on law? Answers to that question could be given by tracing similarities between law and other contested commodities. In what way are they similar, so that the application of non-commodificationist arguments to law is warranted as well? In what way are they different from goods with respect to which we see no problem in their production and distribution according to market standards and the resulting incentive schemes? As will be shown, some of the arguments that have figured prominently in debates about other contested commodities, such as human organs or reproductive capacities, are applicable to legal rules as well.

A. LAW AS A MARKET PRODUCT

'Regulatory competition' denotes a dynamic in which suppliers of legal rules—states as well as arguably non-state entities, which are not the subject of this analysis—engage in competitive behaviour in order to see their legal products have success on an international law market. The analytical appeal as well as the limits of the market analogy in the legal domain are discussed in Chapter 1. The consequence of this dynamic is that from the perspective of participants of such law markets, law is perceived as a market commodity that is subject to the price mechanism in some form or another. In a market setting, production decisions are based on the price signals that suppliers receive via interaction with potential consumers of their product. In a law market setting therefore producers of law will base decisions about the content of legal rules on the price signals coming from the demand side, in the form of preference for one kind of rule over another, or frequently for rules that preserve their freedom more than others.

The commodification of law does not depend on the fact that there is an actual price being paid for law in some objectified form. It need not be as obvious as in the case of tax revenue gained from legal services that tends to be generated in the jurisdiction whose law is chosen for a particular affair or transaction. In many cases, the price mechanism cannot be shown to apply directly.[5] What is left, however, is 'market rhetoric' that serves as a conceptual basis for dealing with commodified goods.[6]

This means that the fact that we think of something or someone in market terms, perhaps as having a certain price or being worth more than something else, being tradable for a certain amount of money or something else, influences the way we conceptualize and value them. Thus, in order for the market analogy to prove analytically useful, a literal price being paid for the use of legal rules need not be present in every instance of regulatory competition. The tendency of market terms to dominate the perspective on a particular good once introduced to them has become known by the term 'crowding out'; it is part of the market's evaluative logic that warrants a closer look.

[5] See section D.

[6] MJ Radin, 'On the Domain of Market Rhetoric' (1992) 15 Harvard Journal of Law and Public Policy 711; MJ Radin, *Contested Commodities* (Harvard University Press 2001) 79–101 (hereafter Radin, *Contested Commodities*). See also E Anderson, *Value in Ethics and Economics* (Harvard University Press 1995).

B. THE EVALUATIVE LOGIC OF THE MARKET

The ultimate measure for ascription of value in a market setting is subjective demand, in the form of expressed preference for particular market goods and services. The value of a good or a service derives from the fact that others want it. When we commodify something, we expose it to this subjectivist evaluative standard and evaluate it accordingly. When we introduce the market as the mechanism to allocate babies to adoptive parents, soon particular qualities in these babies—such as sex, size, colour of skin, hair, and eyes, as well as general health—would show to meet demand preferences more than others (such as, for instance, physical handicaps).

1. THE PRICE MECHANISM

In neoclassical economics, it is assumed that the market mechanism determines the price for which a good is exchanged, but that it does not in any other way affect the good and its (perceived) characteristics.[7] If I sell you my pen for $5, the fact that both of us agreed on this transaction shows that you have a preference for having the pen instead of $5 and I have a preference for having $5 instead of the pen. Judging from this transaction, we might say that the pen is worth $5. If someone else now shows up and buys the pen from you for $10, the pen's worth instantaneously jumps from $5 to $10. However, the price being paid per se does not tell us anything about the value of the pen according to other criteria.[8] In complex situations where value-related attributes are difficult to recognize and to measure, the price mechanism does provide us with a very useful 'proxy' criterion for assessing the

[7] For criticism of this assumption see F Hirsch, *The Social Limits to Growth* (Routledge and Kegan Paul 1976) 84–94.

[8] Hence the saying: 'An economist is someone who knows the price of everything and the value of nothing.' Interestingly, the phrase appears in a slightly different form already in Act III of Oscar Wilde's *Lady Windermere's Fan*:

> CECIL GRAHAM: 'What is a cynic?' *Sitting on the back of the sofa*
> LORD DARLINGTON: 'A man who knows the price of everything and the value of nothing.'

value of something. Indeed, the value neutrality of the market is in part what makes it so appealing as an ordering mechanism, because no (controversial) judgments on the intrinsic value of the goods exchanged have to be made.[9] Whatever people are willing to pay for something, they will have a reason.

The price mechanism, however, is at the same time an imperfect indicator of who values a particular good most, as it reflects not only the willingness but also the ability to pay a particular monetary amount.[10] Other criteria, such as the readiness to queue for something and give up your time, could also be used as an indicator of the value you ascribe to a certain good or activity. This limitation is not always acknowledged by proponents of reliance on the price mechanism as a standard for the distribution of certain goods, such as education or healthcare.

2. CROWDING OUT: CONSEQUENCES OF MARKET EXPOSURE

An alternative conception to markets as 'merely neutral accounting devices for determining and tracking the value of goods'[11] has been discussed by Fred Hirsch as the 'commercialization effect'.[12] When a good is produced and distributed exclusively or predominantly on commercial terms rather than according to other criteria—such as informal exchange, mutual obligation, altruism or love, or feelings of service or obligation—that 'embeddedness' into the market mechanism has an effect on the characteristics of the good itself.

CECIL GRAHAM: 'And a sentimentalist, my dear Darlington, is a man who sees an absurd value in everything, and doesn't know the market price of any single thing.'

[9] MJ Sandel, *What Money Can't Buy: The Moral Limits of Markets* (Palgrave Macmillan 2012) 89, 101.

[10] Sandel (n 9) 32; H Eidenmüller, *Effizienz als Rechtsprinzip* (4th edn, Mohr Siebeck 2015) 116: 'Prices are indicators of subjective valuation.' [translation of the author]; on the privilege of those who can rely on existing economic resources see ibid 117.

[11] D Satz, *Why Some Things Should Not Be for Sale: The Moral Limits of Markets* (OUP 2010) 80.

[12] Hirsch (n 7) 87.

Numerous studies have shown by now that people react differently to goods and practices that are associated with a price compared to those that are not. In his seminal study comparing blood donation schemes in the UK and the US, Richard Titmuss found that paying people to give blood reduced both the quality as well as the quantity of the blood supply available for medical purposes.[13] He concluded that a system relying on the altruistic motivation of voluntary donors was more effective than a commercial market for human blood.

Recent explanations for this phenomenon have been given the telling name 'crowding out effect'.[14] The mere existence and social acceptance of a market influences the norms according to which certain goods are commonly evaluated. The blood that people give to blood banks may gradually shift from being a donation out of a civil commitment to solidarity to something that is sold at a certain price just like any other tradable good.

Or, once a baby market for adoptions has been established and it has been there for some time, the importance of parental love as a standard by which children are valued may fade. The properties of children that have been shown to raise market prices will influence the way children are treated and respected in society and even by their parents.

When subjective demand for baby girls is demonstrably and significantly higher than for boys (or vice versa), social attitudes towards babies that fall into either group can be expected to diverge over time as differences in 'market success' are socially internalized. Suppose someone has two children, a girl and a boy. On the baby market, people would be willing to pay double the price for the girl's adoption compared to the boy's (or vice versa). Surreal as the scenario may appear, it seems to be rather probable

[13] RM Titmuss, *The Gift of Relationship: From Human Blood to Social Policy* (Pantheon 1971); see also BS Frey, *Not Just for the Money* (Edward Elgar Publishing 1997), with an economist's account of how intrinsic motivation may be damaged by the introduction of monetary incentives.

[14] Sandel (n 9) 119: '[I]ntroducing money into a nonmarket setting can change people's attitudes and crowd out moral and civic commitments.'; see also Satz (n 11) 34–5: '[W]e must expand our evaluation of markets, along with the concept of market failure, to include the effects of such markets on the structure of our relationships with one another, on our democracy, and on human motivation.'

that the market mechanism's comparative pricing of these two children would, over time, have some impact on how they are valued by their social and even family environment.

Commercialization and crowding out effects alone, however, provide no sufficient basis for a robust normative argument against commodification. The perceived dominance of market norms casts doubt on the possibility of a continued and stable coexistence between commodified and non-commodified understandings of goods and social interactions.[15] Gift giving is an example for the coexistence of commodified and non-commodified aspects of a social practice. It has been analysed by economic scholars as often producing hugely inefficient outcomes in the many cases in which the gift does not fit with the preferences of the recipient.[16] Many of us, however, would acknowledge that satisfying an existing preference of the recipient is not the only or even the primary purpose of the social practice of gift giving. On the contrary, gifts often perform primarily an expressive function; a gift is a token of the respect and appreciation of the gift giver towards the recipient, and tied to social norms of courtesy. Interestingly, the growing tendency to give money and the market for gift vouchers appears to confirm the crowding out hypothesis. Instead of offering particular gifts, their monetary equivalent is given instead, reducing the practice of gift giving to its monetary dimension without quite having to resort to the perceived profanity of simply giving cash.[17]

If coexistence is necessarily unstable and a temporary stage before crowding out has run its course, once a good or social

[15] On the possibility of such coexistence Radin, *Contested Commodities* (n 6) 102–14.

[16] J Waldfogel, 'The Deadweight Loss of Christmas' (1993) 83 The American Economic Review 1328, which prompted lively discussion, see JA List and JF Shogren, 'The Deadweight Loss of Christmas: Comment' (1998) 88 American Economic Review 1350; BJ Ruffle and O Tykocinski, 'The Deadweight Loss of Christmas: Comment' (2000) 90 American Economic Review 319; SJ Solnick and D Hemenway, 'The Deadweight Loss of Christmas: Comment' (1996) 86 The American Economic Review 1299; J Waldfogel, 'The Deadweight Loss of Christmas: Reply' (1996) 88 The American Economic Review 1306.

[17] Sandel MJ, 'What Money Can't Buy: The Moral Limits of Markets' (1998) The Tanner Lectures on Human Values <http://tannerlectures.utah.edu/_documents/a-to-z/s/sandel00.pdf> accessed 1 August 2018, 104–7.

practice has been subject to commodified or marketized forms of understanding, it 'threaten[s] to decay into a monolithic structure of commodification'.[18]

A caveat is to be noted: the crowding out effect, if real, tells us how people in fact behave when market and non-market reasoning compete as primary standards for the valuation of some good. It tells us that market reasoning tends to be dominant in such face-offs. As a factual claim, however, it does not tell us whether that is good or bad, whether or not such crowding out should be encouraged. It does not in itself contain a reason why a 'monolithic structure of commodification' would warrant a negative normative judgment. Opponents of universal commodification, of course, have tried to pin down reasons why the crowding out effect could be treated not only as an empirical phenomenon that we can extract from people's dealing with goods and social practices, but as something that should be fenced in or avoided in certain cases.

C. CONTESTED COMMODITIES

In 1990, the California Supreme Court had to decide the case of *Moore v Regents of the University of California*;[19] John Moore had been treated at UCLA Medical Center for leukaemia. As part of his therapy, his doctor had removed his spleen and—without Moore's knowledge or consent—had proceeded to use his genetic material further in order to develop a cell line. The doctor was able to sell the material to a private company in exchange for 75,000 shares as well as a considerable amount of money that went to both himself and UCLA.[20] Having discovered what had happened to his spleen, Moore sued on the grounds that his property rights in his genetic material had been violated. The Court ended up rejecting his claim by majority decision, acknowledging

[18] Radin, *Contested Commodities* (n 6) xii.

[19] *Moore v Regents of the University of California* [1990] 271 Cal.Rptr. 146, 51 Cal.3d 120, 793 P.2d 479.

[20] For an extensive discussion of the case see R Warner, 'Does Incommensurability Matter? Incommensurability and Public Policy' (1998) 146 University of Pennsylvania Law Review 1267, 1313–18.

Moore's rights but at the same time emphasizing stronger reasons to allow the socially useful activity of medical research on human cells, even if there is no consent or knowledge of the donor of a particular sample.[21]

The reasoning of the court, balancing Moore's rights in his body parts against the interests of medical research (and business based on that research), was met with emphatic dissent from Justice Mosk[22] quoting a decidedly Kantian[23] line of argument:

> Such research tends to treat the human body as a commodity – a means to a profitable end. The dignity and sanctity with which we regard the human whole, body as well as mind and soul, are absent when we allow researchers to further their own interests without the patient's participation by using a patient's cells as the basis for a marketable product.[24]

Where does the idea that not everything should be subject to the market come from and what are the reasons commonly given for that claim? Not all cases appeal so straightforwardly to our conception of human dignity as the contested sale of human body parts without the affected person's consent. In the following

[21] *Moore v Regents of the University of California* [1990] 271 Cal.Rptr. 146, 51 Cal.3d 120, 793 P.2d 493.

[22] *Moore v Regents of the University of California* [1990] 271 Cal.Rptr. 146, 51 Cal.3d 120, 793 P.2d 515-516: '[O]ur society acknowledges a profound ethical imperative to respect the human body as the physical and temporal expression of the unique human persona. One manifestation of that respect is our prohibition against direct abuse of the body by torture […]. Another is our prohibition against indirect abuse of the body by its economic exploitation for the sole benefit of another person.'

[23] Cf the second formulation of the categorical imperative in I Kant, *Groundwork for the Metaphysics of Morals* (Allen Wood ed and tr, first published 1785, Yale University Press 2002) G 4:429: 'Act so that you use humanity, as much in your own person as in the person of every other, always at the same time as end and never merely as means.'

[24] MT Danforth, 'Cells, Sales, and Royalties: The Patient's Right to a Portion of the Profits' (1988) 6 Yale Law and Policy Review 179, 190; interestingly, the article by Danforth that is quoted by Justices Mosk and Arabian is based on the false assumption that Moore had indeed consented to the further use of his cell material (179), whereas part of the problem was that his consent was *missing*, see A Stanton, 'Forfeited Consent: Body Parts in Eminent Domain' in P J Gibson (ed), *Patenting Lives: Life Patents, Culture and Development* (Ashgate Publishing Limited 2013) 95, 96–7, 112.

sections, we will take a look at three kinds of reasoning that could support scepticism about universal commodification.

1. HISTORICAL ORIGINS: *RES EXTRA COMMERCIUM*

The idea that not everything can or should be treated as a market commodity is far from new to legal scholarship. The term '*res extra commercium*' was used to denote things that could not be exchanged among private individuals for various reasons:[25] *res divini iuris* could not be the objects of private transactions as they were dedicated to the gods (such as temples). Excluded were public goods (*res omnium communes*) as well, most notably natural resources (air, the sea). A third category of *res extra commercium* were formed by *res publicae*—state property in the form non-exclusive goods that were nevertheless exempt from commercial transaction, such as public roads and places, theatres, and rivers. The state was understood to have a particular kind of 'public ownership' over these goods, compatible with their general and non-exclusive usage.[26]

2. DISTRIBUTIVE JUSTICE: ACCESS TO THE GOOD LIFE

One reason why many people think that there should be no baby markets is that they would lead to a redistribution of babies from the poor to those who could afford paying whatever market price for a baby of their liking. This goes against the understanding that having and raising children is a privilege and valuable aspect of human life that should—in principle—be attainable by everyone irrespective of their financial resources. In its core, this argument against baby markets is a version of the fairness objection to liberal market reasoning.

The same has been said about other instances of contested commodification and the issue in general. It is not so much the goods themselves that the debate revolves around—it is their

[25] R Sohm, *The Institutes of Roman Law* (Clarendon Press 1892) 226 §46.

[26] Gaius Institutiones II §1-11; Iustinian Institutiones II.1 §§pr-11.

distribution,[27] our comparative relationship to them, paired with normative considerations such as the idea that there are certain goods that are essential to leading a good life and that everyone should have access to, irrespective of their financial circumstances.[28]

Liberal theorists commonly accept that such inequalities exist and that they may be undesirable from a social justice perspective, but that they are a contingency of social reality that is independent and prior to the workings of the market mechanism. In other words—it is not a fault of the market that, in reality, resources, opportunities and even talent are by no means distributed equally. The problem with contested commodities, the argument continues, is not that they are subject to market exchange, but that background inequalities prevent markets from working properly towards efficient and overall welfare-enhancing scenarios.[29] When we reject markets in human organs such as kidneys as leading to injustice, the problem that we are really referring to is the fact that some people are so poor they find themselves compelled to literally sell parts of themselves, the last thing they have to bring to the market in exchange for other products (such as food) that they may desperately need.

There is truth to this objection insofar as the market mechanism itself is in fact insensitive to issues of distributive justice. This is a characteristic it shares with utilitarian theories in general.[30]

The criticism on the grounds of distributive justice can even be taken further. The market perpetuates the unequal distribution of access to the goods subject to it. When do we find such inequality objectionable? Certainly, there are goods with respect to which unequal distribution of access doesn't bother us at all, such as luxury watches or champagne. With respect to other scarce goods, unequal distribution of access does appear to pose a problem of justice, such as housing, food, and, arguably, reproductive opportunities. What distinguishes one group of goods

[27] Satz (n 11).

[28] Sandel (n 9) 8: 'In a society where everything is for sale, life is harder for those of modest means. The more money can buy, the more affluence (or the lack of it) matters. […] Where all good things are bought and sold, having money makes all the difference in the world.'

[29] Satz (n 11) 5; Landes and Posner (n 1) 339–46.

[30] See Chapter 3.

from the other? Is it something about these goods themselves, our relationship to them, or our relationship to one another? More or less explicit value objectivism translates into the relevance of particular resources that are inevitably part of a good life. We need access to certain goods and services in order to live well. Among these are the goods that commonly appear on the lists of objectivists: housing, food, and the means to satisfy basic human needs and interests.

In political matters, it is more appropriate to discuss the commodification of services instead of goods.[31] The argument, however, is roughly the same: the problem is unequal distribution of access to public services, such as healthcare or education. The looming underlying question is whether healthcare and education should be distributed in the form of public services (accompanied by the argument that as public services it is easier to ensure a minimum threshold of equality of access) or in the form of pure market goods.

Some goods and services are, by nature, unchangeable, unaffected by who owns or uses them. A bar of gold is unchanged by the mechanism by which it is distributed, market, state allocation, or otherwise—its qualities remain unchanged. The primary consequence that market exposure has with regard to these kinds of goods is the price that must be paid in order to gain access to them.

Not all goods and services, however, are unalterable in this way. The consequence of unequal access coordinated by the market mechanism, however, is that suppliers of goods will cater to the interests of those who demonstrate the most effective willingness to pay for them via market exchange. Thus, form, design, and shape of these products will come to reflect the preferences of those who can pay for them, further intensifying unequal distribution.

A profane yet telling example for this simple mechanism can be found in consumer product markets. Manufacturers of premium cars, for example, have started to reform the design and functionalities of their products to cater to the particularities of Asian, particularly Chinese, demand. A small, albeit illustrative,

[31] See Chapter 1.

facet of this change is first the increase in sports cars with rear seats (a contradiction, one might say, to the label 'sports car') so that owners of these cars need not sit next to their driver, a luxury by now less common in Western industrial states. As a result, in premium cars marketed to Chinese consumers, controls for radio, heating, and so on will be located in the rear, where wealthy people with drivers will sit.[32]

As the changing forms of premium cars show, the crucial worry that is related to unequal distribution of access to goods is not only access to the scarce and unchangeable ingredients to a good life, but also inequalities with regard to influence on form, design and functionalities of goods that allow for such modifications in the interests of those that promise to hold the biggest keys to overall market success.

Nevertheless, all in all, at the centre of the debate we find distributive concerns. The worry that feeds them is that the market mechanism per se is insensitive to these considerations, a charge that has been brought forward—as we have already seen—against utilitarianism as well.

3. CORRUPTION OF MORAL CHARACTER

Michael Sandel has laid out what he calls a 'corruption argument' against the commodification of certain goods on the grounds that exposing them to the market mechanism is incompatible with their 'moral character'.[33]

[32] Z Rosenberg, 'Auto Designers Cater to China, the New Giant' (Wired, 18 February 2010) <http://www.wired.com/2010/02/automotive-design-for-china/> accessed 1 August 2018: 'In China, the focus of control shifts from the driver's seat to the passenger or rear seat, where the owner might prefer to sit, as it indicates higher status. Because the rear seat is the position of power, that's where you'll find controls for the radio, heat, sunroof and so forth. In the United States, of course, the driver controls everything.'

[33] The term 'moral character' is not used by Sandel himself, see Sandel (n 17) 100: 'Certain modes of valuation are appropriate to certain goods.'; ibid 94: 'The corruption objection […] points to the degrading effect of market valuation and exchange on certain goods and practices. According to this objection, certain moral and civic goods are diminished or corrupted if bought and sold.'

In a condensed form, the argument can be construed as follows:

1. Exposure to market exchange influences the norms and standards according to which the good exchanged is valued.
2. The moral character of things, practices, and people determines our adequate valuation of them.
3. In some cases, that moral character requires valuation according to norms other than those promoted by market exchange.
4. Therefore, some things should not be exposed to market exchange.

Premise 1 has been discussed in section B.2. The point of the argument's second and third premises may be illustrated with the help of the Nobel Prize example. Of course, it might be possible either to buy a Nobel Prize medal from someone, or to bribe the Nobel committee with an enormous sum into awarding it to a certain person. But that would hardly be the same as winning the Prize for outstanding achievements in science. A large part of the attraction of winning a Nobel Prize lies precisely in the fact that it cannot be bought.[34] Once it became known that the committee could be bribed to sell prizes, this large part of its reputation would presumably vanish. In Sandel's terms, the moral character of the Nobel Prize demands distribution and valuation according to the criterion of scientific achievement and is incompatible with it being a market good that can be had in exchange for money. Establishing a 'Nobel Prize Market' in the sense that scientists could buy the award of the Prize from the committee or buy a medal and title from another scientist would certainly result in a significant change in the way the Prize is seen and valued in society. Would we want that to happen? Probably not. The effect would be 'degrading'.[35]

[34] As noted by S Kelman, *What Price Incentives? Economists and the Environment* (Auburn House Publishing Company 1981) 69: 'Praise that is bought is worth little, even to the person buying it.'

[35] Sandel (n 17) 94; see also, much earlier, M Walzer, *Spheres of Justice: A Defense of Pluralism and Equality* (Basic Books 1983) 97: '[W]e also experience the universality of money as somehow degrading. […] [O]ften enough money fails to represent value; the translations are made, but as with good poetry, something is lost in the process. Hence we can buy and sell universally only if we disregard real values; while if we attend to values, there are things that cannot be bought and sold.'; Kelman (n 34) 30 speaks of 'the diminution of certain positively valued

Whereas the value of some goods would be entirely destroyed, such as is the case with the Nobel Prize, with other goods the picture is not as clear. Why shouldn't there be markets for human organs or babies up for adoption?[36] A purchased heart or liver would work no differently to one distributed by some other scheme, such as a waiting list or a lottery. A purchased baby is still a baby; by being bought and sold it would not lose its meaning and appeal in the same way that a Nobel Prize would.

The corruption argument's second premise holds that the good in question, human babies in this case, is of a (moral) character that makes it unfitting to be treated as a commodity that may be exchanged for a market-determined price. Children, as Sandel argues, are best valued within the conceptual framework of 'parental love'[37] and respect for them as human beings. Treating them as a commodity with a higher or lower price tag depending on race, sex, physical and intellectual abilities, and so on would degrade and disrespect them as persons.[38] For reasons both of principle and of consequence, a market for babies would strike many of us as an instance of a market that is 'toxic to important human values'.[39]

Versions of the corruption argument have been prompted also by the illustrative example of so-called 'Citizenship for Sale' programmes. More than 25 per cent of states worldwide offer programmes by which high-net-worth-individuals are eligible to acquire citizenship or at least permission to reside and work in a particular state.[40] Besides the objection that such programmes exacerbate global inequalities by turning membership in sought after political communities into club goods, access to which

feelings associated with nonmarket relationships and with the down-valuation in the perceived value of certain things when a price is placed on them'.

[36] Landes and Posner (n 1) 323, 347–8.

[37] Sandel (n 9) 12: 'To decide whether to establish a market in babies up for adoption we need to ask what norms should govern the parent-child relationship, and ask whether buying and selling children would undermine those norms.'

[38] Sandel (n 9) 111. [39] Satz (n 11) 3.

[40] For a critical overview regarding Citizenship for Sale programmes see A Shachar, 'Citizenship for Sale' in A Shachar and others (eds), *The Oxford Handbook of Citizenship* (OUP 2017) 789; see also A Shachar and R Hirschl, 'On Citizenship, States, and Markets' (2014) 22 The Journal of Political Philosophy 231.

depends on the ability to pay a certain entrance fee,[41] there is another objection that is based on the moral character of citizenship, in Ayelet Shachar's words:

> Placing a price tag on citizenship signifies a transformation of the criteria of membership from a political to an economic metric, contributing to broader processes of commodification that erode the promise of equality among existing members of the political community.[42]

It is worth adding that the corruption argument against commodification is not simply a version of the argument of unfair background conditions discussed in section C.2. The argument of a lack of reliability of the preferences revealed by market decisions is not an argument against the market mechanism per se: once fair background conditions are established, the objection against inclusion of goods into a market folds. The corruption objection, however, does not fold even on the assumption of an ideal market, as it draws not on the idea of consent, but on the moral character of the good involved.[43]

The strength that the corruption argument derives from its generality and independence from fair background conditions is at the same time a serious weakness. The corruption argument's plausibility depends crucially on a plausible conceptual account of what 'moral character' is, how it is determined, and how it affects our adequate stance towards the bearer of that moral character. Unfortunately, as simple and straightforward as the idea of 'moral character' presents itself to be, it is equally hard to provide it with a reasoned philosophical underpinning. This is a problem with the corruption argument in general. Fundamentally, there are two basic philosophical questions that bear on the operability of the concept. First, what is the 'moral character' of a good? How is its fitting mode of valuation determined? Is it an intrinsic property built into every good that is not susceptible to change? Or does it change with, for example, social attitudes towards the good? Second, how do we know or figure out what that moral character is? Do we recognize it via insight into some objective truth? Or is it the outcome of political and social deliberation?

[41] Shachar (n 40) 804. [42] Ibid 805. [43] Sandel (n 17) 94–5.

Prima facie, both types of answers to these questions combine into a single dilemma. On the first horn, the moral character of something is taken to be part of its 'essential nature', fixed for eternity and unchangeable by social change.[44] The burden of explaining why a certain mode of valuation should be appropriate for a certain good is thereby not in any way alleviated. It is merely being shifted from the notion of 'appropriateness' to the vague concept of an 'essential nature'.[45]

On the dilemma's other horn, we face the danger of 'lapsing into conventionalism' when making the appropriate kind of valuation depend on social practices and meanings that may change over time.[46] According to Sandel, the problem with the conventionalist horn is that the anticommodificationist argument would lose part of its critical appeal. How do we know that the social meanings that are at present predominant are right or true and thereby preferable to other ascriptions of meaning? How are we supposed to know whether they are not completely misguided and will change in the near future?

Faced with the ontological as well as epistemological barriers to determining the 'true moral nature' of things, practices, or relationships, the conventionalist strategy appears comparatively promising. This is not the place to argue in detail against Aristotelian essentialism in all its particular forms; suffice it to say that from a political perspective, it is less of a problem that the force of a conventionalist argument against commodification is limited. Even if we are confined to the particular and relative validity of the moral meaning that things and practices have for us, in a certain community or polity, at a particular time, we still have enough of a basis to plausibly criticize developments that

[44] Sandel (n 17) 106 sees in this horn of the dilemma a 'worryingly Aristotelian aspect, for it depends on attributing to certain social practices a characteristic purpose or end'.

[45] According to GI Cohen, 'Note: The Price of Everything, the Value of Nothing: Reframing the Commodification Debate' (2004) 117 Harvard Law Review 689, 703 the essentialist horn is in danger of falling prey to intuitionism, thus being 'unable to account for what it is about the essence of particular goods that makes their exchange objectionable'.

[46] Sandel (n 17) 106; for an anticommodificationist account based on conventionalist reasoning see Walzer (n 35) chapter 4.

eventually undermine these meanings. We can debate the proper reach of markets based on the empirical observation that their effects of commodification go against our communally shared convictions about the moral meaning of that which is commodified.

4. MARKET VALUATION VERSUS SOCIAL MEANING

When trying to escape from the commodificationist dilemma via the conventionalist route, we must say something about the origin and determinants of the meanings[47] we ascribe to particular goods and practices.

Once in a while, reports surface that politicians or other public figures have been found to have bought themselves academic degrees, either by engaging shady agencies or individuals offering these kinds of 'career services' or by directly bribing institutions who issue such degrees. Public outrage at the immorality of such behaviour can be counted on. What do we find reprehensible in a bought degree? The complaint is that the meaning and function of an academic degree precludes its being bought and sold for money, the predominant currency of the economic sphere. Appropriate criteria for 'earning' such a degree are other standards—demonstrated academic skills, knowledge, and expertise. Buying a degree might work on a micro level, as it enables someone to pretend to be educated and to have certain skills that they in fact do not have. On a macro level, however, assumed to be a common and known practice, it would dissolve the social value of academic degrees. From a Kantian perspective, buying a degree fails to meet the demands of the categorical imperative.[48] The maxim on which buying an academic degree rests instead of properly attaining it, by demonstrated academic achievements, passing of tests, and so on, is self-defeating. The objective of

[47] For a discussion of 'social meaning' and its analytical potential in a political and legal context see L Lessig, 'The Regulation of Social Meaning' (1995) 62 The University of Chicago Law Review 943; L Lessig, 'Social Meaning and Social Norms' (1996) 144 Universitiy of Pennsylvania Law Review 2181; CR Sunstein, 'Social Norms and Social Roles' (1996) 96 Columbia Law Review 903.

[48] Kant (n 23) 30: 'Act only according to that maxim whereby you can at the same time will that it should become a universal law without contradiction'.

enjoying the social value of an academic degree without fulfilling its prerequisites in terms of expertise and skill would become impossible if buying degrees were a universally accepted practice. As a result, commodification of degrees would 'undercut their social purpose as symbols of a certain level of academic achievement as to render them valueless'.[49]

The example of academic degrees illustrates how commodification can be incompatible with the social meaning of a good, as our understanding commits us to different distributive criteria (demonstrated academic skills) than market demand (demonstrated ability and willingness to pay). An interesting question—that cannot be answered here in detail—is to what degree partial commodification of a good can be accepted before contradictions in understanding become virulent.[50] After all, academic degrees do come with some form of 'price tag', not least in the US, where tuition fees at good schools are hefty—and criticized for being so. Nevertheless, we do accept that teachers, researchers, and scientists are paid in cash in order to make a living, even if that kind of compensation fails to fully acknowledge their work's worth.

Another example is political power, which we are inclined to think should not be up for direct sale. Our commitment to noncommodification of political power or, more concretely, of electoral votes, is based on our 'democratic understanding of politics',[51] as Walzer has put it. As is well known, however, money is by far not unknown to the dynamics of politics, as is illustrated by the inflow of funds to electoral campaigns, presidential campaigns in particular. Financial resources have come to play a decisive role in recent US presidential elections, culminating in Barack Obama's 2012 campaign being the first to win the 'money race' by raising in excess of $1 billion over the course of 22 months (Mitt Romney

[49] RP Bellamy, 'Segregating Values: Walzer and the Communitarian Containment of Politics' in RP Bellamy (ed), *Liberalism and Pluralism: Towards a Politics of Compromise* (Routledge 1999) 71.

[50] On the issue of 'incomplete' commodification see Radin, *Contested Commodities* (n 6) 102–14.

[51] Walzer (n 35) 121: 'When money carries with it the control, not of things only but of people, too, it ceases to be a private resource. It no longer buys goods and services on the market; it buys something else, somewhere else, where (given our democratic understanding of politics) buying and selling is ruled out.'

trailing close behind).[52] Hillary Clinton's 2016 campaign broke the record again by raising $1.4 billion, compared to Donald Trump's campaign's $957 million.[53] Time and time again, and especially confronted with such enormous sums, fears are voiced that democracy is being 'corrupted' or 'undermined' by money, resulting in officials that would more adequately be described as 'bought' instead of 'elected'. The negative connotation that underlies the characterization 'corrupted' and 'undermined' points to the fact that the workings of the market mechanism in this sphere are seen as inappropriate, as it interferes with the 'right' way of valuing and distributing goods belonging to that sphere—in this case political office and power.

The idea that the proper valuation of people, things, and social practices may vary across different social spheres (such as the economic, familial, and political sphere) has been eloquently developed by Michael Walzer. In his view, meanings of goods and practices are neither immutable nor universal across spheres and over time. Different kinds of valuation are appropriate in different social spheres, such as the familial, political, or economic spheres. In a family context, the distribution of a scarce resource such as a biscuit (assume there is just one biscuit, but three children) may be fair based on the criterion of desert. Who had the most biscuits during the last days? Who had other sweets today? Who has helped with family work today? In an economic context, however, the concept of desert is much harder to handle, as it appears to contradict other principles of economic reasoning such as efficient allocation of resources: they should be distributed to those who can generate the most welfare from them, with eventual benefits for all. Assume that there is a job vacancy to be filled, with one of three applicants. Relying on who might most deserve to be given the job is plausible if desert is narrowly understood to be a function of the applicant's skills and abilities to fulfil the expectations connected with the particular job. However, that

[52] J Ashkenas and others, 'The 2012 Money Race: Compare the Candidates' *The New York Times* <http://elections.nytimes.com/2012/campaign-finance> accessed 1 August 2018.

[53] A Narayanswamy and others, 'Election 2016: Money Raised As Of Dec. 31' *The Washington Post* (1 February 2017) <https://www.washingtonpost.com/graphics/politics/2016-election/campaign-finance/> accessed 1 August 2018.

these skills and abilities should be the sole criteria used to fill the vacancy can be interpreted in a different way as well. Whatever the job is that needs to be done, the outcome in terms of welfare generation will be greatest if we give it to the person who can make the most of the opportunities offered to him or her. The evaluative standards at work in deciding whom to give a job are clearly different from those at work when deciding which of your children to give that one biscuit to.

Because of the social constitution of goods, Walzer argues that 'distributions are patterned in accordance with shared conceptions of what the goods are and what they are for'.[54] What goods are, how we determine their meaning and purpose, thus depends on the social context in which we deal with them. If distributive criteria and resulting arrangements depend on the characterization of a good that is contextual, they are contextually dependent as well. Thus, there is no such thing as an intrinsically good distribution of a certain good.[55]

Elizabeth Anderson has summarized how different kinds of valuation are appropriate for different social spheres:

> If different spheres of social life, such as the market, the family, and the state, are structured by norms that express fundamentally different ways of valuing people and things, then there can be some ways we ought to value people and things that can't be expressed through market norms. We have to govern their production, circulation, and enjoyment through the norms of other social spheres to value them adequately.[56]

The Walzerian approach to the proper understanding, valuation, and distribution of a good has been criticized on the grounds that the social meaning of a good may be contestable, and with that its appropriate valuation.[57] In fact, many of the goods and

[54] Walzer (n 35) 7.

[55] Walzer (n 35) 8–9: 'Distributive criteria are intrinsic not to the good-in-itself but to the social good. If we understand what it is, what it means to those for whom it is a good, we understand how, by whom, and for what reasons it ought to be distributed. All distributions are just or unjust relative to the social meanings of the goods at stake.'

[56] Anderson (n 6) xiii.

[57] CR Sunstein, 'Incommensurability and Valuation in Law' (1994) 92 Michigan Law Review 779, 791 argues that this is in fact what happens in the background of many disputes about controversial legal issues: 'Some of the most heated disputes

practices with regard to which there is a debate about commodification can be interpreted as being contested precisely in their social meaning.[58] For those who find nothing objectionable in commodification or measurement according to market standards, such as the proponents of adoption markets, a social good such as babies, or the relationship between parents and children may have a different social meaning than for those who adamantly oppose even the thought of markets in this area.[59]

Seen from this angle, the problem is not that commodification leads to an understanding of a good or practice that is contrary to its eternal objective nature.[60] The critical impetus of contrasting the commodification of a particular good or practice with an incompatible understanding of that same good or that of goods closely connected with it does not depend on objectivism regarding the moral values that determine these convictions.

A problem of this approach is that it is difficult to pin down how commodification conflicts with the social meaning of a good if there is no uncontested social meaning of the good in question. It is still possible, however, to uncover and point out inconsistencies in our framework of values and political ideals. The social meaning of particular goods and practices may well be contested among different groups in society, even persistently and ardently so. In order to arrive at a workable understanding of the whole set of goods and practices that form the basis of decent living in society, we must start from some sort of 'minimum conceptual ground' of how we understand the relationship between ourselves and between us and the resources we rely on to flourish. This common ground then serves as a test for the understanding

about law and policy actually turn on the appropriateness of a shift from one kind of valuation to another.'

58 Satz (n 11) 81, taking up Walzer's own example of healthcare (which he thinks must be distributed according to need instead of ability and willingness to pay) and contrasting it with 'serious and long-standing controversies about its meaning'.

59 J Raz, *The Morality of Freedom* (Clarendon Press 1986) 348: 'For many, having children does not have a money price because exchanging them for money, whether buying or selling, is inconsistent with a proper appreciation of the value of parenthood.'

60 See section C.3.

of other goods and practices. Demonstrating incompatibility with our common conceptual core suffices for criticism. Thus, if we are without serious contest committed to a 'democratic understanding of politics', we cannot at the same time undermine precisely that understanding by replacing a central tenet of democratic politics—that is, decision-making by majority vote based on the principle 'one person, one vote'—with a practice of exchanging such votes for sums of money or other advantages.

We have seen that the market, the powerful and efficient distributive mechanism that it is, may not be the ideal way to run the distribution of some goods, as it fails to capture the meaning that these goods have for us and the distributive criteria that follow from these meanings. If we understand access to water and food as a necessary ingredient to a minimally good and worthy life, we are consequently inclined to think that everyone should have access to food and water regardless of their being able to offer something in exchange that others might want. In this way, distributive schemes are connected to the social meaning of a good.[61] Letting food and water be exchanged via unregulated market interaction alone, however, will quickly lead to a situation where our normative conviction that everyone should have access to food and water will not be met.

These aforementioned arguments can broadly be classified along the divide of value objectivism versus relativism or conventionalism. The argument of an unjust distribution of access to valuable components and preconditional resources of a good life depends on an objectivist understanding of these components, in philosophical debate commonly referred to as 'objective list theories' of human well-being. The same philosophical pedigree is shared by the argument of a corruption of a good's 'moral character' that is brought about by its being subject to market interaction. In order to be corruptible, we must have an objectivist understanding of that good's moral character and we must argue for our privileged epistemological position

[61] In contexts where other meanings of food are primarily relevant, such as its being a hostage to the goods or a luxury good for gourmet enjoyment, the distributive consequences are very different: equal access, it appears, is less important in these cases.

regarding this true character. For if we cannot be sure that the moral character we see in a good is its true character, we have no justification to criticize transformative influences on that character as 'corruption'.

The alternative route anchors in the relativist tradition in moral philosophy. We can defer the status and content of values not from some objective and immutable truth but from social experiences. Communal value decisions are the outcome of our asking: how do we want to live together, in a world characterized both by innumerable choice options and at the same time scarcity of key resources?

On this grounding the idea of separate social spheres is built; from that perspective, we can criticize commodification of certain goods as the overreaching of the economic sphere into other spheres that are properly governed by other distributive schemes than the market mechanism. That they should be so governed derives from the meanings of the goods that these spheres contain. Solidarity among family members that is characteristic of the familial social sphere should not be interfered with by the normative matrix of the economic sphere, for example; for to do so would be to compare the incommensurable among the metric of the economic sphere, in blunt words, money. Doing so nevertheless would amount to committing ourselves to a radically different understanding of solidarity as a characteristic of a relationship between people.

In section D, we will see whether the considerations just sketched pertain, in revised form, to law as well and what conclusions we must draw from them if they do.

D. MARKET LOGIC AND THE LAW

Law markets lead to legal rules being treated as commodities. Are the arguments that have been developed against the commodification of other goods, such as human organs, babies, or reproductive capacities, applicable to the law as well?

Their bearing on the commodification of law is limited in a crucial respect: unlike regular products, the debate is not about how physically to distribute legal rules. The problem is not how to determine who has access to how much of a scarce good. Law is not distributed in a physical sense, or at least that is not the issue at hand. It helps to remember that law is more adequately understood as another type of good, that of a service.[62] What we are dealing with, then, is the question of whether law as a political service can or should be subject to the market mechanism, whether it should be commodified into a commercial service.

With respect to other goods, that which makes their commodification contested is the fact that they appear to have a price,[63] that they are associated with a particular amount of a currency (regularly money) for which access to them can be had. In order to analyse legal rules within this framework of contested commodification, we must first ask ourselves whether and how the price mechanism works in this respect. Does law have a price, under circumstances of regulatory competition? In Chapter 1, we discussed several incentives that might motivate state legislators to compete for market success regarding their legal products. The most tangible motivation that could be found is financial in nature: external opt-in creates additional tax revenue, whereas domestic opt-out does the opposite. For the sake of the following discussion, we will assume that this motivation is the crucial one driving regulatory competition on the supply side.

1. LAW AS A PRICE VERSUS THE PRICE OF THE LAW

From a law and economics perspective, mandatory law is a pricing system based on the desirability of particular forms of behaviour. In line with an imperative theory of law, law and economics scholars understand legal rules essentially as creating behavioural obligations backed by sanctions: prices for behaviour deviating from the demands of a particular policy must be high enough so as to result in a sufficient deterrent effect. Price theory is thus used to explain factual behavioural reactions to legal rules as well as to determine prescriptively the design of legal incentives according

[62] See Chapter 1, section A.1.

[63] J O'Neill, *The Market: Ethics, Knowledge and Politics* (Routledge 1998) 127: 'If I care about something, then one way of expressing that care is by refusing to put a price on it.'

to the demands of particular policy goals. Whereas from this point of view law is a price-setting mechanism, under conditions of regulatory competition it is *subject* to that mechanism.

The analogy with other products and services is limited insofar as there is rarely a direct price being paid for use of legal rules as a service provided by the issuing state, with the notable exception of franchise fees being collected by US states, for example, for the 'use' of their company law.[64] Instead, the issue at hand is about the distribution of influence on the service's form: one of the great virtues of markets is that they aggregate individual preferences into a general picture of demand.[65] In demand-driven settings, competitive pressure leads suppliers to adjust their offers to demand preferences, often by imitating the products of particularly successful suppliers. With services, a parallel dynamic can be expected to operate. Successful suppliers will be those who cater to the preferences of potential consumers of their services. Successful legislators will thus be those who offer law of a form that answers to those who can exert most market pressure.

The example of professional sports may illustrate this point.[66] The rules of professional sports, particularly those that are widely broadcast, have in recent times been altered to fit with commercial demands.[67] Scheduling of games (eg the Super Bowl) was moved to the evening hours with higher commercial value as far as broadcasting is concerned; additional breaks were introduced to fit in airtime for commercials; the North American Soccer League even experimented with a rule of mandatory 'shoot outs'

[64] See Chapter 1, section A.4.(b).

[65] See Chapter 2 on the perceived virtues of regulatory competition.

[66] On the (contested) commodification and commercialization of sports see JJ Sewart, 'The Commodification of Sport' (1987) 22 International Review for the Sociology of Sport 171; M Gottdiener, *New Forms of Consumption: Consumers, Culture, and Commodification* (Rowman and Littlefield Publishers 2000); Bellamy (n 46) 81: 'Worries about the imperialism of the market are best seen in terms of a fear that its ethos distorts the incentive structure and nature of certain practices. Games offer a good illustration of this point'.

[67] Sewart (n 63) 173–4 describes extensive rule changes made by the US National Football League Rules Committee in the 1970s in order to increase the game's telegeneity, such as a reduction of penalties to shorter distances, an increase of the player limit, and rescheduling of the Superbowl to the evening hours.

after games that ended in a tie after overtime in order to add 'action' and the expectation of a clear winner to a sport that was perceived as difficult to market.[68]

Just as the rules of a sport can be seen as the 'laws' by which that sport is played, state law can be seen as the rules by which the 'game' of social life is played in a polity. Sticking to the analogy, competitive pressure affects the rules that determine the dynamics of these games. The rules of sports may be altered to fit preferences for more commercial breaks, for fear of losing sponsors otherwise moving their budget to other sports. In the same vein, state law may be amended to fit the interests of those who credibly threaten to generate fiscal revenue in other jurisdictions.

As with the rules of a sports game, the issue is not who gets most of the good 'law' but rather who has the most to say, the most influence, on what form and content legal rules will have. What is 'bought', then, on a law market, is not law as a physical product itself, but rather a certain content of law that will be made generally applicable. From a distributional perspective, the crucial question will be: who has most influence on form and content of legal rules, or more influence *relative* to others?

2. THE MORAL CHARACTER OF LAW

Does the corruption argument apply to the law? That is, is there a case to be made about the moral character of the law being corrupted by its commodity status that is brought about by the development of law markets? In principle, the corruption argument works for any kind of good. This is at the same time both its strength and its weakness. The argument takes a different form in every single case,[69] as it has to be shown that the good concerned is closely tied up with values und norms that do not translate into market terms and that it would amount to a violation of the good's 'moral character' to have those norms crowded out by market reasoning.

[68] Ibid 179. [69] Sandel (n 17) 105–6.

Applied to state law, the corruption argument may be construed in a revised form as follows:

1. Exposure to market exchange influences the norms and standards according to which the good exchanged is valued.
2. The moral character of some things requires valuation according to norms that are not compatible with the norms promoted by market exchange.
3. The moral character of state law is not entirely compatible with the norms promoted by market exchange.
4. Therefore, state law should not be exposed to market exchange.

If the corruption argument works, it (arguably) works for legal rules as well. However, the question that needs an answer for the argument to have any force with respect to the law is: what is the moral character of the law? In order to be able to give a plausible answer to that, it seems that one must first overcome the significant philosophical hurdles posed by the general question ofwhat the moral character of anything is, that presupposes a clear understanding of the meaning of 'moral character', a conceptual problem discussed in section C.3.

The conceptual category of law's 'moral character' is straightforwardly plausible if one shares the general assumptions of natural law theory in a broader sense. In a nutshell, natural law theory is based on the idea that there is an essential connection between law and morality.[70] From this connection, law's status as having universal validity and an immutable true or right content is derived, discoverable by reason, superior to the commands of contingent political de facto authorities. Natural law theory is strongly associated with both classical and medieval thought, most notably by the writings of Aristotle and Cicero, as well as St Thomas Aquinas, Rousseau and more recently by John Finnis.[71]

The idea of law being an expression of and therefore determined by a higher order, such as a deity of some kind, is closely

[70] Natural law theory in an even wider philosophical sense also comprises theories about the nature of morality in general. See LL Weinreb, *Natural Law and Justice* (Harvard University Press 1987).

[71] J Finnis, *Natural Law and Natural Rights* (OUP 2011).

connected with natural law theory in its non-modern forms: in this context, law is sometimes even characterized as being 'sacral'.[72] Whether it is the expression of a divine will, the natural order of the world, or another link of law to a kind of higher order—such a perspective on the law is straightforwardly incompatible with its content being subject to the laws of demand as determined by individual and subjective preference and, correspondingly, strategically tailored demand.[73]

Natural law theory, however, is by far not unrivalled as an explanatory and prescriptive account of law and its claim to authority. Thus, the case against law as a (contested) commodity is stronger if frictions with other accounts of law can be shown as well.

E. SOCIAL MEANING AND FUNCTIONS OF LAW

What is the meaning of 'law'? What does it mean for us that there is a legal rule regarding a certain matter? What is the difference between the situation in which there is an applicable legal rule and one in which there is not? An attempt to answer these questions invariably touches upon the most basic functional qualities of state made legal rules that are the object of this inquiry.

Section C.4 argued for a conceptual link between the meaning that we attribute to a particular good, the shared meaning that has come to establish itself in a community, and the distributive scheme that we regard appropriate with respect to that good. This line of reasoning can be directly applied to the law as well. If, as we have seen, '[t]he meaning or nature of certain goods is such that providing them in this way is inherently inappropriate',[74] we must ask ourselves what the meaning of the law is in order to

[72] On the sacrality of the law in ancient times, with the example of Israelite law in the old testament, JA Soggin, *Introduction to the Old Testament* (3rd edn, Westminster John Knox Press 1989) 164–7.

[73] The reason why arguments based on a theoretical grounding of natural law thought are not further pursued here has been sketched already in the discussion of Aristotelian essentialism that is also part of this family of theories.

[74] R Keat, 'Market Limits and Their Limits' (2012) 28 Economics and Philosophy 251, 255.

know how to appropriately manage its production, distribution, and evaluation, as Joshua Cohen has put it:[75]

> What is unjust, for example, about wealth determining political power in our society is that this violates *our* understanding of *power* – what political power is and what it is good for – not that it conflicts with a *general* presumption in favour of an equal distribution of *all goods*.[76]

In the same vein one can say that what bothers us about de facto mobility of capital exerting pressure and influence on the legislator, to the extent that law is oriented towards capital-owners' preferences, is that this violates our understanding of law, what it is and what it is good for. In this way, what we regard as appropriate norms to judge particular goods is built into our shared understanding of those goods.[77]

What is our shared understanding of the law? Is there one at all? Is law a good that has a social meaning that resists commodification—similar to friendship, love, and Nobel Prizes? Or is it a good that can meaningfully be commodified, such as human organs, but it is contested whether it should be modified?

One way to approach the social meaning that law has for us is this: our understanding of law, the social meaning that it has for us, derives from the societal functions that we expect it to fulfil. A functional perspective on the law thus asks for the purposes and goals that it serves, and for the distinct ways in which it does so (compared to other mechanisms such as public debate). There are countless ways to characterize the functions of particular (bodies of) legal rules on various levels of abstraction.[78] The most salient

[75] Sandel (n 9) 10; see also R Michaels, 'After the Revolution - Decline and Return of U.S Conflict of Laws' in A Bonomi and P Volken (eds), *Yearbook of Private International Law, Vol 11* (Sellier 2010) 11.

[76] J Cohen, 'Spheres of Justice: A Defense of Pluralism and Equality by Michael Walzer' (1986) 83 Journal of Philosophy 457, 459.

[77] Walzer (n 35) 8–9.

[78] As a topic of jurisprudence, however, 'functions' of law in general have received surprisingly little attention from legal scholars. For a notable exception to the otherwise neglect for functions of law see J Raz, *The Authority of Law: Essays on Law and Morality* (Clarendon Press 1979) 163–79. On 'functionalism' as a mainstream method of comparative law, see K Zweigert and H Kötz, *An Introduction to Comparative Law* (Tony Weir tr, 3rd edn, OUP 1998) 34; R Michaels, 'The Functional Method of Comparative Law' in M Reimann and R Zimmermann (eds), *The Oxford Handbook of Comparative Law* (OUP 2006) 339.

dimension of law's functions is perhaps that of 'providing coercive measures'[79] in order to solve conflicts of interest or situations that exhibit the structure of a prisoner's dilemma. Mandatory law putting a sanction on theft of others' property or stating that a certain level of minimum wages must be paid to workers is plausibly interpreted as coercively directing the behaviour of its addressees towards particular policy goals.

This, however, is not the only functional perspective from which the existence of legal rules makes sense; a variety of other functional aspects could be relied upon to justify the existence and particular content of a legal rule:

> Solving recurrent and multiple coordination problems, setting standards for desirable behavior, proclaiming symbolic expressions of communal values, resolving disputes about facts [...] are important functions which the law serves in our society, and those have very little to do with law's coercive aspect and its sanction-providing functions.[80]

Of the functions that Marmor identifies, we will look at two that allow us to circumscribe what we expect legal rules to do in society. First, the resolution of coordination and cooperation problems; second, the expression of communal value decisions that are connected to our shared understanding of how life in a society is to be organized, in all different sorts of respects. As we will see, both these functions commit us to an understanding of the law that is incompatible with it being treated as a market commodity.

[79] A Marmor and A Sarch, 'The Nature of Law', *The Stanford Encyclopedia of Philosophy* (2015) <https://plato.stanford.edu/archives/fall2015/entries/lawphil-nature/> accessed 1 August 2018, Section 1.2: 'Contemporary use of "game theory" in the law tends to show that the rationale of a great variety of legal arrangements can be best explained by the function of law in solving problems of opportunism, like the so-called Prisoner's Dilemma situations. In these cases, the law's main role is, indeed, one of providing coercive measures.'

[80] Ibid Section 1.2.

1. LAW AS ORDER AND STABILIZATION OF EXPECTATIONS

'For law is order'[81] can be taken as a most basic functional definition of law, whether one shares the theoretical outlook of Aristotle or not. Thomas Hobbes offered a similar account of the social role of law, taking its function to be that of creating social order, partly by allowing for a peaceful resolution of disputes.[82] Others have stressed that the existence of rules is a precondition of social cooperation:

> [I]n order to cooperate men must know what behavior will be expected of them and what behavior they may expect from others. [...] For these expectations to be known and fulfilled, there must be rules which are commonly followed.[83]

The functional argument for the existence of law can be read as follows:[84]

1. The characteristic function of law is to maintain order.
2. For a peaceful and stable existence, a society depends on order.
3. Therefore, societies should and do in fact rely on a legal system to achieve order.

From this perspective, providing for order is the main function and legitimizing characteristic of legal rules. There is, of course, ample room for debate about each of these premises, notably

[81] Aristotle, 'Politics' in J Barnes (ed), *Complete Works of Aristotle, Volume 2: The Revised Oxford Translation* (Princeton University Press 2014) Pol. VII 1326a [31-33].

[82] On Hobbes's argument for the necessity of law as a political tool at the hands of the sovereign: T Hobbes, *Leviathan* (first published 1651, Penguin 1985) Part II Ch. 18 238, contrasting the rule of the sovereign by the help of law to 'that dissolute condition of masterlesse men, without subjection to Lawes, and a coercive Power to tye their hands from rapine, and revenge'; see also D Gauthier, *The Logic of Leviathan: The Moral and Political Theory of Thomas Hobbes* (Clarendon Press 1969) 136; BZ Tamanaha, *Law as a Means to an End: Threat to the Rule of Law* (CUP 2006) 2.

[83] GL Dorsey, 'The Necessity of Authority to Freedom' in L Bryson and others (eds), *Freedom and Authority in Our Time: Twelfth Symposium of the Conference on Science, Philosophy and Religion* (Harper and Brothers 1953) 317.

[84] BZ Tamanaha, 'Law', *Oxford International Encyclopedia of Legal History* (2nd edn, OUP 2008) speaking of 'prevailing intuitions that the characteristic function of law is to maintain order'.

about the origins of law. Can legal rules be issued only by institutions of legitimate government? Or by other sources as well? According to Eugen Ehrlich,[85] 'law is an ordering', not necessarily based on state or government institutions—an extremely wide concept of law that encompasses other sources of norms, such as morals, religious practices, and so on, as well.

Why do societies depend on order for long-term flourishing and the promotion of their members' welfare? When caught in a prisoner's dilemma situation, from a game theoretic perspective, the rational thing is not to cooperate in order to maximize our expected gain.[86] One of the purposes of legal rules and their beneficial contribution to social interaction is that they lead people to 'drop their guard'[87] and behave in a way that enables them to find a cooperative exit out of situations calling for strategic non-cooperation.

Even in situations that do not exhibit the structure of a prisoner's dilemma, coordination often would be much costlier absent general and reliably effective rules of conduct. Imagine a world without traffic rules. The benefit of an 'all drive on the right (or left) side of the road' rule is obvious, considering the significant risks and costs associated with cautionary measures in order to avoid head-on collisions (such as driving very slowly at all times). Absent traffic rules, vehicle drivers would be forced to play the 'crossroads game': approaching an intersection of roads, they would speculate about how other drivers will behave. Will

[85] E Ehrlich, *Fundamental Principles of the Sociology of Law, VoL 5* (Transaction Publishers 1936) 24: 'It is not an essential element of the concept of law that it be created by the State, nor that it constitute the basis for the decisions of courts or other tribunals, nor that it be the basis of a legal compulsion consequent upon such a decision. A fourth element remains, and that will have to be the point of departure, i.e. the law is an ordering.'

[86] J Elster, *Rational Choice* (NYU Press 1986) 8–9; the prisoner's dilemma as it presents itself to legislators having to decide on environmental regulation is discussed by R Revesz, 'Rehabilitating Interstate Competition: Rethinking the "Race-to-the-Bottom" Rationale for Federal Environmental Regulation' (1992) 67 New York University Law Review 1210; see also Langille B, 'Competing Conceptions of Regulatory Competition in Debates on Trade Liberalization and Labour Standards' in W Bratton and others (eds), *International Regulatory Competition and Coordination* (Clarendon Press 1996) 479.

[87] T May, *Autonomy, Authority and Moral Responsibility* (Kluwer 1998) 152.

they use precaution and stop before crossing? Should they trust in the risk aversion of others and speed on? General rules such as 'give right of way to those coming from the right' or 'behave according to the signals of traffic lights' stabilize expectations in the behaviour of others that, in the traffic example, enable faster and safer travelling for all.[88]

Stabilization of expectations in the consequences of our own behaviour[89] as well as in the behaviour of others works even counterfactually.[90] Even if we encounter someone who does not act according to these expectations, we need not give them up. The system reacts to such deviations in a way that signals to everyone that they may and should hold on to their expectations. This is the difference between prescriptive norms and mere empirical expectations (eg the expectation that physical objects will gravitate towards the earth when held above ground and left to fall) that must be revised when disappointed.

Different types of law, of course, perform different functions in detail.[91] We will not argue here on the level of these specific functional descriptions of legal rules, although the argument against law markets could be framed in this manner.[92] On a general level,

[88] Ibid 35.

[89] FA Hayek, *The Constitution of Liberty* (Chicago University Press 1960) 156–7: 'The law tells [an individual] what facts he may count on and thereby extends the range within which he can predict the consequences of his actions. [. . .] The law thus serves to enable the individual to act effectively on his own knowledge.'

[90] For the idea that the primary function of law is to 'counterfactually stabilize normative expectations' see N Luhmann, *Law as a Social System* (KA Ziegert tr, F Kastner and others eds, OUP 2004) 147–56; on Luhmann's sociological theory of law see P Zumbansen, 'Spaces and Places: A Systems Theory Approach to Regulatory Competition in European Company Law' (2006) 12 European Law Journal 534, 555–6.

[91] As Luhmann (n 87) 148–9 observes: 'Analytically, one can identify numerous problems and thus numerous functions to which they refer depending on what one wants to compare [. . .] . In this sense, ultimately law also has the function of providing lawyers with income.'

[92] As found eg in L LoPucki, *Courting Failure – How Competition for Big Cases is Corrupting the Bankruptcy Courts* (University of Michigan Press 2005) 258 with respect to competition among US bankruptcy courts: 'The bankruptcy court competition is slowly but surely transferring power over the bankruptcy courts from elected officials to case placers. This ongoing transfer is interfering with two crucial bankruptcy functions: restructuring debt and saving companies.'

more general claims about the function of legal rules can be made. Much of private law fits the functional category of stabilizing expectations, both empirically and counterfactually.[93]

Law markets in large part depend on choice of law options for individuals;[94] these options are typically found in private law (as opposed to eg criminal law). The function of contract law, for example, can be interpreted as offering sample rules for those questions and details of a contract that the parties have not explicitly dealt with during the stage of contract formation, thereby reducing uncertainty.[95] The purpose of dispositive default legal rules, then, is to provide for fair compromise of interests in as many (unforeseen) circumstances as possible. Mandatory provisions of contract law reduce uncertainty as well, insofar as they cannot be opted out of from within the legal system. Their justification, however, typically relies on other considerations as well: protection of the common good or protection of one party to a transaction from adverse effects of its inferior bargaining position. Mandatory provisions of consumer contract law are directed at protecting 'weak' and typically uninformed, less experienced consumers from entering into contracts that do not further their welfare.

In order for mandatory law to become a commodity, the possibility of opt-out must be given. As intra-system opt-out is per definition impossible, inter-system opt-out into another legal regime is the choice at hand, either horizontally into another national regime or vertically into a supranational body such as, for example, the sales law regime offered by the UN Convention on Contracts for the International Sale of Goods (CISG).

[93] F Möslein, *Dispositives Recht: Zwecke, Strukturen und Methoden* (Mohr Siebeck 2011) 290–3.

[94] See Chapter 1, section A.3.(b).

[95] See F Möslein, 'Regulatory Competition between Public and Private Rules' in H Eidenmüller (ed), *Regulatory Competition in Contract Law and Dispute Resolution* (CH Beck 2013) 147, 152: 'Most importantly, however, the provision of rules requires specific knowledge, and their main purpose consists in reducing uncertainty and a lack of information of the addressees.' See also Möslein KM and others, 'Law as a Service – Recht als Dienstleistung: Strategischer Produktivitätsfaktor unternehmerischer Innovation?' (2012) <http://clicresearch.org/wp-content/uploads/downloads/2012/10/23_de_recht_als_dienstleistung.pdf> accessed 1 August 2018, 9.

By engaging in regulatory competition, legislators work against the territoriality principle. Two scenarios of legislative motivation to compete must be distinguished.[96] Whereas proactive competition is based on the objective to achieve opt-in from external consumers, passive or defensive competition, as it has been called, is meant to defend opt-out into other legal regimes paired with internal consequences. Competitive action that is directed at avoiding opt-out in fact protects the territorial links of legal rules. Competing in order to keep people and capital 'at home' is thus directed at preserving legal coherence as defined by territorial criteria.

The more opt-in and opt-out without a physical component occurs, that is, the more individuals and capital are subject to legal regimes that are not the ones of their location, the more interconnections between legal realms will occur.

The mere fact that opt-out is possible, however, reduces its ability to stabilize expectations, for that outcome depends on a rule being applicable. The less we can—generally and in advance—base our expectations on the applicability and effectiveness of legal rules, the less these rules appear to be legitimate in their mandatory and coercive existence. It thus turns out that law markets collide with premise 1 of the functional argument sketched earlier: if a characteristic and legitimizing function of law is to maintain order, then a development that restricts issuers of state law from ensuring that their law comes to application is at the same time an impediment to the fulfilment of that function. Reliable coordination involves a mandatory aspect; if the subjective preferences of all involved in certain matters could be expected to align themselves to the ideal scenario of full cooperation and a lack of free riding, legal rules would be unnecessary.

An empirical hypothesis (hard to verify, admittedly) would be that the growing realization of party autonomy, in the form of choice of law opportunities that are the basis for law markets, affects the ability of state law to maintain order not only theoretically. Gradual changes in terms of legal architecture to the effect that territorial or other objective criteria less and less determine which law applies to a given situation can be expected to

[96] See Chapter 1, section A.5.

influence individuals' attitudes towards legal norms in general. In the traditional picture of largely isolated legal realms with conflicts of laws determined by objective connecting factors, law is perceived as the exogenous normative framework of general rules. In a global marketplace for law, however, with legal rules perceived as commodities to be chosen or disposed of, individuals' disposition to comply with these rules even in situations of conflicting interests should be expected to be lower.

The reasons behind this shift in attitude can be found in the crowding out of traditional social norms governing our perception of legal norms and the behaviour by which we respond. The argument of shifting social norms has been made, for example, with respect to legal regimes governing environmental protection, and the introduction of schemes for the trading of emissions rights:

> Critics claim that emissions trading has damaging effects on social norms by making environmental amenities seem like any other commodity: a good that has its price, to be set through market mechanisms. Thus they suggest that emissions trading systems may have damaging effects on social norms by making people see the environment as something without special claims to public protection.[97]

The argument put forward here is that, by establishing an emissions trading scheme, we change the norms associated with our use of environmental resources. Environmental pollution is no longer seen as repugnant and stigmatized behaviour, but as something you can buy a right to do, thereby 'buying off' moral criticism.

Parallel to this line of reasoning, law markets could be criticized for changing the social norms associated with law. It is no longer seen as the set of universal rules that all have to abide by. Instead, law has been reduced to fixing a price for a certain kind of behaviour under a particular legal regime that comes with its own amenities, such as infrastructure needed for that particular behaviour.

[97] CR Sunstein, 'On the Expressive Function of Law' (1996) 144 University of Pennsylvania Law Review 2021, 2045–6; for a detailed critical discussion of the use of the market mechanism in the field of environmental protection and an analysis of the use of pollution charges see Kelman (n 34), particularly Ch. 2.

2. EXPRESSION OF COMMUNAL VALUE DECISIONS

The example of environmental protection highlights a functional dimension of legal rules that differs from being an instrument for aligning behavioural responses with particular policy goals. Legal rules can be interpreted as saying something other than what kind of behaviour is expected from their addressees. Often, they also convey an expression of value decisions.[98] In the case of environmental protection, prohibitory laws would convey a message that pollution is wrong, whereas an emissions trading scheme instead communicates a price in exchange for which a fixed amount of pollution is right, in the sense that it has been paid for.

In a democratically structured polity, the expressive statements that are embodied in legal rules are communal decisions, with their outcome ideally enjoying widespread agreement.[99] The expressive dimension is more present in some legal rules or bodies than in others. Constitutional provisions on fundamental rights, for example, strongly convey a statement about the importance of particular values, without a direct behavioural imperative. Other examples are anti-discrimination laws, communicating a commitment to social equality; or income tax deductions

[98] R Benabou and J Tirole, 'Laws and Norms' (2011) NBER Working Paper No 17579 <http://www.nber.org/papers/w17579> accessed 1 August 2018, 21: '[L]aw is not merely a price system for bad and good behaviors – it also plays an important role in expressing and shaping the values of society.' See also Anderson (n 6); Sunstein (n 44); Sunstein (n 94); expression of value decisions has been characterized as one instantiation of the larger group of 'symbolic legislation' that is not primarily directed at the enforcement of a legal rule, in terms of behavioural consequences. See G-P Calliess, 'Die Steuerungskrise - jetzt auch im Privatrecht?' in G-P Calliess and others (eds), *Soziologische Jurisprudenz: Festschrift für Gunther Teubner zum 65. Geburtstag* (De Gruyter 2009) 465, 470–1, who describes four types of symbolic legislation: (i) law expressive of basic ethical valuations by the community (eg prohibition of abortion); (ii) laws appellative towards the ethical behaviour of citizens; (iii) 'alibi-legislation' meant to demonstrate authority in situations of crisis; and (iv) 'compromise-legislation' in the form of laws that appease strong feelings on an issue by particular pressure groups, but are designed such that they cannot be properly enforced.

[99] If there is no widespread agreement and acceptance, as there is often with regard to morally sensitive issues, they must be seen as a statement of the democratically dominant majority that has managed to have their views prioritized in the legislative process.

for children, highlighting the importance of family values and intergenerational responsibility.[100] Provisions for a mandatory minimum wage to be paid to workers can be explained not only as an instrument to ensure that workers with comparatively low qualifications can support themselves by their earnings, but as an expression of a commitment to citizen equality. No one should be paid less than a certain amount of money for an hour's work, as that would equate to treating them as a less worthy member of the polity.

What can be said in terms of explanation and justification of the expressive content of legal rules? Two kinds of answers have been given in the past. Proponents of a consequentialist interpretation see communication of value decisions that a legal rule realizes as an instrument to increase that rule's effectiveness in influencing people's behaviour.[101] Empirically, norm compliance is expected to be higher if the norm is supported by expressive content rather than by the threat of sanctions alone. In this vein, Cass Sunstein has characterized the expressive function of law as one aspect of 'norm management'.[102] The idea is that a message about the values realized by norm-conforming behaviour positively influences people's attitudes towards that legal norm, leading to higher rates of compliance.[103] A factual answer to this

[100] NS Arnold, 'Postmodern Liberalism and the Expressive Function of Law' (2000) 17 Social Philosophy and Policy 87, 90.

[101] Ibid 94–7 arguing prescriptively that expressivist concerns alone cannot serve as legitimate reasons for law creation or reform.

[102] Sunstein (n 54) 820–4; Sunstein (n 94); on the lack of integration of expressive concerns into cost benefit analysis RH Pildes and CR Sunstein, 'Reinventing the Regulatory State' (1995) 62 The University of Chicago Law Review 1, 66–75.

[103] Sunstein (n 94) 2045–8; Sunstein (n 44) 965: 'Laws with expressive justifications are most plausibly defended on the ground that they will in fact affect social norms and move them in appropriate directions.' In footnote 233 to that sentence, Sunstein is even more clear, explicitly rejecting 'the use of law to "make statements" independently of consequences', as that would, in his view, 'risk fanaticism and pointlessness'. The advantage he claims for his position is 'shifting debate from basic values to issues that are, at least in principle, subject to empirical testing'. The appeal of a consequentialist approach to law and policy, he rightly observes, is closely related to the appeal of utilitarianism. For a discussion of utilitarianism and its bearing on the merits and problems of regulatory competition see Chapter 3.

empirical claim would be helpful, but is still missing, as Sunstein himself acknowledges.[104]

Others have stressed the relevance and legitimacy of the expressive dimension of law regardless of empirically verifiable consequences in terms of norm efficacy.[105] Influence on behavioural responses to legal rules is not the only answer to explain and justify the expressive message of legal rules. It may be doubtful, for example, whether an anti-discrimination law actually helps those minority groups it aims to protect. The same goes for norms on environmental protection: even if their effectiveness is low, they serve an expressive function towards the members of society.[106] When the criminal ban on flag burning in the US was introduced, instances of flag burning in fact *increased* as a result. Nevertheless, the ban was upheld for the message it sent, despite its consequences.[107]

Be it for its inherent relevance or for its results in terms of behavioural change, it should have become clear that law is expressive of our communal evaluative stance towards the world; as Pildes and Sunstein have put it:

> [E]xpressive or symbolic dimensions of policy are central in many regulatory contexts. They are just as real and significant as other dimensions of policy. Part of what policy-making does is to define, interpret, and create collective understandings and values.[108]

(a) Expressive law and regulatory competition

How exactly does regulatory competition collide with law's expressive function? From the perspective of mobile law consumers, expressive concerns can seldom be expected to be found

[104] Sunstein (n 44) 965: 'Much work remains to be done on these important questions.'

[105] A similar argument, albeit not in terms of legal theory but of utility theory, can be found in R Nozick, *The Nature of Rationality* (Princeton University Press 1994) 28: '[T]he symbolic connection of an action to a situation enables the action to be expressive of some attitude, belief, value, emotion, or whatever.' And '[a] large part of the richness of our lives consists in symbolic meanings and their expression, the symbolic meanings our culture attributes to things or the ones we ourselves bestow' (30).

[106] Ibid 26–35. [107] Pildes and Sunstein (n 99) 69.

[108] Sunstein (n 94) 2045–7.

in the set of considerations that drive either consumer opt-in or opt-out. Particularly in a scenario of opt-in without a physical component, such as choosing the company law of a state without establishing more than the absolute minimum of physical ties to that state (such as a mailbox), expressive concerns play no role for the rational actor. Strategic lawmaking, with an eye to the motivational structure of those that are to be prevented from opting out or induced to opt in, will thus be oriented towards the factors that drive direct or indirect choice of law. Expressive concerns will then be 'sacrificed' for the sake of factors that determine the cost of opting in or refraining from opting out.

In comparison, in a non-competitive setting, the lawmaker has the option to adhere to expressive statements in the law that impose higher prices in terms of behavioural consequences (such as a relatively high minimum wage) without having to fear negative choice signals in return.

The discussion about rules regarding in vitro fertilization (IVF) and other issues of prenatal diagnostics show the dilemma that lawmakers find themselves in. Faced with rapidly growing medical and technical possibilities, societies have been forced to ask themselves how the options that have been developed should be treated, from the age of the woman receiving IVF to the legality of surrogacy and egg donation, the fate of frozen supernumerary embryos, and many other issues. Legal rules restricting the use of these options are typically highly expressive of the value considerations that have led to the ban, relating to the human dignity of mother and embryo, danger of exploitation of surrogate mothers and egg donors, or a perceived threat of the commodification of children and the parent–child relationship.[109]

Prospective parents are mobile; there are countless examples of individuals who have travelled abroad to receive fertility treatment of a sort that is not legally available in their home state. Humans' reproductive preferences thus appear to be strong enough so as to incur the costs of circumventing restrictive rules

[109] For an overview of these issues see Pildes and Sunstein (n 99) 70; for a discussion of procreative autonomy and its implications for reproductive ethics see K Mason, G Laurie, and AM Smith, *Mason and McCall Smith's Law and Medical Ethics* (OUP 2013) Ch. 8.

in their home state by opting into another regime. Competitive pressure on the home state legislator is thus directed at preventing punctual opt-out, more than attracting external opt-in.

Another example is the rate of progressive taxation,[110] or finding a legislative balance between taxation of capital versus earned personal income. A steep increase of tax rates in line with the taxable amount is seen as an expression of a commitment to (re)distributive justice. Similarly, comparatively low levels of taxation on capital gains versus personal income are perceived as unjust. An answer that has been given to these considerations of justice is that competitive capital taxation, even if it is lower than income taxation, may still be preferred, as otherwise capital would be moved out of the jurisdiction altogether (legally or illegally), leading to even less tax revenue in total.

In these situations, the consequentialist argument in favour of law reform is that in the face of factual mobility, at least partially giving in to competitive dynamics will achieve the lesser of two evils. Preventing opt-out by adjusting both the expressive and prohibitory content of a legal rule may, in terms of implementing a polity's value system, be better than taking mobility as a given and sticking with rules that fully retain their expressive content, but become increasingly ineffective. Pure expressivists must reject this argument on the grounds that the effectiveness of a legal rule and its expressive content cannot be weighed against one another.

(b) Which values?

With respect to these issues, preventing regulatory competition by restricting mobility would be the instrument of choice in order to preserve the status quo. Proponents of law markets are right to emphasize that demonstrated legal mobility (with physical side effects) by a critical number of 'law consumers' may serve as an 'accelerator' for much overdue law reform.

Precisely in those fields in which morally sensitive issues and expressive law is affected an argument could prima facie be made

[110] For a general and a historical overview of the debate see E Brake and J Millum, 'Parenthood and Procreation', *The Stanford Encyclopedia of Philosophy* (2018) <https://plato.stanford.edu/archives/spr2018/entries/parenthood/> accessed 1 August 2018, Sections 1 and 2.

in favour of law markets. When social realities and value perceptions change, legal rules should be amended according to these developments. Competitive pressure on legislatures to adapt to these changes may help this process. With regard to these issues and developments, there will of course always be disagreement among different groups in society as to how such changes should be recognized by the legal system at all, and if so to what extent and at what speed—think of same-sex marriage, for example.

In the late eighteenth and early nineteenth centuries, the availability and preconditions for divorce, for example, differed greatly among US states. Whereas in some states such as South Carolina divorce was entirely prohibited until 1949, in others the only recognized ground for divorce was adultery (eg New York).[111] Some states found that good money was to be made from offering a more liberal divorce law, requiring couples to reside in their state for a period of one to three years, having them obtain legal advice, and so on. By the mid-twentieth century, a lively 'divorce scene' had developed in Reno, Nevada, where wealthy individuals enjoyed their expensive lives while waiting for completion of their divorce, which was granted for many reasons that could be proven by unsupported testimony.[112] Nevada's divorce business eventually dried up after 1966, when New York, its main supplier of clients, had given in to competitive pressure and liberalized its own divorce law as well.[113] Since 1975, no-fault divorce without proof has been the rule in all US states.[114]

When the market mechanism arguably 'crowds out' past sets of moral convictions as reflected in state law, we must ask ourselves what the consequences of such crowding out are. There is a case to be made that what comes in afterwards will enjoy more legitimacy in terms of congruence between society's values and the expressive content of law. When people in large numbers move temporarily to other states in order to be divorced according to

[111] EA O'Hara and LE Ribstein, *The Law Market* (OUP 2009) 172.

[112] C Crossen, 'Back When Divorcing Was Hard, Some States Found a Way to Profit', *Wall Street Journal* (New York, 6 August 2007) <http://www.wsj.com/articles/SB118635505489588702> accessed 1 August 2018.

[113] O'Hara and Ribstein (n 110) 172.

[114] M Grossberg, 'Balancing Acts: Crisis, Change, and Continuity in American Family Law 1890–1990' (1994) 28 Indiana Law Review 273.

a more liberal law, it should come as no surprise that other states are influenced in their deliberation about law reform regarding preconditions of divorce.

What we should keep in mind, however, is that from the 'expressive perspective', it matters where such shifts come from, how they are determined and by whom. In an ideal democratic world, expressive content of legal rules is eventually bound to a decision by the sovereign, not to pressure by individual opt-out.[115] Of course, legal adaptation to changed realities in terms of value perceptions is necessary; but acceleration of this process by establishing law markets is bought by a decrease in (democratic) legitimacy of the results that follow.

(c) Mobility for some, mandatoriness for others

Another aspect of the functioning of legal rules in a market setting is noteworthy. Whether legal rules are perceived as an inescapable normative framework that communicates binding value decisions of the respective community, or the offering of an infrastructure bundle that comes with a certain price tag, crucially depends on the costs associated with opting out of the law in question. As described in Chapter 1, the differentiation between choice of law that is or is not accompanied by physical relocation of individuals or financial or other resources is only a matter of degree in terms of the costs of changing from one legal environment to another. Typically, physical components of that choice increase costs. The incentive structure, however, is essentially the same.

From this it follows that, from the demand perspective, the greater the advantages to be expected from legal arbitrage are, the less switching costs will figure in the eventual cost–benefit calculation. Large volume entities will therefore be more likely to engage in arbitrage than small volume individuals, for whom the costs of opt-out will often be prohibitively high.[116] Individuals who have to pay taxes on their average personal income in Sweden will rarely contemplate relocating to Switzerland in order to choose a tax law of their liking.

[115] See Chapter 5, section A.

[116] M Galanter, 'Why the "Haves" Come out Ahead: Speculations on the Limits of Legal Change' (1974) 9 Law and Society Review 95.

From the perspective of those below the level of beneficial arbitrage opportunities, the law market with its alternative offerings is only a theoretical occurrence. The functioning of legal rules will thus be different for two groups of addressees: those for whom choice makes no economic sense, and those for whom it does. In light of the features of generality and universality that are commonly associated with at least mandatory state law, this divide is not what should be worked towards. The divide is equally difficult to reconcile with the expressive function of law discussed already. If law is to express communal decisions about which values should be realized and how and to what comparative extent in case of conflicts, having some perceive these decisions as binding and others as a mere commodity on offer cannot properly work in the long term.

(d) Philosophical externalities of regulatory competition

The anti-commodificationist argument against law markets that builds upon our understanding of legal rules, the functions they fulfil, and the values they communicate within a political system could also be interpreted as an argument about 'philosophical externalities'[117] of law's own commodification.

The fact that market logic crowds out other values could be interpreted as a meta-level externality. There are 'costs' in terms of the hindered realization of other values that cannot adequately be considered within the market paradigm. These external costs do not enter into the calculation when assessing the merits of regulatory competition from a perspective within that paradigm. They could be called externalities as well: costs that are borne by others who did not choose to incur them. They are thus not considered correctly in the utilitarian calculus that market adherents most often presuppose.

The argument could also be put in functional terms. Instead of values whose realization is crowded out by the prevalence of market demand we could focus on a shift in the purposes that legal rules are there to serve. The functions of stabilizing expectations and expressing values are, from this perspective, crowded

[117] On the economic argument from resulting externalities see Chapter 2, section B.1.(b).

out by its serving as an instrument for pricing behaviour. In fully fledged Tieboutian law markets,[118] legislators treat their legal rules primarily as part of the infrastructure bundle they offer to mobile consumers. Crowding out then happens not on the level of particular values and political principles, but with regard to the functional description of law.

3. LAW MARKETS AND SPHERES OF JUSTICE

With a view to the idea of separate spheres of justice that determine the appropriate way of valuing people and things, the criticism of law markets can be put in Walzerian terms as well.

The political upshot of spherical justice is a concern with the preservation of 'sphere autonomy'.[119] The evaluative standards of one sphere must be prevented from 'taking over' evaluation in other spheres. In many contemporary cases, it is the economic sphere whose standards and evaluative criteria are perceived to reach over into other dimensions of social life, such as the social, familial, or political spheres. As a side effect, its currency invades almost all spheres, enabling people to buy goods without being entitled to them according to other normative criteria, as market distributions are a function of ability and willingness to pay.[120] As we demand that other spheres be protected from being sucked into the dynamics of market exchange, we express a conviction that 'the morality of the bazaar belongs in the bazaar'[121] and an intuitive 'concern that the market sector not be permitted to encroach further into the private nonmarket or the government sectors'.[122]

[118] CM Tiebout, 'A Pure Theory of Local Expenditure' (1956) 64 Journal of Political Economy 416.

[119] JJ Thorndike and DJ Ventry, *Tax Justice: The Ongoing Debate* (Urban Institute Press 2002) use the term 'integrity'.

[120] Radical capitalists would, of course, emphatically contest this claim. Success and reward in market settings is the deserved outcome of 'intelligence, resolution, hard work, and a willingness to take risks', as portrayed by Walzer (n 35) 121.

[121] G Gilder, *Wealth and Poverty: A New Edition for the Twenty-First Century* (Regnery Publishing 2012) 101.

[122] Walzer (n 35) 109.

Law markets, the argument goes, amount to a violation of evaluative sphere autonomy, by subjecting the creation of an instrument that belongs to the political sphere to the criteria of the economic sphere.

In the context of contested commodification of other goods, such as babies, education, or political office, an interesting function of law is highlighted. In these contexts, legal rules are called for as a 'bulwark' against the dominant and 'contagious'[123] tendencies of the market sphere.[124] Blocked exchanges regarding these goods are necessary in order to prevent their commodification, to protect the values we associate with these goods—human dignity and parental love with babies, equality of opportunity with education, citizen equality and democracy with political office—from the dynamic of the market and its evaluative focus on the ability and willingness to pay in the currency of money. Law's role then is to provide protection of other social spheres from 'market imperialism', to delineate one evaluative sphere from another and ensure that the currency of one does not enable success in all. The argument runs parallel to Hans-Werner Sinn's claim that law markets undermine the function of law to prevent market failure.[125] When law markets are established, competitive pressure on legislatures leads to a situation in which creation and reform of legal rules follows the logic of the market sphere. Protection and sphere delineation are undermined.

The strongest criticism of the commodification of law itself in the course of regulatory competition lies in its societal functions that are incompatible with its commodity status. To expose the law to the market mechanism is to focus exclusively or primarily on certain functions, thereby neglecting and eventually compromising others, such as the law as an expression of communal value decisions. When we allow regulatory competition to unfold, we must be clear that over time the functions that we

[123] Kelman (n 34) 55; see also the discussion of the 'crowding-out effect' in section B.2.

[124] Radin, *Contested Commodities* (n 6) 13: 'What is the role of law in underwriting and expressing the humanistic culture that can support democracy?'

[125] Radin, *Contested Commodities* (n 6) 173, Ch. 3.

can expect the law to perform as a social and political ordering instrument will change.

F. CONCLUSION

This chapter does not aim to offer a conclusive argument as to why there should be no regulatory competition at all. The aim is, rather, to offer a philosophical framework for thinking about the commodification of law and its consequences that are brought about by states perceiving themselves as suppliers of market goods in the form of law.

One conclusion is that regulatory competition is incompatible with our understanding of law, in particular with respect to two of its functions.[126] First, law is a political instrument, intended to establish and maintain social order in large groups, mainly by stabilizing expectations. Law's ability to perform this function, however, is built upon its binding character that is not dependent on individual choice (without which competitive markets could not exist). Second, law can be seen as a social form that expresses and helps to realize political decisions. Among them are decisions about the values and principles that should ideally determine how social and political life is organized, on various levels of abstraction. In other words, legal norms reflect decisions about how we want to live together, from basic civil rights in the constitution to withdrawal rights of consumers in long-distance contracts. Under conditions of regulatory competition, however, there is a case to be made that some of these normative considerations would in case of conflict be 'crowded out' by the imperatives of success in a global law market. In line with their commodity status, legal rules would come to reflect primarily the interests of those on whose positive choice their application in fact depends, consistency with the overall normative framework of a polity not guaranteed.

What follows from this lack of consistency alone is not that regulatory competition is necessarily bad, but only that we cannot hold on to our perception of law as characterized in this chapter

[126] Recognizing that there are many other appropriate functional descriptions of legal rules, some of which may as well be affected by the emergence of regulatory competition, positively or negatively.

and at the same time accept competitive dynamics with regard to law itself to unfold in a growing number of regulatory fields.

Which of the incompatible perceptions of law should be given preference is a question that cannot be answered comprehensively at this point. It depends on the understanding of the good life, particularly the good political and social life that one embraces. There is no, and in hardly any polity will ever be, an uncontested and entirely coherent answer to these matters.

6

CONCLUSION

A. SUMMARY OF CRITICAL ARGUMENTS

We have seen that regulatory competition and law markets appear problematic from a number of theoretical angles. Chapter 2 illustrates that the economic case for regulatory competition as a process for the discovery of efficient legislative products is inconclusive. Chapter 3 lays out principled objections to utilitarian assumptions underwriting the promise of regulatory competition that translate into direct criticism. Chapter 4 focuses on frictions with regard to structural features of political systems and the principles and values embodied therein, such as democracy, political autonomy, and authority. Chapter 5 argues that law's status as a market commodity collides with our functional understanding of mandatory legal rules, particularly with respect to law as one of the primary political instruments to create order and enable long-term cooperative behaviour among members of the polity and as an expression of political value decisions, of ideals that we accept as a basis for our shared lives.

Looking at all these tensions between regulatory competition and our traditional understanding of law and the state and its functions tells us nothing yet about what particular policy consequences are to be drawn from our diagnosis. After all, regulatory competition as a factual phenomenon is the logical effect of legal diversity and mobility, which are themselves factual phenomena as well. When factual developments apparently do not fit well into an existing political and legal architecture, one can think of two kinds of reaction. First, shaping reality so that it conforms better with present normative structures. Second, adapting the normative structure so that new factual developments are adequately dealt with.

In our case, the first route would require removing the preconditions of regulatory competition. Should we, for a start, harmonize more actively and dispose of choice-of-law opportunities, both physical and legal? In an increasingly globalized world that is held together by a growing portion of transnational transactions, restricting physical and legal mobility may seem to be an overly simple and inappropriate answer.

The second route would require amending our understanding of what democratic principles, state autonomy, and political authority require, and to what extent legal rules serve to stabilize expectations and express communal value decisions.

That such amendment may be impossible to avoid entirely becomes clear when we see regulatory competition as a phenomenon that has, in many fields, not been deliberately brought about by politicians following the advice of policy advisers trained in Chicago. Instead, to a large extent it is a consequence of factual global developments that are commonly summarized under the broad term 'globalization'.

B. REGULATORY COMPETITION AS A SYMPTOM OF GLOBALIZATION

In the course of the global integration of both political and economic spheres, the nation state has lost some of its relevance. National law is no longer the primary source of authority over a given territory.[1] What does this mean for the implicit methodological nationalism of contemporary political theory? And what does it mean for state law as the state's primary ordering instrument? At first sight, its freedom to set political priorities may seem untouched:[2] National legislators remain free to issue laws of

[1] EA O'Hara and LE Ribstein, *The Law Market* (OUP 2009) 217: 'The globalization of business has profoundly undermined the territorial basis of lawmaking'; see also A Peters, 'The Competition between Legal Orders' (2014) 3 International Law Research 42, 48: '[G]lobalisation and global governance have called into question the traditional monopoly position of the State as the provider of law.'

[2] Ibid 45; H Eidenmüller, 'The Transnational Law Market, Regulatory Competition, and Transnational Corporations' (2011) 18 Indiana Journal of Global Legal Studies 707, 730; see also Chapter 4, section A.1.(b).

whatever content; yet the reach of those laws, their steering function, and their impact have become smaller.

Regulatory competition is one symptom of the changes that this development has given rise to. Engaging in competition is one of the answers available to nation states facing increasing stages of political and economic integration.[3] The 'competition state'[4] has been contrasted to the traditional conception of the welfare state that derived its legitimacy as a 'demarketizing institution' from guaranteeing a good life for its citizens by providing public goods and keeping various kinds of markets in check. Processes of globalization have led to many states understanding themselves more as 'competition states', in a global arena that lays the ground for competition for mobile capital.[5] Nation states try to attract and retain capital by providing a friendly environment for capital that has connected itself with their territory. From a domestic perspective, 'new public management' seeks to rebuild state administration along the lines of market structures and private firms, with the aim of a 'service state' that offers administrative products.[6]

[3] DM Andrews, 'Capital Mobility and State Autonomy: Toward a Structural Theory of International Monetary Relations' (1994) 38 International Studies Quarterly 193, 199: '[The] features of the emerging international structure include improved communications and information technologies as well as new financial mechanisms. Together, these features have enhanced the capacity of capital asset-holders to evade the jurisdiction of unfriendly regulators. States must therefore be increasingly sensitive to changes in the regulatory policies of their neighbors, since they are now effectively competing for the right to regulate capital. The general thrust of this new competitive dynamic has been for states to accommodate the preferences of market actors by liberalizing (or in other words, lowering) their regulatory standards.'

[4] PG Cerny, 'Globalization and the Changing Logic of Collective Action' (1995) 49 International Organization 595.

[5] See R Palan, 'Recasting Political Authority: Globalization and the State' in RD Germain (ed), *Globalization and its Critics* (Palgrave Macmillan 2000) 139, 158: '[I]ndividuals and companies increasingly feel comfortable in choosing their country of residence instrumentally. […] By implication, the state is seen no longer as the political voice of the people but as a provider of the means of accumulation.'

[6] J Kersten, 'Wettbewerb zwischen Hoheitsträgern' in H Kube and others (eds), *Leitgedanken des Rechts – Paul Kirchhof zum 70. Geburtstag* (CF Müller 2013) 845, 846.

Globalization per se is not a normative concept. It does not tell us whether the developments and outcomes that we vaguely denote by that term are good or bad. At the same time, we cannot turn back the clock and undo the development of the world towards integration, interwovenness, and interdependency of economic and political spheres. We can, however, from our current perspective, think about what law's role in these processes is and should be. Should it be a 'motor of change' or rather the opposite, guarding state and society against the untamed dynamics of global markets? Legal rules mirror political processes. Their creation and content are, after all, subject to political decisions.

With this in mind, we may ask ourselves whether or not we want to use the law as an enforcer of global integration. For if we create the conditions for regulatory competition, mainly by making legal mobility less costly in terms of time, money, and other resources, we will be oiling the machine of globalization that has generated demand for such mobility in the first place. These questions cannot satisfactorily be answered from the perspective of one single nation state. The issue seems to boil down to the question of what we think the role of the state is in a globalized world, and what the purposes and functions of the legal rules that it issues are.

C. LAW AND THE STATE: PHILOSOPHICAL AND CULTURAL DIFFERENCES

In the end, attitudes towards regulatory competition appear to correspond with convictions regarding the state—its purpose and justification. More particularly, optimism about contemporary democratic states' ability to promote the well-being of all relevant actors significantly influences the assessment of alternative forms of ordering, as the market mechanism is one.[7]

[7] On the dependency of an assessment of tax competition in light of optimism regarding the democratic state W Schön, 'Der "Wettbewerb" der europäischen Steuerordnungen als Rechtsproblem' in J Pelka (ed), *Europa- und verfassungsrechtliche Grenzen der Unternehmensbesteuerung* (Dr Otto Schmidt 2000) 191, 203; see also G Bachmann, *Vertikaler Regulierungswettbewerb im europäischen Gesellschaftsrecht* (Dr Otto Schmidt 2012) 28.

1. INDIVIDUAL WELL-BEING

Diverging accounts of the state's purpose need not even be the end point of this discussion. For we can further ask why there are diverging views about what legitimizes the existence of state structures. Can we find common conceptual ground from which these views diverge? The most straightforward common denominator is the good human life that the state is there to promote. This is a normative concept: as a social and political institution, the state derives its claim to authority and legitimacy from contributing to the good life of its citizens.

There are many questions to be asked about this intuitively appealing line of reasoning. Answers to these questions, what constitutes the good human life, and by what political means it is best achieved fall in three broad categories. First, subjectivist accounts that tie the good life to the desires (or preferences) of the affected individual. As noted in Chapter 3, when economists talk about welfare, implicitly or explicitly, they rely on this kind of conception of the good human life.[8] Second, mental states as the decisive basis for human well-being have regained considerable attention in recent times (so-called hedonic theories), as economists and psychologists have started focusing on human 'happiness', or 'subjective well-being'.[9] Third, objective-good theories of human well-being have argued for particular components of a good human life, of what makes humans flourish, and a life worth living that is independent from individual epistemic or motivational access.[10]

[8] See Chapter 3, section A.1 and M Adler, *Well-Being and Fair Distribution: Beyond Cost-Benefit Analysis* (OUP 2012) 156: 'A preference-satisfaction account of well-being has long been the dominant view within economics.'; for a detailed discussion of varieties of subjectivism in (welfare) economics see J O'Neill, *The Market: Ethics, Knowledge and Politics* (Routledge 1998) 38–52.

[9] For a discussion see Adler (n 8) 156. These approaches will not be further discussed in the following, as their ascent is fairly recent and not directly related to variations in the evaluation of regulatory competition.

[10] Martha Nussbaum's and Amartya Sen's scholarship on certain decisive 'capabilities' that make for an inalienable basis of human flourishing points in this objectivist direction; for an overview see M Nussbaum and A Sen (eds), *The Quality of Life* (Clarendon Press 1993).

The main difference between conceptions of well-being that is of present interest is the divide between subjectivist and objectivist accounts of what, ultimately, makes life worth living. Adherence to one or the other conception of the good human life certainly influences one's view of purpose and legitimacy of the state. For proponents of desire theories, the state is easier to justify in the form of a 'minimal state' that confines itself to offering a necessary frame for the continued satisfaction of individual preferences. From an objectivist perspective, sympathy for a robust welfare state that ideally guarantees the realization of the good life for ideally all its citizens comes much easier, if necessary by means of coercion (eg redistribution of resources) or paternalist measures (overriding an individual's preferences for his or her own good).

Differences in the understanding of the good life and the purpose and legitimacy of the state lead to different understandings of purpose and functions of law. Subjectivist theories of well-being point in the direction of understanding law as a state instrument for social control and coordination of citizen behaviour that must be sparsely employed in its mandatory form so as not to hamper individual preference satisfaction more than absolutely necessary. Objectivist theories, however, tend to be more sympathetic to the coercive dimension of legal rules, to the benefit of the rights of other persons, the common good, political values and principles, or even the well-being of those who are directly affected (legal paternalism).

In the end, varying conceptions of the state and its law that are related to competing conceptions of the bases of human well-being 'trickle down' to the issue of regulatory competition. From a subjectivist perspective, regulatory competition is to be welcomed as one symptom of a state of the legal world in which individuals have room for choice of the law that best promotes their own idea of a good life. It is thus conducive to the satisfaction of individual preferences and consequently to be welcomed in principle. From an objectivist perspective, however, regulatory competition appears as a threat to the demands of the components of an objectively good life.[11]

[11] Peters (n 2) 47 argues to this effect with reference to values embodied in constitutional provisions: '[L]awyerly examination needs to assess and evaluate the benefits of that competition process with a view at legal criteria which do not

2. CULTURAL TRADITIONS

The differences in philosophical accounts of the functions and grounds of legitimacy of the state and its law and their relationship to the market mechanism that have been outlined here can even be traced into cultural and geographical divergences. Simon Deakin has interpreted diverging attitudes towards regulatory competition among US and European politicians and scholars as stemming from differences in the fundamental approach to the relation of state and market as competing ordering mechanisms:

> At a fundamental level, the debate between European and American approaches is one of the prevailing conceptions of the relationship between regulation and the market. The US literature, particularly the standard law and economics approach, views regulation as external interference in private ordering, to be justified only where a clear market failure can be demonstrated. By contrast, the predominant European approach has been to see regulation, and the legal system more generally, as constituting the market order, an approach that is compatible with the idea that regulatory and market forces will more often complement than oppose each other.[12]

It thus comes as no surprise that regulatory competition tends to be judged more favourably in an Anglo-Saxon and particularly US-American context, in which political and philosophical culture are closer to the utilitarian tradition than, by comparison, legal culture and scholarship in continental Europe. The Anglo-Saxon understanding of the 'minimal state' that preserves individual liberty to the greatest extent possible demands other approaches to law and policy than a robust conception of a 'welfare state' that is more directly involved in realizing for its citizens the components of a good life.[13]

necessarily coincide with personal preferences of individuals, such as capacity of the competition process to secure respect of legal (and even constitutional) principles, namely security, freedom, and equality.'

[12] S Deakin, 'Legal Diversity and Regulatory Competition: Which Model for Europe?' (2006) 12 European Law Journal 440, 454.

[13] The functions of law are seen differently from these angles as well, see for a rejection of the expressive function of law NS Arnold, 'Postmodern Liberalism and the Expressive Function of Law' (2000) 17 Social Philosophy and Policy 87, 90: 'Classical liberals believe that the legitimate functions of government are limited to protecting people's fundamental rights, providing public goods, and

3. AGREEING TO DISAGREE

The aim of the chapters in this book, particularly Chapters 3, 4, and 5, has been to uncover tensions between what we think law is and does and what it is there for, and the idea that legislators compete against each other in order to 'sell' their legal products to as many law customers as possible.

The arguments presented in these chapters are meant to contribute to a clearer picture of the incompatibilities between the theoretical pedigree of regulatory competition—the assumptions we must accept in order to see its promises and its appeal—and other sets of beliefs and commitments that shape our thinking about law and the state.

Some of the criticisms developed may make more sense from the perspective of some legal cultures than others. Yet, even then, it may be helpful to know why it is more specifically that there is disagreement about the normative assessment of a factual phenomenon that all legislators have to deal with in some way.

dealing with externalities. For classical liberals, making statements, even if the statements are politically correct from their perspective, is not a proper function of the state or its laws.' For a comparative discussion of Anglo-Saxon and European approaches to the welfare state see G Esping-Andersen, *The Three Worlds of Welfare Capitalism* (John Wiley & Sons 2013).

BIBLIOGRAPHY

Adams Z and Deakin S, 'Freedom of Establishment and Regulatory Competition' in D Chalmers and A Arnull (eds), *The Oxford Handbook of European Union Law* (OUP 2015) 537–61.

Adler M, *Well-Being and Fair Distribution: Beyond Cost-Benefit Analysis* (OUP 2012).

Anderson E, *An Expressive Theory of Rational Action in Value* (Harvard University Press 1993).

Anderson E, *Value in Ethics and Economics* (Harvard University Press 1995).

Anderson E, 'Democracy: Instrumental vs Non-Instrumental Value' in T Christiano and J Christman (eds), *Contemporary Debates in Political Philosophy* (Wiley-Blackwell 2009) 213–27.

Andrews DM, 'Capital Mobility and State Autonomy: Toward a Structural Theory of International Monetary Relations' (1994) 38 International Studies Quarterly 193–218.

Aristotle, 'Politics' in J Barnes (ed), *Complete Works of Aristotle, Volume 2: The Revised Oxford Translation* (Princeton University Press 2014).

Armbrüster C, 'Englischsprachige Zivilprozesse vor deutschen Gerichten?' (2011) 44 Zeitschrift für Rechtspolitik 102–4.

Armour J, 'Share Capital and Creditor Protection: Efficient Rules for a Modern Company Law' (2000) 63 Modern Law Review 355–78.

Arneson R, 'Perfectionism and Politics' (2000) 111 Ethics 37–63.

Arneson R and Anderson E (2009), 'The Supposed Right to a Democratic Say' in T Christiano and J Christman (eds), *Contemporary Debates in Political Philosophy* (Wiley-Blackwell 2009) 197–227.

Arnold NS, 'Postmodern Liberalism and the Expressive Function of Law' (2000) 17 Social Philosophy and Policy 87–109.

Arrow KJ, *Social Choice and Individual Value* (2nd edn, Yale University Press 1963).

Ashkenas J and others, 'The 2012 Money Race: Compare the Candidates', *The New York Times* <http://elections.nytimes.com/2012/campaign-finance> accessed 1 August 2018.

Avi-Yonah RS, 'Globalization, Tax Competition, and the Fiscal Crisis of the Welfare State' (2000) 113 Harvard Law Review 1573–676.

Ayres I, 'Filling Gaps in Incomplete Contracts: An Economic Theory of Default Rules' (1989) 99 Yale Law Journal 87–130.

Bachmann G, *Vertikaler Regulierungswettbewerb im europäischen Gesellschaftsrecht* (Dr Otto Schmidt 2012).

Bachmann G and others, *Regulating the Closed Corporation* (De Gruyter 2014).

Bachmann G and Richter H, 'Contracting Co-Determination: The SE-Directive as a Model?' in H Eidenmüller (ed), *Regulatory Competition in Contract Law and Dispute Resolution* (CH Beck 2013) 187–98.

Baird D and Rasmussen R, 'Beyond Recidivism' (2006) 54 Buffalo Law Review 343–63.

Barnard C, 'Regulating Competitive Federalism in the European Union? The Case of EU Social Policy' in J Shaw (ed), *Social Law and Policy in an Evolving European Union* (Hart Publishing 2000) 49–70.

Bebchuk LA, 'Federalism and the Corporation: The Desirable Limits on State Competition in Corporate Law' (1992) 105 Harvard Law Review 1435–510.

Becht M, Mayer C, and Wagner HF, 'Where Do Firms Incorporate? Deregulation and the Cost of Entry' (2008) 14 Journal of Corporate Finance 241–56.

Bellamy RP (ed), *Liberalism and Pluralism: Towards a Politics of Compromise* (Routledge 1999).

Bellamy RP, 'Segregating Values: Walzer and the Communitarian Containment of Politics' in RP Bellamy (ed), *Liberalism and Pluralism: Towards a Politics of Compromise* (Routledge 1999) 67–89.

Benabou R and Tirole J, 'Laws and Norms' (2011) NBER Working Paper No 17579 <http://www.nber.org/papers/w17579> accessed 1 August 2018.

Berger KP, 'Abschied von der Privatautonomie im unternehmerischen Geschäftsverkehr? Zum Differenzierungsgebot im AGB-Recht' [2006] Zeitschrift für Wirtschaftsrecht 2149–57.

Birks P and McLeod G (trs), *The Institutes of Justinian* (Duckworth 1987).

Birmingham RL, 'Breach of Contract, Damage Measures, and Economic Efficiency' (1970) 24 Rutgers Law Review 273–92.

Blackaby N and others (eds), *Redfern and Hunter on International Arbitration* (6th edn, OUP 2015).

Bobbio N, *The Future of Democracy* (Polity Press 1987).

Bohman J and Rehg W, 'Introduction' in J Bohman and W Rehg (eds), *Deliberative Democracy: Essays on Reason and Politics* (MIT Press 1997) ix–xxx.

Bonacich E and Wilson JB, *Getting the Goods: Ports, Labor, and the Logistics Revolution* (Cornell University Press 2008).

Brachert S and Dietzel A, 'Editorial: Deutsche AGB – Rechtsprechung und Flucht ins Schweizer Recht' [2005] Zeitschrift für das gesamte Schuldrecht 441.

Brake E and Millum J, 'Parenthood and Procreation', *The Stanford Encyclopedia of Philosophy* (2018) <https://plato.stanford.edu/archives/spr2018/entries/parenthood/> accessed 1 August 2018.

Bratton WW and McCahery JA, 'Regulatory Competition, Regulatory Capture and Corporate Self-Regulation' (1995) 73 North Carolina Law Review 1861–948.

Bratton WW and McCahery JA, 'The New Economics of Jurisdictional Competition: Devolutionary Federalism in a Second-Best World' (1997) 86 The Georgetown Law Journal 201–78.

Bratton W and others, 'Introduction: Regulatory Competition and Institutional Evolution' in W Bratton and others (eds), *International Regulatory Competition and Coordination* (Clarendon Press 1996) 1–55.

Braun R and others, 'Does Charter Competition Foster Entrepreneurship? A Difference-in-Difference Approach to European Company Law Reforms' (2013) 51 Journal of Common Market Studies 399–415.

Brennan G and Buchanan JM, *The Power to Tax: Analytic Foundations of a Fiscal Constitution* (CUP 1980).

Brown JG, 'Competitive Federalism and Legislative Incentives to Recognize Same-Sex Marriage' in W Bratton and others (eds), *International Regulatory Competition and Coordination* (Clarendon Press 1996) 271–74.

Bruns A, *Haftungsbeschränkung und Mindesthaftung* (Mohr Siebeck 2003).

Bundesnotarkammer and others (eds), 'Law Made in Germany: Global, Effective, Cost-Efficient' (2014) <https://www.lawmadeingermany.de/Law-Made_in_Germany_EN.pdf> accessed 1 August 2018.

Calliess G-P, 'Die Steuerungskrise - jetzt auch im Privatrecht?' in G-P Calliess and others (eds), *Soziologische Jurisprudenz: Festschrift für Gunther Teubner zum 65. Geburtstag* (De Gruyter 2009) 465–79.

Cary WL, 'Federalism and Corporate Law: Reflections Upon Delaware' (1974) 83 Yale Law Journal 663–705.

Cerny PG, 'Globalization and the Changing Logic of Collective Action' (1995) 49 International Organization 595–625.

Charny D, 'Competition among Jurisdictions in Formulating Corporate Law Rules: An American Perspective on the Race to the Bottom in the European Communities' (1991) 32 Harvard International Law Journal 423–56.

Charny D, 'Regulatory Competition and Labour Law Standards' in DC Esty and D Geradin (eds), *Regulatory Competition and Economic Integration: Comparative Perspectives* (OUP 2001) 311–29.

Christiano T, *The Constitution of Equality: Democratic Authority and Its Limits* (OUP 2008).

Christiano T, 'Democracy' in C McKinnon (ed), *Issues in Political Theory* (OUP 2012) 80–102.

Christiano T, 'Democracy', *The Stanford Encyclopedia of Philosophy* (2015) <https://plato.stanford.edu/archives/fall2018/entries/democracy/> accessed 1 August 2018.

Christman J, 'Autonomy in Moral and Political Philosophy', *The Stanford Encyclopedia of Philosophy* (2018) <https://plato.stanford.edu/archives/spr2018/entries/autonomy-moral/> accessed 1 August 2018.

Cohen GI, 'Note: The Price of Everything, the Value of Nothing: Reframing the Commodification Debate' (2004) 117 Harvard Law Review 689–710.

Cohen J, 'Spheres of Justice: A Defense of Pluralism and Equality by Michael Walzer' (1986) 83 Journal of Philosophy 457–68.

Coleman JL, 'Efficiency, Utility, and Wealth Maximization' (1979) 8 Hofstra Law Review 509–51.

Collins H, 'Regulatory Competition in International Trade: Transnational Regulation through Standard Form Contracts' in H Eidenmüller (ed), *Regulatory Competition in Contract Law and Dispute Resolution* (CH Beck 2013) 121–41.

Cooter RD and Ulen TS, *Law and Economics, International Edition* (6th edn, Prentice Hall 2012).

Crossen C, 'Back When Divorcing Was Hard, Some States Found a Way to Profit', *Wall Street Journal* (New York, 6 August 2007), <http://www.wsj.com/articles/SB118635505489588702> accessed 1 August 2018.

Cumming DJ and MacIntosh JG, 'The Role of Interjurisdictional Competition in Shaping Canadian Corporate Law' (2000) 20 International Review of Law and Economics 141–86.

Curzon-Price V, 'Fiscal Competition and the Optimization of Tax Revenues for Higher Growth' in A Bergh and R Höijer (eds), *Institutional Competition* (Edward Elgar Publishing 2008) 155–81.

Dahl R, 'Can International Organizations be Democratic? A Skeptic's View' in I Shapiro and C Hacker-Cordón (eds), *Democracy's Edges* (CUP 1999) 19–36.

Daines R, 'Does Delaware Law Improve Firm Value?' (2001) 62 Journal of Financial Economics 525–58.

Dammann J and Hansmann H, 'Globalizing Commercial Litigation' (2008) 94 Cornell Law Review 1–71.

Danforth MT, 'Cells, Sales, and Royalties: The Patient's Right to a Portion of the Profits' (1988) 6 Yale Law and Policy Review 179–202.

Davies RB and Vadlamannati KC, 'A Race to the Bottom in Labor Standards? An Empirical Investigation' (2013) 103 Journal of Development Economics 1–14.

Deakin S, 'Legal Diversity and Regulatory Competition: Which Model for Europe?' (2006) 12 European Law Journal 440–54.

Deakin S, 'Regulatory Competition After Laval' (2007) 10 Cambridge Yearbook of European Legal Studies 581–609.

Deakin S and Wilkinson F, 'Rights v Efficiency? The Economic Case for Transnational Labor Standards' (1994) 23 Industrial Law Journal 289–310.

Devereux MP, Lockwood B, and Redoano M, 'Do Countries Compete over Corporate Tax Rates?' (2008) 92 Journal of Public Economics 1210–35.

Donahue JD, *Disunited States* (Basic Books 1997).

Dorsey GL, 'The Necessity of Authority to Freedom' in L Bryson and others (eds), *Freedom and Authority in Our Time: Twelfth Symposium of the Conference on Science, Philosophy and Religion* (Harper and Brothers 1953).

Easson A, 'Taxing International Income', in RE Krever (ed), *Tax Conversations: A Guide to the Key Issues in the Tax Reform Debate: Essays in Honour of John G Head* (Kluwer Law International 1997) 415–45.

Easterbrook FH, 'Federalism and European Business Law' (1994) 14 International Review of Law and Economics 125–32.

Economic and Financial Affairs Council, 'Conclusions of the ECOFIN Concil Meeting on 1 December 1997 concerning taxation policy' (Information) 98/C 2/01.

Ehrlich E, *Fundamental Principles of the Sociology of Law, VoL 5* (Transaction Publishers 1936).

Eidenmüller H, 'Free Choice in International Company Insolvency Law in Europe' (2005) 6 EBOR 423–47.

Eidenmüller H, 'Wettbewerb der Insolvenzrechte' (2006) 35 Zeitschrift für Unternehmens- und Gesellschaftsrecht 467–88.

Eidenmüller H, 'Die GmbH im Wettbewerb der Rechtsformen' (2007) 36 Zeitschrift für Unternehmens- und Gesellschaftsrecht 168–211.

Eidenmüller H, 'Abuse of Law in the Context of European Insolvency Law' (2009) 6 European Company and Financial Law Review 1–28.

Eidenmüller H, 'Recht als Produkt' (2009) 64 Juristenzeitung 641–53.

Eidenmüller H, 'The Transnational Law Market, Regulatory Competition, and Transnational Corporations' (2011) 18 Indiana Journal of Global Legal Studies 707–49.

Eidenmüller H, 'What Can Be Wrong with an Option? An Optional Common European Sales Law as a Regulatory Tool' (2013) 50 Common Market Law Review 69–84.

Eidenmüller H, *Effizienz als Rechtsprinzip* (4th edn, Mohr Siebeck 2015).

Eidenmüller H, 'Collateral Damage: Brexit's Negative Effects on Regulatory Competition and Legal Innovation in Private Law' (2018) ECGI Working Paper No 403/2018 <https://ssrn.com/abstract=3171973> accessed 1 August 2018.

Eidenmüller H, Engert A, and Hornuf L, 'Incorporating under European Law: The Societas Europaea as a Vehicle for Legal Arbitrage' (2009) 10 European Business Organization Law Review 1–33.

Eidenmüller H, Grunewald B, and Noack U, 'Minimum Capital in the System of Legal Capital' in M Lutter (ed), *Legal Capital in Europe, ECFR Special Volume 1* (De Gruyter 2006) 17–41.

Eidenmüller H, Hornuf L, and Reps M, 'Contracting Employee Involvement: An Analysis of Bargaining over Employee Involvement Rules for a Societas Europaea' in H Eidenmüller (ed), *Regulatory Competition in Contract Law and Dispute Resolution* (CH Beck 2013) 155–86.

Eidenmüller H and Stark J, 'Behavioral Economics and Private International Law' in J Basedow and others (eds), *European Encyclopedia of Private International Law* (Edward Elgar Publishing 2017) 171–79.

Eisenberg T and Miller GP, 'The Flight to New York: An Empirical Study of Choice of Law and Choice of Forum Clauses in Publicly-Held Companies' Contracts' (2009) 30 Cardozo Law Review 1475–512.

Elster J, *Rational Choice* (NYU Press 1986).

Enriques L, 'EC Company Law and the Fears of a European Delaware' (2004) 15 European Business Law Review 1259–74.

Enriques L and Gelter M, 'Regulatory Competition in European Company Law and Creditor Protection' in H Eidenmüller and W Schön, *The Law and Economics of Creditor Protection* (TMC Asser Press 2008) 421–57.

Enriques L and Macey JR, 'Creditors Versus Capital Formation: The Case against the European Legal Capital Rules' (2001) 86 Cornell Law Review 1165–204.

Ertman MM and Williams JC (eds), *Rethinking Commodification: Cases and Readings in Law and Culture* (NYU Press 2005).

Esping-Andersen G, *The Three Worlds of Welfare Capitalism* (John Wiley & Sons 2013).

Estlund D, 'Debate: On Christiano's the Constitution of Equality' (2009) 17 Journal of Political Philosophy 241–52.

Esty DC and Geradin D (eds), *Regulatory Competition and Economic Integration: Comparative Perspectives* (OUP 2001).

Faria JAE, 'Der Wettbewerb zwischen den Rechtsordnungen' (2015) 65 Anwaltsblatt 104–9.

Fischel D, 'The "Race to the Bottom" Revisited: Reflections on Recent Developments in Delaware's Corporation Law' (1982) 76 Northwestern University Law Review 913–45.

Finnis J, *Natural Law and Natural Rights* (OUP 2011).

Fitzroy FR and Kraft K, 'Co-Determination, Efficiency and Productivity' (2005) 43 British Journal of Industrial Relations 233–47.

Foot P, *Natural Goodness* (OUP 2001).

Frederick S, Loewenstein G, and O'Donoghue T, 'Time Discounting and Time Preference: A Critical Review' (2002) 40 Journal of Economic Literature 351–401.

Frey BS, *Not Just for the Money* (Edward Elgar Publishing 1997).

Fried C, *Contract as Promise: A Theory of Contractual Obligation* (first published 1935, 2nd edn, OUP 2015).

Flessner A, 'Deutscher Zivilprozess auf Englisch – Der Gesetzentwurf des Bundesrats im Lichte von Staatsrecht, Grundrechten und Europarecht' (2011) 11 Neue Juristische Online Zeitschrift 1913–24.

Fuchs AE, 'Autonomy, Slavery, and Mill's Critique of Paternalism' (2001) 4 Ethical Theory and Moral Practice 231–51.

Gabor B, *Regulatory Competition in the Internal Market* (Edward Elgar Publishing 2013).

Galanter M, 'Why the "Haves" Come out Ahead: Speculations on the Limits of Legal Change' (1974) 9 Law and Society Review 95–160.

Garrett G, 'Global Markets and National Politics: Collision Course or Virtuous Circle?' (1998) 52 International Organization 787–824.

Gauthier D, *The Logic of Leviathan: The Moral and Political Theory of Thomas Hobbes* (Clarendon Press 1969).

Gelter M, 'The Structure of Regulatory Competition in European Corporate Law' (2005) 5 Journal of Corporate Law Studies 247–84.

Gelter M, 'Tilting the Balance between Capital and Labor? The Effects of Regulatory Arbitrage in European Corporate Law on Employees' (2010) 33 Fordham International Law Journal 792–857.

Genschel P, Kemmerling A, and Seils E, 'Accelerating Downhill: How the EU Shapes Corporate Tax Competition in the Single Market' (2011) 49 Journal of Common Market Studies 585–606.

Genschel P, Rixen T, and Uhl S, 'Die Ursachen des europäischen Steuerwettbewerbs' (2007) 48 Politische Vierteljahresschrift 297–320.

Gerhardt M, 'Consumer Bankrupty Regimes in the US and Europe: Further Effects and Implications of the Crisis' (2009) CEPS Working Paper No 318 http://ssrn.com/abstract=1438511, accessed 1 August 2018.

Gerken L, 'Introduction' in L Gerken (ed), *Competition among Institutions* (Palgrave Macmillan 1995) x–iv.

Gerken L, 'Institutional Competition: An Orientative Framework' in L Gerken (ed), *Competition among Institutions* (Palgrave Macmillan 1995) 1–31.

Gerken L (ed), *Competition among Institutions* (Palgrave Macmillan 1995).

Giegerich T, 'Wettbewerb von Rechtsordnungen' (2009) 69 Veröffentlichungen der Vereinigung der Deutschen Staatsrechtslehrer 57–105.

Gilder G, *Wealth and Poverty: A New Edition for the Twenty-First Century* (Regnery Publishing 2012).

Giridharadas A, 'Silicon Valley Roused by Secession Call' *New York Times* (28 October 2013) <http://www.nytimes.com/2013/10/29/us/silicon-valley-roused-by-secession-call.html?_r=0>, accessed 1 August 2018.

Goetz CJ and Scott RE, 'Liquidated Damages, Penalties and the Just Compensation Principle: Some Notes on an Enforcement Model and a Theory of Efficient Breach' (1977) 77 Columbia Law Review 554–94.

Gossen HH, *The Laws of Human Relations and the Rules of Human Action Derived Therefrom* (first published 1845, MIT Press 1983).

Gottdiener M, *New Forms of Consumption: Consumers, Culture, and Commodification* (Rowman and Littlefield Publishers 2000).

Green L, *The Authority of the State* (Clarendon Press 1988).

Green L, 'Legal Obligation and Authority', *The Stanford Encyclopedia of Philosophy* (2012) <http://plato.stanford.edu/archives/win2012/entries/legal-obligation/>, accessed 1 August 2018.

Griffin J, *Well-Being: Its Meaning, Measurement, and Moral Importance* (Clarendon Press 1986).

Grossberg M, 'Balancing Acts: Crisis, Change, and Continuity in American Family Law 1890–1990' (1994) 28 Indiana Law Review 273–328.

Häberle P, *Europäische Rechtskultur: Versuch einer Annäherung in zwölf Schritten* (Suhrkamp 1997).

Habersack M, 'Grundsatzfragen der Mitbestimmung in SE und SCE sowie bei grenzüberschreitender Verschmelzung' (2007) 171 Zeitschrift für das gesamte Handels- und Wirtschaftsrecht 613–43.

Hansson SO and Grüne-Yanoff T, 'Preferences', *The Stanford Encyclopedia of Philosophy* (2018) <https://plato.stanford.edu/archives/sum2018/entries/preferences/> accessed 1 August 2018.

Hare RM, 'Ethical Theory and Utilitarianism' in A Sen (ed), *Utilitarianism and Beyond* (CUP 1982) 23–38.

Harsanyi JC, 'Individual Utilities and Utilitarian Ethics' in A Diekmann and P Mitter (eds), *Paradoxical Effects of Social Behavior* (Physica-Verlag 1986) 1–12.

Hayek FA, 'The Use of Knowledge in Society' (1945) 35 The American Economic Review 519–30.

Hayek FA, *The Constitution of Liberty* (Chicago University Press 1960).

Hayek FA, 'Competition as a Discovery Procedure' (MS Snow tr, first published 1968, 2002) 5 Quarterly Journal of Austrian Economics 9–23.

Heinrich-Böll-Stiftung (ed), *Der Wert öffentlicher Güter* (Heinrich-Böll-Stiftung 2015).

Henzler HA, 'The New Era of Eurocapitalism' (1992) 70 Harvard Business Review 57–67.

Herzog L, *Inventing the Market: Smith, Hegel, and Political Theory* (OUP 2013).

Herzog L, 'Markets', *The Stanford Encyclopedia of Philosophy* (2018) <https://plato.stanford.edu/archives/fall2017/entries/markets/> accessed 1 August 2018.

Hicks JR, 'The Foundations of Welfare Economics' (1939) 49 The Economic Journal 696–712.

Hirsch F, *The Social Limits to Growth* (Routledge and Kegan Paul 1976).

Hirschman AO, *Exit, Voice, and Loyalty: Responses to Decline in Firms, Organizations and States* (Harvard University Press 1970).

Hirschman AO, 'Exit, Voice and the State' (1978) 31 World Politics 90–107.

Hobbes T, *Leviathan* (first published 1651, Penguin 1985).

Hurka T, *Perfectionism* (OUP 1993).

Jeffery RJ, *The Impact of State Sovereignty on Global Trade and International Taxation* (Kluwer 1999).

Kahan M, 'Legal Capital Rules and the Structure of Corporate Law: Some Observations on the Difference Between European and US Approaches' in K Hopt and E Wymeersch (eds), *Capital Markets and Company Law* (OUP 2003) 145–49.

Kahan M and Kamar E 'The Myth of State Competition in Corporate Law' (2002) 55 Stanford Law Review 679–749.

Kaldor N, 'Welfare Propositions of Economics and Interpersonal Comparisons of Utility' (1939) 49 The Economic Journal 549–52.

Kane E, 'Interaction of Finanical and Regulatory Innovation' (1988) 78 The American Economic Review 328–34.

Kant I, *Groundwork for the Metaphysics of Morals* (Allen Wood ed and tr, first published 1785, Yale University Press 2002).

Kaplow L and Shavell S, *Fairness Versus Welfare* (Harvard University Press 2002).

Keat R, 'Market Limits and Their Limits' (2012) 28 Economics and Philosophy 251–63.

Kelman S, *What Price Incentives? Economists and the Environment* (Auburn House Publishing Company 1981).

Kersten J, 'Standortmarketing für die Bundesrepublik– verfassungsrechtliche Rahmenbedingungen und verwaltungsrechtliche Steuerung der Werbung für den Investitions- und Wirtschaftsstandort Deutschland' [2008] Verwaltungsarchiv 30–45.

Kersten J, 'Wettbewerb der Rechtsordnungen?' in J Isensee and P Kirchhof (eds), *Handbuch des Staatsrechts, VoL XI* (CF Müller 2013) §233, 305–31.

Kersten J, 'Wettbewerb zwischen Hoheitsträgern' in H Kube and others (eds), *Leitgedanken des Rechts – Paul Kirchhof zum 70. Geburtstag* (CF Müller 2013) 845–51.

Kersten J and Battis U, *Standortmarketing im Bundesstaat* (Duncker and Humblot 2008).

Kieninger E-M, *Wettbewerb der Privatrechtsordnungen im Europäischen Binnenmarkt* (Mohr Siebeck 2002).

Kirchhof P, 'Freiheitlicher Wettbewerb und staatliche Autonomie – Solidarität' (2005) 58 ORDO 39–45.

Klöhn L, *The Case for Market-Mimicking Supranational Corporate Forms in Europe* (2012) <http://ssrn.com/abstract=2021061> accessed 1 August 2018.

Klöhn L, 'Supranationale Rechtsformen und vertikaler Wettbewerb der Gesetzgeber im europäischen Gesellschaftsrecht' (2012) 76 Rabel Journal of Comparative and International Private Law 276–315.

Kocaoglu K, *A Comparative Bibliography: Regulatory Competition on Corporate Law* (Georgetown University Law Center 2008).

Koetz H, 'The Jurisdiction of Choice: England and Wales or Germany?' (2010) 6 European Review of Private Law 1243–57.

Krugman P, 'Competitiveness: A Dangerous Obsession' (1994) 73 Foreign Affairs 28–44.

Kymlicka W, *Contemporary Political Philosophy: An Introduction* (OUP 2002).

Landes EM and Posner RA, 'The Economics of the Baby Shortage' (2002) 7 The Journal of Legal Studies 323–48.

Landes EM and Posner RA, 'Adjudication as a Private Good' (1979) 8 The Journal of Legal Studies 235–84.

Langille B, 'Competing Conceptions of Regulatory Competition in Debates on Trade Liberalization and Labour Standards' in W Bratton and others (eds), *International Regulatory Competition and Coordination* (Clarendon Press 1996) 479–90.

Legrand P, 'Pre-Contractual Disclosure and Information: English and French Law Compared' (1986) 6 Oxford Journal of Legal Studies 322–52.

Lessig L, 'The Regulation of Social Meaning' (1995) 62 The University of Chicago Law Review 943–1045.

Lessig L, 'Social Meaning and Social Norms' (1996) 144 Universitiy of Pennsylvania Law Review 2181–89.

Lindseth PL, 'Democratic Legitimacy and the Administrative Character of Supranationalism: The Example of the European Community' (1999) 99 Columbia Law Review 628–738.

Lischek J and Mahnken V, 'Vertragsverhandlungen zwischen Unternehmen und AGB – Anmerkungen aus der Sicht der Praxis' [2007] Zeitschrift für Wirtschaftsrecht 158–63.

List JA and Shogren JF, 'The Deadweight Loss of Christmas: Comment' (1998) 88 American Economic Review 1350–55.

Little IMD, *A Critique of Welfare Economics* (Clarendon Press 1957).

LoPucki L, *Courting Failure – How Competition for Big Cases is Corrupting the Bankruptcy Courts* (University of Michigan Press 2005).

LoPucki L and Doherty J, 'Bankruptcy Fire Sales' (2007) 106 Michigan Law Review 1–59.

Luhmann N, *Law as a Social System* (KA Ziegert tr, F Kastner and others eds, OUP 2004).

Lutter M (ed), *Legal Capital in Europe*, ECFR Special Volume 1 (De Gruyter 2006a).

Lutter M, 'Legal Capital of Public Companies in Europe – Executive Summary of Considerations by the Expert Group on "Legal Capital in Europe"' in M Lutter (ed), *Legal Capital in Europe*, ECFR Special Volume 1 (De Gruyter 2006b) 1–14.

MacDougall GDA, 'The Benefits and Costs of Private Investment from Abroad: A Theoretical Approach' (1960) 22 Bulletin of the Oxford University Institute of Economics and Statistics 189–211.

MacMillan C, 'Brexit, Business and Trade: The Impact of Brexit upon English Contract Law' (2016) 27 King's Law Journal 420–30.

Mankowski P, 'Rechtskultur' (2009), 64 Juristenzeitung 321–31.

Marmor A and Sarch A, 'The Nature of Law', *The Stanford Encyclopedia of Philosophy* (2015) <https://plato.stanford.edu/archives/fall2015/entries/lawphil-nature/> accessed 1 August 2018.

Marquand D, *Parliament for Europe* (Jonathan Cape 1979).

Mason K, Laurie G, and Smith AM, *Mason and McCall Smith's Law and Medical Ethics* (OUP 2013).

Mason R, 'Citizenship Taxation' (2016) 89 Southern California Law Review 169–239.

May T, 'The Concept of Autonomy' (1994) 31 American Philosophical Quarterly 133–44.

May T, *Autonomy, Authority and Moral Responsibility* (Kluwer 1998).

Mény Y, 'De la démocratie en Europe: Old Concepts and New Challenges' 41 Journal of Common Market Studies 1–13.

Michaels R, 'The Functional Method of Comparative Law' in M Reimann and R Zimmermann (eds), *The Oxford Handbook of Comparative Law* (OUP 2006) 339–82.

Michaels R, 'After the Revolution – Decline and Return of U.S Conflict of Laws' in A Bonomi and P Volken (eds), *Yearbook of Private International Law, VoL 11* (Sellier 2010) 11–30.

Michaels R, 'Make or Buy – a Public Market for Legal Transplants?' in H Eidenmüller (ed), *Regulatory Competition in Contract Law and Dispute Resolution* (CH Beck 2013) 27–44.

Mill JS, 'Considerations on Representative Government' in JM Robson (ed), *Essays on Politics and Society, Collected Works of John Stuart Mill, VoL XIX* (first published 1861, University of Toronto Press/Routledge and Kegan Paul 1977) 371–577.

Mill JS, *Principles of Political Economy* (S Nathanson ed, first published 1848, Hackett Publishing 2004).

Monopolkommission, *Sondergutachten Systemwettbewerb* (Nomos 1998).

Moore GE, *Principia Ethica* (first published 1903, CUP 1993).

Morreau M, 'Arrow's Theorem', *The Stanford Encyclopedia of Philosophy* (2016) <https://plato.stanford.edu/archives/win2016/entries/arrows-theorem/> accessed 1 August 2018.

Möslein F, *Dispositives Recht: Zwecke, Strukturen und Methoden* (Mohr Siebeck 2011).

Möslein F, 'Regulatory Competition between Public and Private Rules' in H Eidenmüller (ed), *Regulatory Competition in Contract Law and Dispute Resolution* (CH Beck 2013) 147–54.

Möslein KM and others, 'Law as a Service - Recht als Dienstleistung: Strategischer Produktivitätsfaktor unterne-hmerischer Innovation?' (2012) <http://clicresearch.org/wp-content/uploads/downloads/2012/10/23_de_recht_als_dienstleistung.pdf> accessed 1 August 2018.

Mülbert P and Birke M, 'Legal Capital – Is There a Case Against the European Legal Capital Rules?' (2002) 3 EBOR 695–732.

Murphy DD, 'The Business Dynamics of Global Regulatory Competition' in D Vogel and R Kagan (eds), *Dynamics of Regulatory Change: How Globalization Affects National Regulatory Policies* (University of California Press 2004) 84–117.

Murphy DD, *The Structure of Regulatory Competition: Corporations and Public Policies in a Global Economy* (OUP 2006).

Musgrave PB and Musgrave RA, 'Fiscal Coordination and Competition in an International Setting' in CE McLure (ed), *Influence of Tax Differentials on International Competitiveness* (Kluwer Law and Taxation Publishers 1990) 61–86.

Narayanswamy A and others, 'Election 2016: Money Raised As Of Dec. 31' *The Washington Post* (1 February 2017) <https://www.washingtonpost.com/graphics/politics/2016-election/campaign-finance/> accessed 1 August 2018.

Nielsen K, *Equality and Liberty: A Defense of Radical Egalitarianism* (Rowman and Littlefield Publishers 1984).

Nozick R, *Anarchy, State, and Utopia* (Basic Books 1974).

Nozick R, *The Nature of Rationality* (Princeton University Press 1994).

Nussbaum M and Sen A (eds), *The Quality of Life* (Clarendon Press 1993).

O'Hara O'Connor EA, 'Jurisdictional Competition for Dispute Resolution: Courts versus Arbitration' in H Eidenmüller (ed), *Regulatory Competition in Contract Law and Dispute Resolution* (CH Beck 2009) 428–41.

O'Hara EA and Ribstein LE, 'From Politics to Efficiency in the Choice of Law' (2000) 67 University of Chicago Law Review 1151–232.

O'Hara EA and Ribstein LE, *The Law Market* (OUP 2009).

O'Neill B, 'A Minimum Standard for Debt Discharge in Europe?' [2014] The Commercial Law Practicioner 156–63.

O'Neill J, *The Market: Ethics, Knowledge and Politics* (Routledge 1998).

Ogus A, 'Competition between National Legal Systems: A Contribution of Economic Analysis to Comparative Law' (1999) 48 International and Comparative Law Quarterly 405–18.

Ogus A, 'The Economic Approach: Competition between Legal Systems' in E Örücü and D Nelken (eds), *Comparative Law: A Handbook* (Hart 2007) 155–67.

Olney W, 'A Race to the Bottom? Employment Protection and Foreign Direct Investment' (2013) 91 Journal of International Economics 191–203.

Olson M, *The Logic of Collective Action* (Harvard University Press 2009).

Orbach B, 'What is Regulation?' (2012) 30 Yale Journal on Regulation Online 1–10.

Organization for Economic Co-Operation and Development, *Harmful Tax Competition: An Emerging Global Issue* (OECD Publications 1998) <https://www.oecd-ilibrary.org/taxation/harmful-tax-competition_9789264162945-en> accessed 1 August 2018.

Organization for Economic Co-Operation and Development, Addressing the Tax Challenges of the Digital Economy, Action 1 – 2015 Final Report (OECD Publications 2015) <http://www.oecd.org/tax/addressing-the-tax-challenges-of-the-digital-economy-action-1-2015-final-report-9789264241046-en.htm> accessed 1 August 2018.

Oxford English Dictionary Online, 'Market' (June 2018) <http://www.oed.com/view/Entry/114178?rskey=odMicM&result=1&isAdvanced=false> accessed 1 August 2018.

Palan R, 'Recasting Political Authority: Globalization and the State' in RD Germain (ed), *Globalization and Its Critics* (Palgrave Macmillan 2000) 139–63.

Peters A, 'The Competition between Legal Orders' (2014) 3 International Law Research 45–65.

Pfeifer T, 'Flucht ins schweizerische Recht' in FC Genzow, B Grunewald, and H Schulte-Nölke (eds), *Zwischen Vertragsfreiheit und*

Verbraucherschutz – Festschrift für Friedrich Graph von Westphalen (Dr Otto Schmidt 2010) 555–68.

Philpott D, 'Sovereignty', *The Stanford Encyclopedia of Philosophy* (2014) <https://plato.stanford.edu/archives/sum2016/entries/sovereignty/> accessed 1 August 2018.

Pigou AC, *The Economics of Welfare* (first published 1920, Palgrave Macmillan 2013).

Pildes RH and Sunstein CR, 'Reinventing the Regulatory State' (1995) 62 The University of Chicago Law Review 1–129.

Pogge T, 'Creating Supra-National Institutions Democratically: Reflections on the European Union's "Democratic Deficit"' (1997) 5 The Journal of Political Philosophy 163–82.

von Pommern-Peglow M, 'Deutsche Zivilgerichte im internationalen Wettbewerb' [2015] Zeitschrift für Rechtspolitik 178–81.

Posner R, 'Utilitarism, Economics and Legal Theory' (1979) 8 The Journal of Legal Studies 103–40.

Posner R, *Economic Analysis of Law* (first published 1973, 9th edn, Wolters Kluwer Law and Business 2014).

Radin MJ, 'On the Domain of Market Rhetoric' (1992) 15 Harvard Journal of Law and Public Policy 711–31.

Radin MJ, *Contested Commodities* (Harvard University Press 2001).

Raz J, *The Authority of Law: Essays on Law and Morality* (Clarendon Press 1979).

Raz J, *The Morality of Freedom* (Clarendon Press 1986).

Raz J, 'The Problem of Authority: Revisiting the Service Conception' (2006) 90 Minnesota Law Review 1003–44.

Rehberg M, 'Spezifika des Systemwettbewerbs' in EV Towfighand and others (eds), *Recht und Markt: Wechselbeziehungen zweier Ordnungen* (Nomos 2009) 29–52.

Revesz R, 'Rehabilitating Interstate Competition: Rethinking the 'Race-to-the-Bottom' Rationale for Federal Environmental Regulation' (1992) 67 New York University Law Review 1210–54.

Richman PB, *Taxation of Foreign Investment Income: An Economic Analysis* (John Hopkins Press 1963).

Ringe W-G, 'Corporate Mobility in the European Union - a Flash in the Pan? An Empirical Study in the Success of Lawmaking and Regulatory Competition' (2013) 10 European Company and Financial Law Review 230–67.

Roe MJ, 'Delaware's Competition' (2003) 177 Harvard Law Review 588–646.

Romano R, 'Law as a Product: Some Pieces of the Incorporation Puzzle' (1985) 1 Journal of Law, Economics and Organization 225–83.

Romano R, *The Genius of American Corporate Law* (The AEI Press 1993).

Rosenberg Z, 'Auto Designers Cater to China, the New Giant' (Wired, 18 February 2010) <http://www.wired.com/2010/02/automotive-design-for-china/> accessed 1 August 2018.

Ruffle BJ and Tykocinski O, 'The Deadweight Loss of Christmas: Comment' (2000) 90 American Economic Review 319–24.

Rühl G, *Statut und Effizienz* (Mohr Siebeck 2011).

Rühl G, 'Choice of Law by the Parties' in J Basedow, K J Hopt, and R Zimmermann (eds), *Max Planck Encyclopedia of European Private Law* (OUP 2012) 190–4.

Rühl G, 'The Choice of Law Framework for Efficient Regulatory Competition in Contract Law' in H Eidenmüller (ed), *Regulatory Competition in Contract Law and Dispute Resolution* (CH Beck 2013) 287–303.

Sacco R, 'Legal Formants: A Dynamic Approach to Comparative Law (Installment II of II)' (1991) 39 American Journal of Comparative Law 343–401.

Sandel MJ, 'What Money Can't Buy: The Moral Limits of Markets' (1998) The Tanner Lectures on Human Values <http://tannerlectures.utah.edu/_documents/a-to-z/s/sandel00.pdf> accessed 1 August 2018.

Sandel MJ, *What Money Can't Buy: The Moral Limits of Markets* (Palgrave Macmillan 2012).

Satz D, *Why Some Things Should Not Be for Sale: The Moral Limits of Markets* (OUP 2010).

Saunders L, 'So How Much Did He Really Save?' *Wall Street Journal* (New York, 18 May 2012) <http://www.wsj.com/articles/SB10001424052702303360504577410571011995562> accessed 1 August 2018.

Schleicher D, 'What if Europe Held an Election and No One Cared?' (2011) 52 Harvard International Law Journal 109–61.

Schneewind JB, *The Invention of Autonomy: A History of Modern Moral Philosophy* (CUP 1998).

Schön W, 'Der "Wettbewerb" der europäischen Steuerordnungen als Rechtsproblem' in J Pelka (ed), *Europa- und verfassungsrechtliche Grenzen der Unternehmensbesteuerung* (Dr Otto Schmidt 2000) 191–226.

Schön W, 'Playing Different Games? Regulatory Competition in Tax and Company Law Compared' (2005) 42 Common Market Law Review 331–65.

Schön W, 'Leichter auf die Anklagebank' (2014) 02 EY TAX & LAW Magazine <https://www.tax.mpg.de/fileadmin/TAX/docs/TL/WS/EY_BEPS.pdf> accessed 1 August 2018.

Schram S, *After Welfare: The Culture of Postindustrial Social Policy* (NYU Press 2000).

Schumann C-D, 'Plan eines zentralen Gerichtshofs für die Anerkennung von Schiedssprüchen – Was ist daraus geworden?' (1993) 39 Recht der internationalen Wirtschaft 701–2.

Schumpeter J, *Capitalism, Socialism and Democracy* (Harper 1975).

Schwenzer I and Whitebread C, 'International B2B Contracts – Freedom Unchained?' (2015) 4 Penn State Journal of Law and International Affairs 33–46.

Sengenberger W, 'Labour Standards: An Institutional Framework for Restructuring and Development' in W Sengenberger and D Campbell (eds), *Creating Economic Opportunities: The Role of Labour Standards in Industrial Restructuring* (International Institute for Labour Studies 1994) 3–42.

Sewart JJ, 'The Commodification of Sport' (1987) 22 International Review for the Sociology of Sport 171–92.

Shachar A, 'Citizenship for Sale' in A Shachar and others (eds), *The Oxford Handbook of Citizenship* (OUP 2017) 789–814.

Shachar A and Hirschl R, 'On Citizenship, States, and Markets' (2014) 22 The Journal of Political Philosophy, 231–57.

Singer P, *Democracy and Disobedience* (OUP 1973).

Sinn H-W, 'The Selection Principle and Market Failure in Systems Competition' (1997) 66 Journal of Public Economics 247–74.

Sinn H-W, *The New Systems Competition* (John Wiley & Sons 2003).

Sinn S, 'The Taming of Leviathan: Competition among Governments' (1992) 3 Constitutional Political Economy 177–96.

Smith A, *An Inquiry into the Nature and Causes of the Wealth of Nations* (RH Campbell and AS Skinner eds, first published 1776, OUP 1979).

Smith SN, 'On the Economic Rationale for Codetermination Law' (1991) 16 Journal of Economic Behavior and Organization 261–81.

Soggin JA, *Introduction to the Old Testament* (3rd edn, Westminster John Knox Press 1989).

Sohm R, *The Institutes of Roman Law* (Clarendon Press 1892).

Solnick SJ and Hemenway D, 'The Deadweight Loss of Christmas: Comment' (1996) 86 The American Economic Review 1299–305.

Solum LB, 'Legal Theory Lexicon: It Takes a Theory to Beat a Theory' (2015) <http://lsolum.typepad.com/legaltheory/2015/07/legal-theory-lexicon-it-takes-a-theory-to-beat-a-theory.html> accessed 1 August 2018.

Spector H, 'Autonomy' in G Gaus and R D'Agostina (eds), *The Routledge Companion to Social and Political Philosophy* (Routledge 2013) 573–84.

Stanton A, 'Forfeited Consent: Body Parts in Eminent Domain' in P J Gibson (ed), *Patenting Lives: Life Patents, Culture and Development* (Ashgate Publishing Limited 2013) 95–120.

Stewart A, 'Covenant Marriage: Legislating Family Values' (1999) 32 Indiana Law Review 509–36.

Stigler GJ, 'Competition' in SN Durlauf and LE Blume (eds), *The New Palgrave Dictionary of Economics* (Springer 2008) 51–57.

Sun J-M and Pelkmans J, 'Regulatory Competition in the Single Market' (1995) 33 Journal of Common Market Studies 67–89.

Sunstein CR, 'Incommensurability and Valuation in Law' (1994) 92 Michigan Law Review 779–861.

Sunstein CR, 'On the Expressive Function of Law' (1996) 144 University of Pennsylvania Law Review 2021–53.

Sunstein CR, 'Social Norms and Social Roles' (1996) 96 Columbia Law Review 903–68.

Tamanaha BZ, *Law as a Means to an End: Threat to the Rule of Law* (CUP 2006).

Tamanaha BZ, 'Law', *Oxford International Encyclopedia of Legal History* (2nd edn, OUP 2008).

Teichmann C, 'Verhandelte Mitbestimmung für Auslandsgesellschaften' (2009) 30 Zeitschrift für Wirtschaftsrecht 1787–88.

Thaler RH and Benartzi S, 'Save More Tomorrow™: Using Behavioral Economics to Increase Employee Saving' (2004) 112 Journal of Political Economy 164–87.

The Law Society of England and Wales, 'England and Wales: The jurisdiction of choice' (2007) <http://www.eversheds.com/global/de/what/publications/books.page> accessed 1 August 2018.

The Law Society of England and Wales, 'Enland & Wales: Global Legal Centre' (2016) <https://www.lawsociety.org.uk/policy-campaigns/documents/global-legal-centre-leaflet/> accessed 1 August 2018.

Thoma I, 'Public Policy (Ordre Public)' in J Basedow and others (eds), *European Encyclopedia of Private International Law* (Edward Elgar Publishing 2017) 1453–60.

Thorndike JJ and Ventry DJ, *Tax Justice: The Ongoing Debate* (Urban Institute Press 2002).

Tiebout CM, 'A Pure Theory of Local Expenditure' (1956) 64 Journal of Political Economy 416–24.

Titmuss RM, *The Gift of Relationship: From Human Blood to Social Policy* (Pantheon 1971).

Trachtman JP, 'International Regulatory Competition, Externalization, and Jurisdiction' (1993) 34 Harvard International Law Journal 47.

United Nations Conference on Trade and Development, *Review of Maritime Transport 2017* (United Nations 2017).

Van den Bergh R, 'Subsidiarity as an Economic Demarcation Principle and the Emergence of European Private Law' (1998) 5 Maastricht Journal of European and Comparative Law 129–52.

Van der Elst C and Vermeulen E, 'The Dutch Private Company: Successfully Relaunched?' (2013) ECGI Law Working Paper No 215/2013 <http://ssrn.com/abstract=2267522> accessed 1 August 2018.

Vishnubhakat S, 'Reconceiving the Patent Rocket Docket: An Empirical Study of Infringement Litigation 1985-2010' (2011) 11 The John Marshall Review of Intellectual Property Law 58–82.

Vogel K, *Taxation of Cross-Border Income, Harmonization, and Tax Neutrality under European Community Law* (Kluwer Law and Taxation Publishing 1994).

Vogenauer S, 'Regulatory Competition through Choice of Contract Law and Choice of Forum in Europe: Theory and Evidence' (2013) 21 European Review of Private Law 13–78.

Vogenauer S, 'Regulatory Competition through Choice of Contract Law and Choice of Forum in Europe: Theory and Evidence' in H Eidenmüller (ed), *Regulatory Competition on Contract Law and Dispute Resolution* (CH Beck 2013) 227–84.

Vogenauer S and Hodges C, *Civil Justice Systems in Europe* (Hart 2016).

Wagner G, 'The Economics of Harmonization: The Case of Contract Law' (2002) 39 Common Market Law Review 995–1023.

Wagner G, 'Dispute Resolution as a Product: Competition between Civil Justice Systems' in H Eidenmüller (ed), *Regulatory Competition in Contract Law and Dispute Resolution* (Beck 2013) 347–422.

Wagner G, 'The Dispute Resolution Market' (2014) 62 Buffalo Law Review 1085–158.

Waldfogel J, 'The Deadweight Loss of Christmas' (1993) 83 The American Economic Review 1328–36.

Waldfogel J, 'The Deadweight Loss of Christmas: Reply' (1996) 88 The American Economic Review 1306–8.

Waldron J, *Law and Disagreement* (OUP 1999).

Walzer M, *Spheres of Justice: A Defense of Pluralism and Equality* (Basic Books 1983).

Warner R, 'Does Incommensurability Matter? Incommensurability and Public Policy' (1998) 146 University of Pennsylvania Law Review 1267–325.

Weber M, *Economy and Society: An Outline of Interpretive Sociology, Vol I* (University of California Press 1978).

Weber M, *Economy and Society: An Outline of Interpretive Sociology, Vol II* (University of California Press 1978).

Wehberg H, 'Pacta Sunt Servanda' (1959) 53 The American Journal of International Law 775–86.

Weinreb LL, *Natural Law and Justice* (Harvard University Press 1987).

White K, 'Covenant Marriage: An Unnecessary Second Attempt at Fault-Based Divorce' (2010) 61 Alabama Law Review 869–90.

Wilde O, *Lady Windermere's Fan* (I Small ed, first published 1892, Bloomsbury Publishing 1999).

Williams B, 'A Critique of Utilitarianism' in JJC Smart and B Williams (eds), *Utilitarianism: For and Against* (CUP 1973) 75–150.

Winter RK, 'State Law, Shareholder Protection, and the Theory of the Corporation' (1977) 6 Journal of Legal Studies 251–92.

Wolff RP, *In Defense of Anarchism* (University of California Press 1970).

Wolff RP, *The Conflict between Authority and Autonomy* (Basil Blackwell 1990).

Woolcock S, 'Competition among Rules in the European Market' in W Bratton and others (eds), *International Regulatory Competition and Coordination* (Clarendon Press 1996) 289–321.

Zimmer D, 'Zwischen Theorie und Empirie: Zur Konkurrenz der Gesetzgeber im Gesellschaftsrecht' in G Bitter and others (eds), *Festschrift für Karsten Schmidt zum 70. Geburtstag* (DR Otto Schmidt 2009) 1789–803.

Zumbansen P, 'Spaces and Places: A Systems Theory Approach to Regulatory Competition in European Company Law' (2006) 12 European Law Journal 534–56.

Zweigert K and Kötz H, *An Introduction to Comparative Law* (Tony Weir tr, 3rd edn, OUP 1998).

INDEX

ability to pay, 170, 171
adoption, 125, 130, 145–46
alternative dispute resolution, *see* dispute resolution
altruism, 129–30
anarchism, 117
Anderson Elisabeth, 145
arbitrage, 25–26, 36
arbitration, 51–52
Aristotle, 152, 156
asylum law, 33–34
asymmetry
  of bargaining power, *see* bargaining power
  of influence, 67–69, 94
  of information, *see* information: asymmetries
authority
  concept, 115–16
  legal, 115–16
  political, *see* political authority
autonomy
  personal, 104–5, 121
  political, 7, 105, 176
  state, *see* state autonomy

baby market, 125, 126–27, 130, 134, 145–46
B2B
  choice of law, 45–46
  standard terms review, 45–46
bankruptcy law, *see* insolvency law
bargaining
  collective, 46–47
  power, 42–43, 159
base erosion and profit shifting (BEPS) project, 35–36
battle of the brochures, 31–32, 45, 55–56
behavioural economics, 73–74
Bobbio Norberto, 92–93
Brandeis Justice, 63–64
Brexit, 21, 38–39, 45–46
bundling, 25, 29, 68–69, 168

capabilities approach, 179
categorical imperative, 88–89
centre of main interest (COMI), 49–50
charter competition, 27, 37–41, 94–95
children, 165
choice of forum, 25–26, 48–50, 51–53
choice of law
  in contract law, 44–46
  costs, 23–25
  opt-out, *see* opt-out
  options, 10–11, 22, 23–24, 29–30, 65, 159, 160–61, 175–76
Christian ethics, 88
Cicero Marcus Tullius, 152
citizenship taxation, 25, 34–35
civil law systems, 27
co-determination
  mandatory, 41–43
  in the Societas Europaea, 43
coercion, 180
collective action problems, 74, 120
commercialization, *see* commodification
commodification
  of citizenship, 139–40
  contested commodities, *see* contested commodities
  corruption, 137–38
  crowding out effect, *see* crowding out effect
  and distributive justice, 134–137
  of law, 7, 126, 148–49, 169, 171
  of political power, 143–44
  res extra commercium, 134
Common European Sales Law (CESL), 46

common good, 75, 92–93, 159, 180
common law systems, 27
company law, 23, 34, 37–43
charter competition, *see* charter competition
creditor protection, *see* creditor protection
Delaware, *see* Delaware
minimum capital requirements, *see* minimum capital requirements
comparability
cardinal, 79
interpersonal utility, 79, 89
ordinal, 79
competition
charter, *see* charter competition
concept, 15–16
creative destruction, 59
discovery of efficient solutions, 58–59, 175
and efficiency, *see* efficiency
regulatory, *see* regulatory competition
competition law, 2
compliance, 163–64
constitutional constraints, 97, 124, 180
consumer contracts, 53
contested commodities, 7, 125, 132–33
contracts
consumer, *see* consumer contracts
cross-border, 20
efficient breach, *see* efficient breach in contract law
pacta sunt servanda, 82, 87–88
sanctity of, 82
contract law, 28–29, 44–46
conventionalism, 141–142, 147
cooperation, 76–77, 100–1, 155
corporate governance, 41–42, 71
corporate law, 23, 37–43
corruption, 137–38
costs
mobility, *see* mobility costs
of economic goods, 13
of production, 9–10
cost-benefit analysis, 168
creditor protection, 39–40, 63–64, 87
crowding out effect, 7, 127, 129–32, 151, 172
culture, 54–55, 83, 100, 181

Delaware, 14, 27, 37–38
democracy
decision-making, 22–23, 92, 110, 111–12, 146–47
deficit, *see* democratic deficit
deliberative process, 93–94, 111–12
egalitarian commitments of, 92, 101, 102–3, 171
electoral campaign, 26
instrumentalist justification, 102
intrinsic justification, 102
legislative process, 93, 114
legitimacy, 65, 95, 100–1, 113–14, 168
majority rule, *see* majority rule
meaning, 92
one person, one vote, 103, 146–47
parliamentary, *see* parliament
political ideal, 7, 103, 176
representative, 95
transparency, 113–14
democratic deficit, 93–94, 100–1
dignity, *see* human dignity
dispute resolution, 51–54
arbitration, *see* arbitration
mediation, *see* mediation
distributive justice, 42–43, 79, 113, 135, 166
divorce, 167

e-commerce, 20
economies of scale, 28–29
education, 83, 129, 136, 171
efficiency
breach of contract, *see* efficient breach in contract law
increase by competition, 58–59
Kaldor-Hicks criterion, *see* Kaldor-Hicks efficiency
Pareto-optimality, 41–42
efficient breach
in contract law, 82
in insolvency law, 88–89
Ehrlich Eugen, 156–57
emigration law, 21

employee representation, *see* co-determination
employment, 18
enforcement, 48
English law
corporate law, 23, 60–61
competitiveness, 31–32
contract law, 45–46, 68–69
environmental regulation, 1, 65, 161, 162, 164
equality
among citizens, 162–63, 171
and democracy, *see* egalitarian commitments of democracy
as a political principle, 124
and utilitarianism, 75, 79
European Court of Justice, 23
European Union, 15–16, 109
European Union law
and corporate law, 38–39
and economic efficiency, 96–97
fundamental freedoms, *see* fundamental freedoms
Treaty of Lisbon, 97
exit, 20, 22–23, 76
expressive function
of gift giving, 131
of law, *see* functions of law
externalities, *see* external effects
external effects, 18, 65–66, 169

fairness, 79
federalism
competitive, 19, 97
as a political system, 19, 58
Finnis John, 152
flags of convenience, 1–2, 63–64
flourishing, *see* well-being
forum shopping, 25–26
free rider problem, 120, 160
French law, 27, 50
functions of law
coordination, 10, 160, 172
expressive, 162–69, 171–72, 176
social, 7, 75, 153–55, 156–61, 176–77
solution of conflict, 154–55
stabilization of expectations, 157–58, 169–70, 172, 176
fundamental freedoms, 20, 23, 38–39, 47–48, 96–97

German law, 27, 31–32, 40–41, 45–46, 50, 54–55, 60–61, 97, 109–10
gift giving, 131
globalization, 8, 175–78
good life, *see* well-being

happy sadist problem, 77–78
harmonization, 99, 100–1, 175–76
Hayek Friedrich von, 58–59, 60
healthcare, 83, 129, 136
hedonic theories, 179
Hirsch Fred, 129
Hirschman Albert, 22–23, 29, 76
Hobbes Thomas, 61, 156
human dignity, 78, 88, 165, 171
human flourishing, *see* well-being
hyperbolic discounting, 73–74

immigration law, 21
imperialism, 56
incentives to compete
economic, 27–30
of legislators, 2, 9, 15, 25–27, 29
information
asymmetries, 61
discovery by competition, 61
in Tiebout model, 17, 18
infrastructure, 83–84, 160, 167
insolvency law
centre of main interests (COMI), *see* cenre of main interests
European Insolvency Regulation (EIR), 49–50
residual debt discharge, *see* residual debt discharge
US, 48–49
integrity, 78
invisible hand, 75
in vitro fertilization (IVF), 165
Irish law, 51
jurisdictional competition, *see* regulatory competition
justice
distributive, *see* distributive justice
spheres of, 144–46, 170–71
utilitarianism, 75

Kaldor-Hicks efficiency, 58–59
Kant Immanuel, 88–89

labour law
minimum wage, 1, 46–47, 162–63
standards, 46–48, 63–64
Landes Elizabeth, 51–52, 125
language, 53–54
law
commodification, *see* commodification of law
enforcement, *see* enforcement
functions of, *see* functions of law
mandatory, *see* mandatory law
moral character of, *see* moral character of law
non-state/private origin, 16–17
price, *see* price of law
reform, 60, 166
as a product, 7, 10–11, 12–15
as a public good, *see* public good
sacrality of, 152
as a service, 12–13
and social change, 178
social meaning, *see* social meaning
statutory, 15–16
supranational, *see* supranational law
law market
and commodification of law, *see* commodification of law
concept, 10, 11–12
competitive element, 10–11
dialectical phenomenon, 23
and regulatory competition, *see* regulatory competition
legal innovation, 29
legal products, *see* law as a product
legal services, 27–29
Leviathan state, 61, 67, 69
majority rule
versus demand rule, 92–101
devolutionary erosion of, 99–101
evaluative neutrality, 92–93
indirect erosion of, 95–98
method of collective decision-making, 92
pragmatic appeal, 92–93, 101
mandatory law, 2–3, 24, 66–67, 159, 169, 180
market
for babies, *see* baby market
and commodification, *see* commodification
commodities, *see* commodities
competitive, 9–10
concept of, 9–10
evaluative logic of the, 7, 128
external effects/externalities, *see* external effects
failure, 63–67, 171, 181
for law, *see* law market
moral limits of, *see* contested commodities
price mechanism, *see* price mechanism
race to the bottom, *see* race to the bottom
three-pole concept, 9–10
value neutrality of the, 92–93, 128–29
marriage, 20, 120
and divorce, *see* divorce
same-sex, 166–67
tourism, 33–34
mediation, 51–52
minimum capital requirements, 23, 39–40, 60–61
mobility
capital, 20–21, 84, 87, 154, 177
corporate, 65
costs, 20–21, 22–23, 25, 28–29, 55, 76, 84, 168, 178
cross-border, 96–97
legal, 22–25, 166
physical, 17, 19–21, 25
of production factors, 20
money, 79, 131
moral
character, 138, 140–41
character of law, 151–53
conventionalism, *see* conventionalism
relativism, *see* relativism

natural law theory, 152–53
neutrality 92–93, 128–29

offshore companies, 27–28
opt-out, 24–25, 159–60, 164–65
Organisation for Economic Co-Operation and Development (OECD), 35–36, 109

Pareto optimality, 41–42
parliament, 11, 93–95, 97, 101
patent law, 52–53
paternalism, 59, 120, 180
perfectionism
 Aristotelian, 119
 paternalism, 120
 and political authority, *see* perfectionist accounts of political authority
political authority
 concept, 115–16
 legitimacy, 117, 118
 perfectionist accounts of, 116, 118–22
 proceduralist accounts of, 116, 117, 122–23
 service conception, 119–20, 121
 stability, 117
political obligations, 116
Posner Richard, 51–52, 125
power
 bargaining, *see* bargaining power
 parliamentary, 93–94
 political, 103, 143–44, 154
preferences
 illegitimate, 86
 satisfaction of, 179–80
price
 law as, 149–50, 165
 of law, 149–50, 168
 mechanism, 126–27, 128–29
primacy of politics, 98, 108, 109, 176–77
prisoner's dilemma, 74, 157
private goods, 13–14, 83
private international law, 10–11, 22
 choice of law options, *see* choice of law options
 ordre public, *see* ordre public
 Rome I Regulation, *see* Rome I Regulation
procedural law, 54–55
public goods, 13–14, 17, 83, 87, 177
public interest, 75
public international law, 19–20, 21
public law, 23–24
public management, 177

race to the bottom, 38, 63–64
race to the top, 5
Raz Joseph, 119–20, 121
redistribution, 180
regulatory competition
 concept of, 10–11
 economic incentives, 27–30
 efficiency, 5, 29
 empirical evidence, 2, 31–33
 horizontal, 15–16
 negative, 33–34
 passive/defensive, 30–31, 56, 160
 philosophical externalities, 7–8
 political incentives, 26–27
 preconditions, 8, 18–25
 price mechanism, *see* price mechanism
 proactive, 30–31, 160
 race to the bottom, *see* race to the bottom
 race to the top, *see* race to the top
 selection principle, *see* selection principle
 supranational framework, 99–101
 utilitarianism, 6
 vertical, 15–16
relativism, 147–48
reproduction, 120, 126, 135–36, 165
residual debt discharge, 50–51, 87–89
rights
 constitutional, 160
 individual, 77–78
Rousseau Jean Jacques, 152

safety, 83
Sandel Michael, 137
seasteading movement, 21
secession, 21
selection principle, 66–67
service state, 177
Sinn Hans Werner, 4, 66–67, 70, 171
Smith Adam, 75

social functions of law, *see* functions of law
social meaning
of law, 7, 153–55
of a practice, 145–48
Societas Europaea (SE), 15–16, 43
solidarity, 88, 130, 148
spheres of justice, *see* justice, spheres of
spill over effects, *see* external effects
stabilization of expectations, 157–58, 169–70, 172, 176
standard contract terms, 45–46
state
authority, *see* political authority
autonomy, *see* political autonomy
justification, 178–79
legitimacy of the, 178–79, 180
minimal, 180, 181
service, *see* service state
welfare, *see* welfare state
state autonomy
concept, 104–5, 176
democratic decision-making, 111
formal, 107–8, 176–77
in public international law, 105
substantive, 107–8, 176–77
St Thomas Aquinas, 152
Sunstein Cass, 163–64
supranational law, 2–3
Swiss Law, 22–23, 45–46, 168
systems competition, 10–11

taxation
capital, 166
income, 166, 168
progressive, 166
tax competition, 34, 35–37, 83–87, 89
tax justice, 85–86, 166
tax law, 34–37
tax reform, 113
territoriality principle, 19–20, 22, 47–48, 160, 176–77
Tiebout model, 17–18, 62
Titmuss Richard, 130
transactions, *see* contracts
Treaty of Versailles, *see* Versailles Treaty

United Nations (UN), 15–16, 109
United States law, 21, 167
utilitarianism
Anglo-Saxon tradition, 181
efficient breach of contract, 82
individual rights, 77–78
(distributive) justice, 75, 79–80
legal, 74–75
rule, 78
special relationships, 81–82
utility
declining marginal, 80
interpersonal comparisons, *see* comparability

value
communal decisions, 162–64, 176
conventionalism, *see* conventionalism
objectivism, 135–36
Versailles Treaty, 47–48
vertical regulatory competition, *see* regulatory competition, vertical
voice, 22–23, 76
voting with one's feet, 17, 20

Walzer Michael, 143–45
Weber Max, 115–16
welfare
and behavioural economics, 73–74
increase by competition, 57
irrationality, 73
versus perfectionist theories, 122
satisfaction of subjective preferences, 58–59, 72, 179
utilitarianism, 124
welfare state, 87, 177, 180, 181
well-being
objective conception of, 73, 119, 147–48, 179–80
subjective conception of, 72, 179–80
willingness to pay, 170, 171

www.ingramcontent.com/pod-product-compliance
Lightning Source LLC
LaVergne TN
LVHW010320220926
848484LV00004BB/812
* 9 7 8 0 1 9 8 8 3 9 4 9 1 *